TEACHING FASHION STUDIES

TEACHING FASHION STUDIES

EDITED BY
HOLLY M. KENT

BLOOMSBURY VISUAL ARTS
LONDON · NEW YORK · OXFORD · NEW DELHI · SYDNEY

BLOOMSBURY VISUAL ARTS
Bloomsbury Publishing Plc
50 Bedford Square, London, WC1B 3DP, UK

BLOOMSBURY, BLOOMSBURY VISUAL ARTS and the Diana logo are trademarks of Bloomsbury Publishing Plc

First published in Great Britain 2018

Copyright © Holly M. Kent and contributors, 2018

Holly M. Kent has asserted her right under the Copyright, Designs and Patents Act, 1988, to be identified as Editor of this work.

For legal purposes the Acknowledgments on p. x constitute an extension of this copyright page.

Cover design: Dani Leigh
Cover image © Shutterstock

All rights reserved. No part of this publication may be reproduced or transmitted in any form or by any means, electronic or mechanical, including photocopying, recording, or any information storage or retrieval system, without prior permission in writing from the publishers.

Bloomsbury Publishing Plc does not have any control over, or responsibility for, any third-party websites referred to or in this book. All internet addresses given in this book were correct at the time of going to press. The author and publisher regret any inconvenience caused if addresses have changed or sites have ceased to exist, but can accept no responsibility for any such changes.

A catalogue record for this book is available from the British Library.

Library of Congress Cataloging-in-Publication Data
Names: Kent, Holly M., 1981- editor.
Title: Teaching fashion studies / edited by Holly Kent.
Description: London, UK ; New York, NY : Bloomsbury Academic, 2018. | Includes bibliographical references and index.
Identifiers: LCCN 2018009622 | ISBN 9781350022874 (hb) | ISBN 9781350022881 (pb) | ISBN 9781350022904 (eBook) | ISBN 9781350022898 (ePDF)
Subjects: LCSH: Fashion–Study and teaching. | Fashion–Research–Methodology.
Classification: LCC GT511 .T44 2018 | DDC 391.0071–dc23 LC record available at https://lccn.loc.gov/2018009622

ISBN: HB: 978-1-350-02287-4
PB: 978-1-350-02288-1
ePDF: 978-1-350-02289-8
eBook: 978-1-350-02290-4

Typeset by Integra Software Services Pvt. Ltd.

To find out more about our authors and books visit www.bloomsbury.com.
and sign up for our newsletters.

CONTENTS

List of Figures ix
Acknowledgments x

PART ONE INTRODUCING *TEACHING FASHION STUDIES* 1

Introduction: "Teaching Fashion Studies in an Interdisciplinary Context" 3
Holly M. Kent, University of Illinois-Springfield

PART TWO RESEARCH METHODS AND THEORIES IN FASHION STUDIES 7

1. Fashion Theory Review 9
   Alexandra van den Berg Christensen, Independent Scholar

2. Undergraduate Research in the Fashion Studies Classroom 17
   Sarah Wiggins, Bridgewater State University

3. Inspiration in the Past: Database Searches to Build Fashion History Knowledge 25
   Sara Marcketti, Jennifer Farley Gordon, and Charity Calvin Armstead, Iowa State University

PART THREE FASHION FORECASTING AND TREND PREDICTION 31

4. Trend Forecasting, Taste and Fashion Production 33
   Jay McCauley Bowstead, London College of Fashion and Lili Golmohammadi, Goldsmiths, University of London

5. Fashion Forecasting: Critical Thinking and Analyses for Trends 43
   Alyssa Dana Adomaitis, The New York City College of Technology, City University of New York

6 Identifying Apparel and Accessory Trends 53
Katherine Schaefer, Columbia College Chicago

PART FOUR FASHION MERCHANDISING, MANAGEMENT, AND MARKETING 59

7 The Fashion Formula: A Product Development Project 61
Michele Granger, Missouri State University

8 The Importance of Understanding the Market Value of Historical Costume 69
Patricia Dillon, New York University and Putnam Art Advisors & Consultants

9 Retail Anthropology 77
Shipra Gupta, University of Illinois-Springfield

10 Fashioning a Successful Business 83
Michele Granger, Missouri State University

PART FIVE CONSTRUCTION-, DESIGN-, AND OBJECT-BASED PROJECTS 93

11 The Slow Approach to Seeing 95
Ingrid Mida, Ryerson University

12 Object Analysis and Adaptation for the Current Fashion Market 103
Diane Maglio, Berkeley College

13 Understanding Fashionable Figures Via Paper Corset Models 113
Alexandra van den Berg Christensen, Independent Scholar

14 Overcoming the Challenges of Distance Learning in Historical Costume Studies 123
Patricia Dillon, New York University and Putnam Art Advisors & Consultants

15 *Project Runway*: Second-Hand Clothing Challenge 131
Anna Green, Michigan State University

16 Developing Construction and Design Skills Through Application of Science, Technology, Engineering, and Math (STEM) 141
Jody Aultman and Sara Marcketti, Iowa State University

17 Exercises in Critiquing Fashion's Classic Styles in the Design Studio 149
Alice Payne and Kiara Bulley, Queensland University of Technology

PART SIX DIVERSITY AND IDENTITY 157

18 Intersectionality Map Assignment 159
Anya Kurennaya, Parsons School of Design

19 Analyzing Representations of Feminist Aesthetics in Print Media 167
Elizabeth Stigler, University of Kansas

20 The "Vintage Black Glamour" Showcase: Developing Media Literacy and Cultural Competency 175
Mel Michelle Lewis, Saint Mary's College of California

21 Discussing Difference in Students' Fashion Blogs 183
Holly M. Kent, University of Illinois-Springfield

PART SEVEN ETHICS AND SUSTAINABILITY 191

22 Weighing Up Sustainable Fashion 193
Alice Payne, Queensland University of Technology

23 Thinking About Cultural Appropriation and Indigenous Fashion 201
Amanda Sikarskie, University of Michigan-Dearborn

24 A Systemic Analysis of the Ethics of Fast Fashion Consumerism and a Call to Sustainability 209
June-Ann Greeley, Sacred Heart University

PART EIGHT EMBODIMENT AND DAILY FASHION PRACTICES 219

25 An Exercise in Reflecting on Daily Dress Practices 221
Anya Kurennaya, Parsons School of Design

26 Experiencing the Clothed Body in Public Space 229
Laura Snelgrove, Parsons School of Design

27 Fashioning Dress from the Rag Trade to the Runway 237
Eileen Boris, University of California, Santa Barbara

PART NINE HISTORY AND LITERATURE 247

28 Making Models to Understand Ancient Greek Historic Costume 249
Diana Saiki, Ball State University

29 Putting the "I" in Iconography: Projects on Queen Elizabeth I's Royal Image 257
Catherine Howey Stearn, Eastern Kentucky University

30 Analyzing the Social Functions of Dress in Different Historical Eras 265
Amber M. Chatelain, Eastern Kentucky University

31 Costume in Historical Context 273
Catherine Bradley, McGill University

32 Culture and Clothes in Premodern Literature 283
Patricia Lennox, Gallatin School, New York University

Discipline Guide 291
Author Biographies 293
Index 297

LIST OF FIGURES

11.1 Pink and gold changeable silk cape with black satin and chiffon ties. Ryerson Fashion Research Collection FRC2014.07.158, gift of the Suddon-Cleaver Collection 98

11.2 Pencil drawing of cape (Ryerson FRC2014.07.158) with continuous line by Ingrid Mida, 2017 99

11.3 Pencil drawing of cape (Ryerson FRC2014.07.158) with nondominant hand by Ingrid Mida, 2017 100

13.1 Paper model of late 1880s corset, constructed by students in the author's Fashion History class 118

13.2 Paper model of late 1820s corset, constructed by students in the author's Fashion History class 118

16.1 Jody Aultman one-fourth design of Reflected Symmetry, 2011. Photo courtesy of author's private design collection 146

16.2 Jody Aultman reflected design of Reflected Symmetry, 2011. Photo courtesy of author's private design collection 146

18.1 Susan Kaiser's model of intersectionality among subject positions 165

22.1 Example of brand garment cards to hand out (image: Alice Payne) 196

ACKNOWLEDGMENTS

It is something of a truism for editors to open their acknowledgments by noting that, if they were to thank every person who made their book possible, that list of thank-yous would be a book-length manuscript in its own right. That is certainly the case for *Teaching Fashion Studies*, a book which is possible only because of the hard work of many people—each and every one of whom I am very grateful to, and for.

This book quite literally could not exist without the remarkable scholars and educators who contributed their chapters (and many hours) to the project. The work they've done here, and that they do in their classrooms, is vital to the field of fashion studies, and I am honored they choose to be part of this volume. Many thanks are also due to the entire team at Bloomsbury Publishing. I am very grateful for all of the time, care, and attention which Frances Arnold, Hannah Crump, Georgia Kennedy, and Pari Thomson gave to the project through all of its different stages, the copy editors who read the manuscript with such discerning and meticulous eyes, and the anonymous readers who offered such valuable feedback.

At my home institution of the University of Illinois-Springfield (UIS), I greatly benefited from receiving a course release during the 2015–2016 year to work on this project. My colleague Michael Murphy spent more hours than I know he could readily spare talking me through the many complexities and joys of assembling an edited collection. I have also had the great privilege of teaching my course on US fashion history several times in my career at UIS, and all of my students pushed me to think in new ways about what fashion means, and how we as educators can teach it most effectively (as well as just consistently being delights to talk with, and to learn from).

As *Teaching Fashion Studies* took shape, I also greatly benefited from presenting on fashion studies pedagogy at the conferences of the American Historical Association, the Costume Society of America, the National Women's Studies Association, the Rural Women's Studies Association, and the Seneca Falls Dialogues. The insights of my copanelists and our audiences at these conferences were invaluable in helping to develop this book and its conversations about teaching fashion in interdisciplinary classrooms.

And last but certainly not the least, I am very grateful to the people in my life who helped, supported, and encouraged me as *Teaching Fashion Studies* made its way from idea to book. Meagan Cass, Christianne Gadd, and Shannon O'Brien, especially, listened to me talk about book things more than any person should reasonably be expected to listen to anyone talk about anything, and Nancy Kent and Douglas Kent deserve particular thanks for always encouraging me to pursue—and to wear—what I loved.

PART ONE
INTRODUCING *TEACHING FASHION STUDIES*

INTRODUCTION: "TEACHING FASHION STUDIES IN AN INTERDISCIPLINARY CONTEXT"

Holly M. Kent, University of Illinois-Springfield

Like many parts of culture that have traditionally been associated with female-identified and LGBTQ people, fashion has a long history of being dismissed as trivial, frivolous, and unworthy of serious consideration or study. Since fashion is inevitably tied to the body, ideals of beauty, and practices of self-adornment, it has also frequently been coded as shallow and insubstantial—as a silly diversion, rather than as a significant indicator (and an important creator) of the mores, ideals, and cultural practices of a particular time and place. While the teaching of fashion, dress, and style has made significant inroads into the academy in recent years, fashion studies has nonetheless not yet been fully incorporated into many college and university classrooms.[1] *Teaching Fashion Studies* addresses itself to instructors involved in this work, providing them with exercises, assignments, and approaches to bringing fashion studies into courses based in a range of different disciplines. Learning about fashion, dress, and style, as the chapters in this book demonstrate, offers students invaluable opportunities to connect the theoretical with their daily lives and experiences, to consider complex ethical issues and questions, and to learn how to effectively conduct independent research.

This book is centered on several key approaches to, and themes within, the teaching of fashion studies: interdisciplinarity, diversity, and a commitment to engaging students with many different learning styles. As pedagogical theory and studies have long demonstrated, there is not one ideal, set way for individuals to learn. Traditional educational models (which involve students in passively listening to an authoritative, seemingly-all-knowing instructor) are frequently not effective in energizing students to actively participate in their classrooms, in making students feel inspired to learn more about course topics, or in enabling students to see the relevance and importance of course material to their own lives and experiences.[2] Each of the exercises in this book draws on a range of learning styles (visual, aural, verbal, and kinesthetic), to enable different students to approach fashion studies in ways productive for them. These assignments also encourage students to develop their creativity and to bring their distinctive perspectives and abilities into the classroom, empowering them to more fully, richly enter into course subject matter.

The other core principles at the center of this book are interdisciplinarity and diversity. Within the academy, disciplinary boundaries are often as limiting as they are clarifying, drawing artificial divisions between fields of study that are, in reality, profoundly interconnected.[3] A fundamentally interdisciplinary field, fashion studies has many distinct, but interrelated, subfields—in design; business; history; sociology; and women, gender, and sexuality studies (to name but a few)—which frequently coexist side by side, but separately. This book is structured to encourage new approaches to interdisciplinary teaching, divided into sections that offer multiple perspectives on teaching specific themes in fashion studies. In addition, each chapter contains thoughts and suggestions about how its assignment could be used in a range of classrooms in different disciplines. While exercises in construction, for example, might most commonly be associated with fashion design courses, it is also of great value for fashion history students to actively reflect on the concrete realities of how garments are created. While assignments centered on ethical questions about cultural appropriation in fashion might most frequently be associated with ethnic studies or sociology courses, fashion design students also benefit from reflecting on how this complex topic will impact their future work as designers. *Teaching Fashion Studies* aims to increase these kinds of interdisciplinary conversations, in a wide array of different courses.

And finally, diversity is a central concern of the exercises in this book. Stereotypically associated with wealthy, Western, cisgendered, thin, female-identified people, fashion, dress, and style impact the lives of (and are themselves fundamentally transformed by) people of all different races, ethnicities, nationalities, genders, and sexualities.[4] Considering how the fashion system undermines and upholds existing hierarchies is a key consideration of *Teaching Fashion Studies*. This book's exercises help students to reflect on how different individuals and groups experience dress in their daily lives, how the fashion economy impacts those who participate and labor in it, and the potential that a global fashion media has to reaffirm (as well as to destabilize) existing ideals about beauty and the body. Considering how diverse individuals and groups interact with, shape, and are impacted by fashion culture facilitates students' ability to analyze complex questions about how personal, regional, national, and global identities and systems are created and challenged.

Much like fashion itself, approaches to teaching fashion studies are ever evolving. In an increasingly global, interconnected world, which is constantly changing along cultural, economic, political, and technological lines, new questions consistently arise for instructors working in fashion studies, about how to have their students engage in complex reflections on the many different meanings of fashion in the contemporary world. The exercises and assignments contained in this book thus constitute not a final, definitive word about how to teach and study fashion, but rather the beginning of an ongoing, ever-enriching conversation about how classrooms can be productive spaces for learning about the complicated roles that fashion plays in the lives of nations, cultures, and individuals.

Notes

1. For recent examples of how fashion studies and fashion studies research have become a more significant, sustained presence within the academy, please see Yuniya Kawamura, *Doing Research in Fashion and Dress: An Introduction to Qualitative Methods* (New York: Bloomsbury Academic, 2011); and Ingrid Mida and Alexandra Kim, *The Dress Detective: A Practical Guide to Object-Based Research in Fashion* (New York: Bloomsbury Press, 2015).
2. For reflections on the value of more diverse, active pedagogies in the classroom, see Alice Y. Kolb and David A. Kolb, "Learning Styles and Learning Spaces: Enhancing Experiential Learning in Higher Education," *Academy of Management Learning & Higher Education* 42 (June 2005): 193–212; Maureen J. Lage, Glenn J. Platt, and Michael Treglia, "Inverting the Classroom: A Gateway to Creating an Inclusive Learning Environment," *The Journal of Economic Education* 31, no. 1 (Winter 2000): 30–43.
3. For more on broader reflections on the value, and the challenges, of interdisciplinary teaching, please see Rebecca S. Nowacek, "Why Is Being Interdisciplinary So Very Hard to Do?: Thoughts on the Perils and Promise of Interdisciplinary Pedagogy," *College Composition and Communication* 60, no. 3 (February 2009): 493–516; and Charlotte Woods, "Researching and Developing Interdisciplinary Teaching: Towards a Conceptual Framework for Classroom Communication," *Higher Education* 54, no. 6 (December 2007): 853–866.
4. For overall reflections on the importance of bringing multiple forms of diversity into classrooms and pedagogical approaches, please see Beverly M. John, "The Politics of Pedagogy," *Teaching Sociology* 31, no. 4 (October 2003): 375–382; and Rosa Hernández Sheets, *Diversity Pedagogy: Examining the Role of Culture in the Teaching-Learning Process* (New York: Pearson, 2004).

Bibliography

John, Beverly M. "The Politics of Pedagogy." *Teaching Sociology* 31, no. 4 (October 2003): 375–382.

Kawamura, Yuniya. *Doing Research in Fashion and Dress: An Introduction to Qualitative Methods*. New York: Bloomsbury Academic, 2011.

Kolb, Alice Y., and David A. Kolb. "Learning Styles and Learning Spaces: Enhancing Experiential Learning in Higher Education." *Academy of Management Learning & Higher Education* 42 (June 2005): 193–212.

Lage, Maureen J., Glenn J. Platt, and Michael Treglia. "Inverting the Classroom: A Gateway to Creating an Inclusive Learning Environment." *The Journal of Economic Education* 31, no. 1 (Winter 2000): 30–43.

Mida, Ingrid, and Alexandra Kim. *The Dress Detective: A Practical Guide to Object-Based Research in Fashion*. New York: Bloomsbury Press, 2015.

Nowacek, Rebecca S. "Why Is Being Interdisciplinary So Very Hard to Do?: Thoughts on the Perils and Promise of Interdisciplinary Pedagogy." *College Composition and Communication* 60, no. 3 (February 2009): 493–516.

Sheets, Rosa Hernández. *Diversity Pedagogy: Examining the Role of Culture in the Teaching-Learning Process*. New York: Pearson, 2004.

Woods, Charlotte. "Researching and Developing Interdisciplinary Teaching: Towards a Conceptual Framework for Classroom Communication." *Higher Education* 54, no. 6 (December 2007): 853–866.

PART TWO

RESEARCH METHODS AND THEORIES IN FASHION STUDIES

Introduction

Fashion studies is a fundamentally diverse, interdisciplinary field, comprised of educators from a wide range of different theoretical backgrounds, who utilize multiple methodological approaches in their teaching work. As varied as fashion studies educators' academic training and specific fields of scholarly expertise are, there are nonetheless key approaches, perspectives, and ideas valuable for all fashion studies students (regardless of their disciplinary focus) to be exposed to. This section offers educators guidance about how to effectively introduce students to central ideas in fashion studies theory and practice. The chapters in these sections provide examples of how educators can help students analyze core concepts in fashion studies theory and develop the skills fashion studies scholars require to effectively conduct independent research.

In her chapter, Alexandra van den Berg Christensen discusses how to enable students to better understand the significance of several key theorists, from a range of different eras, disciplines, and intellectual perspectives, for the fashion studies field. Christensen's exercise demonstrates how to have students undertake close readings of theorists such as Herbert Blumer, Georg Simmel, Thorsten Veblen, and Agnes Brooks Young, and define and analyze concepts including collective taste, conspicuous consumption, and fashion cycles. Having students engage in careful analyses of these scholars and concepts helps students consider larger questions about the origins and dissemination of fashion trends and the importance of gender and class in fashion culture and dress studies.

Sarah Wiggins's chapter provides a valuable model of how fashion studies educators can help students develop the skills and confidence required to effectively undertake independent research projects in the field. Wiggins details the different steps involved in students' process of developing original research, including locating a mentor, assessing primary and secondary sources, crafting effective research questions, productively giving and receiving feedback, writing, editing, and creating scholarly presentations. Mastering these varied skillsets enable students develop as active learners, and as knowledge creators in fashion studies.

In their chapter, Sara Marcketti, Jennifer Gordon, and Charity Calvin Armstead consider how to help students better understand the connections between historic and contemporary fashions. A vital way for students to make these connections is by undertaking research into fashion-oriented academic databases, which feature a range of primary sources in fashion history. Marcketti, Gordon, and Calvin's work discusses how to teach students how to most effectively locate and reflect on primary sources in historic fashion and how to draw on a rich range of online resources available in doing so. All of this section's chapters provide dynamic models of how fashion studies scholars across disciplines can help students build their skills in independent research and put key concepts from fashion studies theory into practice.

1
FASHION THEORY REVIEW

Alexandra van den Berg Christensen,
Independent Scholar

Contextualization

A fashion history course should begin with a review of fashion theory. This establishes a foundation of scholarly thought to support subsequent learning and discussion, as well as laying out the techniques, theories, and methods useful in the field. It provides students with a working vocabulary and allows them to see where their own ideas fall in a broader intellectual landscape. Academic courses in history begin with historiography. Dissertations and theses require a review of relevant literature and methods. A class focusing on a specific field of history should be no different. The study of fashion is becoming more accepted as an academic endeavor, and we must find our historiographical and methodological roots in order to ensure sustained development in the field of fashion history.

Dress history has its own pedigree, although its recognition as a legitimate field of study is only a few decades old. Studies of clothing and fashion date from the fifteenth century, beginning with collections of illustrations depicting local and "foreign" people in their respective garb. By the late nineteenth century, these glossaries had been replaced by histories of individual garments and social science theories that attempted to define what fashion was and why it existed. "La mode" had been considered a feminine frivolity at best and the root of myriad social ills at worst, but by the mid-twentieth century, society began to value clothing as an admirable form of self-expression, and by the end of that century and the beginning of the next, its study was likewise validated as an important tool for studying societies and people.

This process of legitimization coincided with the rise of several intellectual trends in the study of history as a whole: social history, which deepens the study of history to include the social and cultural trends evolving alongside the traditional timeline of kings and wars; microhistory, which narrows the focus of research onto individual moments and figures; and global history, which connects the stories of nations to reveal a vast network of interdependencies. Dress history has proven itself to be a versatile field with wide-ranging applications in each of these genres. The study of fashion sheds light on understudied and otherwise invisible populations, hints at the corporeality and the daily life of individuals, and connects the cultures of the world through interlocking consumption patterns and the common pursuit of novelty. There is no better time for historians to unpack the meanings and methods behind the clothing people wore and the changing flux of fashion.

Beyond the purely descriptive study of clothing, there are two fundamental questions to be asked about the nature of fashion. First, what *is* fashion? Second, why and how does it continually change? The ideas and debates surrounding these questions are excellent starting points in a class considering its history or its influence on culture.

Fashion is more than simply the wearing of garments (though the word is often appropriated to describe just that). Scholars have defined it as a system of change in clothing that is, in concise terms, rapid, socially motivated, and inspired by the "other." This explanation of the fashion system is juxtaposed with another type of vestimentary system, often called the "customary" or "hierarchical" system in which clothing styles, changing only slowly, are prescribed from above according to one's rank or class. Applying these starkly opposing definitions has proved problematic, not least because the fashion system, so described, is rather Eurocentric. As Beverly Lemire and Giorgio Reillo lamented: "Global history has not yet tackled the issue of fashion, and it is regrettable that prominent theorists of fashion's evolution still claim it was an exclusively western development, western in origins, in its evolution" (Lemire and Reillo, 2008: 887). Furthermore, this definition of fashion has led historians to claim wildly different eras for fashion's initial emergence. Depending on the writer, fashion came into being during the Victorian era, with the Industrial Revolution, at the end of the French Revolution, or with the birth of the Renaissance.

Recent scholarship has challenged the long-held belief that fashion is inherently Western and recent. Antonia Finnane asserts that "Europe's historical experience of fashion should not be allowed to negate China's," and her book, *Changing Clothes in China*, paves the way for a study of global fashion history on its own terms (Finnane, 2008: 15). Odile Blanc, applying the cultural requirements for a fashion system to her era of expertise, argues that the experience of the Crusades and the resulting cultural exchange initiated a European fashion system in the eleventh century (Blanc, 2002: 157–172). These new analyses suggest that as more evidence of historical consumption patterns from different eras and areas is uncovered, fashion might be found growing alongside. Students of the history of dress should be familiar with the definition of the fashion phenomenon in order to recognize it whenever and whenever it appears.

The mechanics of fashion have likewise been explained and reexplained by numerous theorists. Sociological, economic, psychoanalytic, and quantitative analyses all attempt to explain the mysteries of la mode. What makes people discard (and even begin to loathe) a recently beloved style in favor of something new? Does fashion evolve toward something? Is it cyclical or random? Is fashion the impulse of society, the result of creative genius, or merely another manifestation of the pendulum swings history seems subject to? Do fashions work their way down from the rich and powerful to the lower classes or vice versa? Is fashion devised by one authoritative personality or collectively agreed upon? These questions give depth to the study of clothing, linking the simple *what* to a complex and fascinating web of *why*s. The exercise outlined in this chapter aims to expose students to a few of these fashion theories. By reviewing and analyzing many different explanatory articles, students will learn relevant vocabulary, practice critical thinking, and build a theoretical basis for understanding the fashion system.

The format is an article review writing assignment paired with in-class presentations and discussion. I chose four articles from the late nineteenth to the mid-twentieth century for my students to read, write about, and discuss. They each expound different theories about the mechanics of the fashion system. These writings are interesting not only as examples of varied ideas but also as primary documents—artifacts from different time periods and intellectual standpoints. Georg Simmel plays the part of distant ethnographer and gives a very misogynist, classist analysis of changes in fashion. Thorsten Veblen is an economist looking at the desire for prestige through money and goods as the engine that drives change in fashion. Agnes Young is a historian who argues that fashion change is an autonomous cycle of thirty-year phases, uninfluenced by historical events. Hebert Blumer looks through the lens of twentieth-century fashion production, and concludes that successful fashion is the winning interpretation of a culture's communal yearning for the future.

These are, of course, not the only important writings on fashion theory during these time periods. Instructors can feel free to swap out or add articles that they consider more or additionally valuable to their specific curriculum. One variation might be to focus on the definition of fashion, rather than its process. Instructors could assign articles that attempt to apply the definition of fashion to a particular time and place. Suggested works by A.L. Kroeber, J.C. Fluegel, Quentin Bell, and Rene Koenig are found in the bibliography. Case studies such as these will show how controversial it has been to pinpoint a so-called "birth of fashion" and will require students to think carefully about the variety of circumstances in which fashion might flourish or falter. Ultimately, this exercise will work with any set of articles that present a range of views and ideas.

The study of fashion would be a purely aesthetic exercise without an understanding of the social, economic, and cultural influences at play. This assignment asks students to study, analyze, and then explain several key theories that will provide them with the fundamental vocabulary, arguments, and perspectives necessary to begin looking critically at the history of clothing. The combination of individual study and team teaching helps cement this learning.

Appropriate courses and course levels for the assignment: Fashion history courses (in either national or global contexts); women, gender, and sexuality studies courses; history of consumption and trade courses; fashion industry courses.

Appropriate class size: This exercise has been effective in a class of twenty to twenty-five students, with five or six of them studying each of the four articles outlined in this exercise, but it can be adapted easily to other circumstances, such as a large lecture with smaller discussion sections or even to an online course.

Estimated time required: The take-home assignment can be completed in a week. The in-class portion will take about forty-five to sixty-five minutes, with ten minutes for in-group discussion, five to ten minutes per group presentation, and fifteen minutes of class discussion time at the end.

Required materials: The instructor must provide students with a digital or hard copy of the articles to be read and the assignment handout. Students will need to be able to type out and print or email their reviews to the instructor. Space for breakout groups and a whiteboard, blackboard, or other surface to write on in the classroom will facilitate presentations and discussion.

Learning goals

- How to write an article review for a theoretical text.
- Explore different theories of why and how fashion exists in society.
- Understand the paradigms that influenced key theories of fashion as well as our own theories and ideas about fashion culture.
- Expand vocabulary for talking about fashion and its changes, cycles, and influences.

Assessment

Two types of assessment are built into this assignment. The written article review will be handed in and graded by the instructor for analytical content. The group presentation will be assessed through peer comprehension. Because one of the purposes of the presentation is to teach classmates about the theories they did not study, successful presentations will result in the class as a whole being able to describe the four theories and discuss them comparatively. The instructor may wish to offer students a formal grade for the presentations, based on this outcome.

Guidelines for instructors

I have used this as the first assignment of the semester and found it very effective. Divide the class into four groups (or another number equal to the number of articles chosen for review). Hand out the readings (giving every student within a group the same article) and the assignment worksheet. Before looking at the articles, lead the class in a group brainstorm about the definition of fashion or the reasons fashions change. Instructors may wish to use some of the questions from the assignment worksheet to guide this brainstorm, but should invite answers based on the experiences and opinions of the students. The readings are approachable enough for students to analyze without prerequisites, especially if they have already begun thinking about the question of fashion from their own perspectives.

Introduce each article, and explain the assignment. Make sure students know how to write an article review. If this type of writing is new to them, take the time to explain the purpose and content of such an essay. The most common mistake is that the student merely summarizes the article rather than analyzing it, so the assignment worksheet includes a list of questions for students to ponder as they read, helping them ask more challenging questions of the texts. It should be emphasized to the students at the beginning of the assignment that critical thinking and analysis are the primary focus of a review and should take up the bulk of the writing. I have typically asked my students to write briefly (about three pages), but adapt the assignment to the skill level and learning goals of your class (i.e., assigning a longer review in a writing-heavy course).

Once the written part of the assignment has been completed by the class, it is time for the in-class element. Begin by drawing a table on the board with a row for each article and columns for the following themes:

Who is the author?	Fashion is …	Why	How	Who	What do you think?
Simmel-					
Veblen-					
Young-					
Blumer-					

The column headings refer to the questions from the fashion review worksheet, briefly outlined here:

1. Who is the author? Provide information about the time frame and background of the author.
2. Fashion is … How does the author define fashion?
3. Why does fashion exist? Why does it continually change?
4. How does fashion change; that is, what is the mechanism?
5. Who is fashionable? Who directs fashion change? Who participates in fashion and how?
6. What do you think? What aspects of the author's argument do you agree with or disagree with and why?

Separate the class into the four article groups, and give them ten minutes to compare notes and organize themselves to present their findings to the class. The presentations should touch on each of the topics written on the board, and the students should fill in the table with information as they discuss each point. As each group presents its findings, encourage questions from the rest of the class and draw attention to useful phrases and vocabulary. Once the groups are finished, lead the class in a summary discussion, drawing out observations about the differences and similarities between the four theories. By the end of this exercise, the entire class should have a general understanding of the main theses and key points of each of the essays.

Copy of the assignment

Fashion theory review paper—due on _____

- Blumer, Hebert, "Fashion: From Class Differentiation to Collective Selection," pp. 275–291.
- Simmel, Georg, "Fashion," pp. 541–552. (Stop at "not completely enslaved within.")
- Veblen, Thorsten, "Dress as an Expression of Pecuniary Culture," pp. 118–131
- Young, Agnes Brooks, "Chapter VIII: The Second Tubular Cycle," pp. 21–27, 115–133.

Read your assigned fashion theory article. Write a three-page review/response of the article. Your paper should be composed of a brief summary of the author's key points, followed by your analysis of and response to the author's arguments. I suggest summarizing for a page and analyzing for two pages.

The following are some questions to consider. Don't feel obligated to answer each question directly, but let them guide you as you read and respond.

1. Who is the author? When was the article written? What is the author's background? What assumptions does the author rest his/her argument on?
2. How does the author define fashion? Is fashion a positive or a negative thing to this author? What makes you think so?
3. Why does fashion exist? Why does it continually change? What is the cause of its evolution?
4. How does the fashion change? What is the mechanism of change?
5. Who is fashionable? Who is responsible for fashion change? Who participates in fashion and how?
6. What do you think about this theory? Does it make sense? Why or why not? What aspects of the author's argument do you agree with or disagree with and why? How do you or do you not see this theory playing out in modern sartorial habits?

Final thought: How do you think this theory will help us in our studies in the coming semester?

Formatting guidelines

Three pages
Times New Roman, twelve-point font
Double spaced
One-inch margins

Student name and title of article in top left corner
No bibliography necessary
Refrain from the use of personal pronouns

Typical results and reflections on the assignment

- Students are generally good at summarizing the articles in their papers and to their peers, and even though summary is not the focus of the assignment, a solid understanding of the main ideas of each of the four theories is extremely beneficial. Group presentations help to define key phrases and new terms in fashion theory, such as "conspicuous consumption," "fashion cycle," and "collective taste," and this new vocabulary is very useful for students to draw upon for the remainder of the course.
- In their written analysis, students often note that many aspects of each of these theories ring true to their own experiences. Even the more outdated essays, such as those of Veblen and Simmel, include familiar elements. Finding these similarities helps students connect to the past on a personal level, adding insight to their study of different historical paradigms.
- Throughout the rest of the course, students were asked to test the theories by applying them to different circumstances as we studied them. I often found opportunity to ask questions such as "Do you think Young's fashion theory would apply here, or do you see evidence of historical determinism?" These types of questions started profitable discussions about the processes involved in the fashion we were studying.
- Some of the most satisfying moments came when students critically discussed their own paradigms in class discussion, putting their thought processes on the table for observation. This assignment can be a starting point for additional analysis, allowing students to develop their own theories and paradigms of fashion theory.
- It appears to be a common belief that modern fashion is somehow free of the social constraints that our predecessors labored under. A good discussion of these fashion theories helps to place our fashion paradigms of today in the context of paradigms from past eras; and with this perspective, it is harder for students to claim immunity to social influence when it comes to their own fashion choices and decisions.

Bibliography

Bell, Quentin. *On Human Finery*. New York: Schocken Books, 1976.
Blanc, Odile. "From Battlefield to Court: The Invention of Fashion in the Fourteenth Century." In *Encountering Medieval Textiles and Dress*, edited by Desiree Koslin and Janet Snyder, 157–172. New York: Palgrave Macmillan, 2002.

Blumer, Hebert. "Fashion: From Class Differentiation to Collective Selection." *The Sociological Quarterly* 10, no. 3 (Summer 1969): 275–291.

Finnane, Antonia. *Changing Clothes in China: Fashion, History, Nation*. New York: Columbia University Press, 2008.

Fluegel, J.C. *The Psychology of Clothes*. London: Hogarth Press, 1950.

Heller, Sarah-Grace. "Introduction." In *Fashion in Medieval France*, Rochester, NY: D.S. Brewer, 2007.

Koenig, Rene. *A La Mode: On the Social Psychology of Fashion*. Trans. F. Bradley. New York: The Seabury Press, 1973.

Kroeber, A.L. "On the Principle of Order in Civilization as Exemplified by Changes of Fashion." *American Anthropologist* 21, no. 3 (July–September, 1919): 235–263.

Lemire, Beverly, and Giorgio Reillo. "East & West: Textiles and Fashion in Early Modern Europe." *Journal of Social History* 41, no. 4 (Summer 2008): 887–916.

Simmel, Georg, "Fashion." *American Journal Sociology* 62, no. 6 (May 1957): 541–558.

Taylor, Lou. *Establishing Dress History*. Manchester: Manchester University Press, 2004.

Taylor, Lou. *The Study of Dress History*. Manchester: Manchester University Press, 2002.

Veblen, Thorsten. "Dress as an Expression of the Pecuniary Culture." In *The Theory of the Leisure Class*, 118–130. New York: New Modern Library, 1953.

Young, Agnes Brooks. *Recurring Cycles of Fashion, 1760–1937*. New York: Harper & Row, 1937.

2
UNDERGRADUATE RESEARCH IN THE FASHION STUDIES CLASSROOM

Sarah Wiggins, Bridgewater State University

Contextualization

The following assignment, an undergraduate research project, was featured in an honors second-year seminar on the history of fashion. It introduces undergraduate students to the study of the history of fashion as an academic discipline and demonstrates that the field is engaging, creative, and intellectual. Students became active learners by conducting independent research on a fashion topic of their choosing, writing an essay, and delivering a public presentation. The course aims to reveal how clothing shaped the lives of individuals and communities in the past, and students investigate this concept collectively in class and independently as researchers. By conducting research, students further understand how scholars approach the history of fashion. Students pose their own questions and build expertise on the design and function of garments, past and present.

The assignment, which incorporates the entire length of the course, provides an opportunity for students to apply basic research skills to the field of fashion studies. By undertaking this assignment, students can address questions such as: how do I choose a research topic related to clothing? How do I work with a mentor and engage in productive conversation on interpreting fashion? Where do I find proper primary and secondary sources related to fashion studies? How do I construct an argument and integrate sources? These questions are approached through class discussion, peer review, and faculty guidance. The instructor mentors the students outside of the classroom, thus taking extra time to encourage students to look at fashion in an innovative manner by emphasizing in greater detail how a particular topic has been approached by researchers and encourage the students to think of new avenues of interpretation. Students receive feedback on their writing from their peers and the instructor. Student peer review initiates informal discussion among peers on the fashion topics that each individual is pursuing, allowing students to teach each other. By the end of the project, students have a better understanding of the field of fashion studies and how scholarship is produced and disseminated.

This assignment design draws from the insights of teacher-scholars, such as Katherine Gottschalk's and Keith Hjortshoj's *The Elements of Teaching Writing* and John C. Bean's *Engaging Ideas.* Gottschalk and Hjortshoj offer a chapter on designing a research assignment that explains how to structure the project with an emphasis on proposals, drafts, peer reviews, presentations, and instructor feedback, including individual meetings.[1] Bean also offers advice on scaffolding a research project and conducting peer review.[2] While these texts assist in general assignment design techniques, a research project based on the history of fashion provides its own unique challenges for students. As Karen Harvey has noted, the study of material culture opens up a visual field of object enquiry for historians who generally analyze textual sources.[3] Fashion research therefore challenges students to consider looking at objects from the past and "reading" them. It is a worthwhile endeavor for undergraduate students who may have limited education in the visual arts.

The history of fashion covers a range of avenues for consideration, including thinking about design throughout the decades; production and dissemination of clothing and textiles; legacies of individual designers; and gendering of objects, body image, class, sexuality, and politics. Students delve into these topics throughout the semester and examine the development and recycling of fashion over time. Although traditional in its approach, conducting research allows students to study the subject of fashion with greater depth over a sustained period of time. The secondary sources on a topic provide additional reading material for the student and introduce theories in the field while visual primary sources encourage students to inspect clothing thoughtfully. With one garment, a student can evaluate an object and the historical forces behind it, learning the interconnected elements of fashion.

Appropriate courses and course levels for the assignment: This assignment was conducted in an undergraduate honors history course, but it can be applied to any course where the instructor wants students to develop basic research skills. Fashion studies is an interdisciplinary field, and the assignment can be modified for any specific discipline. The level appropriate for this exercise extends from sophomore to senior students.

Appropriate class size: This assignment suits a class with ten to fifteen students. A class that exceeds that number would be difficult to manage due to the time needed for mentorship outside of the classroom.

Estimated time required: The assignment runs the length of the semester and includes time inside and outside of the classroom.

Required materials: The use of online databases for items such as journal articles and visual primary sources, including paintings, photographs, and museum objects, through an institution's library remains important. Access to an archive or museum exhibits on clothing and textiles is not required but ideal.

Learning goals

- Learning to analyze primary sources related to clothing, visual and textual.
- Learning to read and interpret theories from secondary reading material on the history of fashion.
- Creating a better understanding of fashion history through reading multiple academic sources.
- Improving writing through editing and revising essays with peer review.
- Enhancing speaking skills with delivering a public presentation and articulating the language and ideas related to fashion studies.
- Building a research relationship with a faculty mentor and sharing ideas about the field.

Assessment

Students will be evaluated on their ability to identify and analyze appropriate primary and secondary sources. Student writers should demonstrate that a visual source, such as a photograph, originates from and illustrates the clothing of a specific time period while being able to comment on this source descriptively and analytically. Primary sources should be integrated with academic secondary sources, especially peer-reviewed journal articles and monographs, and students should display a grasp of the historical narrative of fashion history and the specific debates that surround their specialized topic. Students therefore need to demonstrate that they can think critically and broadly about fashion, and the content should reveal an understanding of the subject and an ability to engage in visual interpretation of clothing and recognition of design within historical context. To ensure that students learn that research and writing is a process that requires frequent revision and feedback, students are assessed on participation in peer review and mentor meetings. The public presentation should be cohesive and relatable to the audience, with appropriate visual cues that illustrate the clothing and the period of time that it represented. Through speaking skills that incorporate eye contact, volume, and pace, the student should be able to verbally deconstruct the historical significance of fashion and lead discussion on the subject.

Guidelines for instructors

The assignment is a semester-long project culminating in a fifteen-page essay. The research and writing is scaffolded to allow the student to maintain an organized schedule. The student first brings to class an abstract describing the fashion topic along with a bibliography so that sources can be identified early in the semester. The instructor needs to ensure that students can identify appropriate secondary sources and that primary sources in the form of photography, paintings, or museum objects provide examples of clothing that students can evaluate. Students then begin writing the essay in installments, and bring two copies of their rough draft to designated class sessions for peer review. One copy of the essay is for the peer review session, while the second copy is for the instructor. The students spend a portion of the class (depending on the length of the rough draft) engaged in reading and giving feedback on another student's rough draft. The instructor will need to prepare guiding questions for peer review, so that students can understand what to recognize while editing an essay. The instructor also reads the rough drafts and gives feedback to the students during the week following peer review to help prepare students for the next session. The student therefore develops skills over time on how to write about and interpret a primary source. Presentations can be delivered in class or outside of the classroom at an event.

The project can be organized on a weekly basis depending on the length of a given semester. The following example covers fourteen weeks:

- Week 2 or 3: Meet with mentor to discuss research topic
- Week 4: Students submit topic abstract and bibliography
- Week 5: Meet with mentor to discuss sources
- Week 6: Peer review session for essay introduction
- Week 7: Meet with mentor to discuss introduction and research progress
- Week 8: Peer review session for five pages of rough draft
- Week 9: Meet with mentor to discuss five pages of writing and research progress
- Week 10: Peer review session for ten pages of rough draft
- Week 11: Meet with mentor to discuss ten pages of writing and research progress
- Week 12: Peer review session for fifteen pages of rough draft
- Week 13: Meet with mentor to discuss fifteen pages of writing and final adjustments
- Week 14: Public presentation of research and submission of final essay

Discussion questions: For peer review, students can be given prompts for editing such as identifying the thesis, incorporating a literature review, integrating sources, paragraph and sentence structure, clarity, citation, and any additional item that the instructor wants to emphasize. The questions will be dependent upon the page length of the rough draft.

Cautionary advice for instructors

- The assignment schedule is demanding for both students and instructors. Anticipate some students not being able to attend every mentor meeting during your office hours due to other responsibilities. Communication through email may serve as an alternative, although a face-to-face meeting and discussion help the student to process academic material with the instructor.

- Students need to be coached on the importance of revision and the need to be critical in evaluating other students' work. Students should understand that delivering constructive criticism is helpful for their peers. Instructors can explain that one's own writing improves through editing others' work and that the world of professional academic publishing involves peer review. Students understand that they are modeling the academic community.

- Students require guidance on identifying proper primary and secondary sources. The internet can pose challenges with discerning quality material.

- Presenting one's research publicly can generate anxiety for students. It is helpful for the instructor to give tips on how one can try to combat fears attached to public speaking and answering questions from an audience. Mentorship involves coaching students on how to convert written research material into an oral presentation along with how to appropriately field audience questions.

- Research needs may require financial resources. Check to see if your institution supports undergraduate research through small grants to purchase books or other research materials or funds to travel to museums, archives, or conferences.

Copy of the assignment

Fashion research project

For this assignment, you will write a research essay relating to the history of fashion. You will select your own topic, and your essay will be based upon original research that you will conduct, using primary and secondary source materials. You will conduct this research throughout this entire semester and be required to submit components of your work as designated in the course schedule. You will submit a topic abstract and bibliography, and rough drafts for peer review. I will serve as your mentor throughout the semester, and you will meet with me on a regular basis to discuss your progress. In order to receive full credit for this assignment, you must turn in your work on the days listed in the schedule, participate in the peer review sessions, meet with me consistently, and deliver a presentation. Sources for research should feature at least two primary sources, including images such as paintings, photography, and images of museum objects, and four secondary sources in academic article or book format. The essay must be fifteen full pages in length, typed, and double-spaced and use Times New Roman font and twelve-point font size, and the pages must be numbered. Citations must be in footnote form and follow the *Chicago Manual of Style* guidelines.

You will present your research either in class or as part of a campuswide research symposium, as available. We will work on the elements of preparing a research presentation and how to speak on the topic of fashion during the semester and in your individual mentoring meetings with me.

Typical results and reflections on the assignment

- The majority of students were able to keep up with the demanding workload of this assignment and responded positively to the way that the essay is structured with peer review sessions. Students are intimidated with the project at the beginning of the semester, especially if they do not have a fashion background, but once they begin their work and build upon their writing in increments, their confidence grows.

- Although not all students proved sophisticated in their analysis of primary and secondary sources, they were still given a taste of how to read secondary texts and learn the narrative history of fashion as it is related to their topic. For primary sources, which were mostly visual, they learned to look at clothing more carefully and pay attention to the details of design and think more critically about historical concepts.

- The requirement for students to present their research to an audience proved effective. Students experienced a sense of accomplishment and increased confidence in facing the speaking hurdle and discussing fashion with a larger audience, thus providing greater legitimacy and reward for a semester's work.

- The most successful element of this assignment was mentorship. I believe that students' writing improved as a result of engaging in individual meetings. As an instructor, it was satisfying to get to know my students better so that I could attend to their academic needs and watch them grow intellectually. The time dedicated to meeting with individuals was not as overwhelming as expected because students visited during my office hours and the small class size made it manageable.

Notes

1   Katherine Gottschalk and Keith Hjortshoj, *The Elements of Teaching Writing: A Resource for Instructors in All Disciplines* (Boston: Bedford/St. Martin's Press, 2004), 104–120. For instruction on peer review, see 72–75.

2   John C. Bean, *Engaging Ideas: The Professor's Guide to Integrating Writing, Critical Thinking, and Active Learning in the Classroom* (San Francisco: Jossey-Bass, 2001), 212–213, 222–225. I am also indebted to my colleagues at Bridgewater State University for sharing their writing pedagogies. I would also like to thank the Bridgewater State University Office of Teaching and Learning for financial support related to this project and Holly M. Kent for her editorial guidance. A version of this chapter was presented at the 2016 Symposium: Fashion and the Body at the College of Design, University of Minnesota.

3   Karen Harvey, "Introduction: Practical Matters," in *History and Material Culture: A Student's Guide to Approaching Alternative Sources*, ed. Karen Harvey (London: Routledge, 2009), 1–23, especially 2–8.

Bibliography

Bean, John C. *Engaging Ideas: The Professor's Guide to Integrating Writing, Critical Thinking, and Active Learning in the Classroom*. San Francisco: Jossey-Bass, 2001.

Bedikian, Sonia A. "The Death of Mourning: From Victorian Crepe to the Little Black Dress." *Omega: Journal of Death & Dying* 57 (2008): 35–52. doi: 10.2190/OM.57.1.c.

Doan, Laura. "Passing Fashions: Reading Female Masculinities in the 1920s." *Feminist Studies* 24 (1998): 663–700.

Gottschalk, Katherine, and Keith Hjortshoj. *The Elements of Teaching Writing: A Resource for Instructors in All Disciplines*. Boston: Bedford/St. Martin's Press, 2004.

Harvey, Karen, ed. *History and Material Culture: A Student's Guide to Approaching Alternative Sources*. London: Routledge, 2009.

Laver, James. *Costume and Fashion: A Concise History*. 5th edn. New York: Thames and Hudson, 2012.

Nead, Lynda. "The Layering of Pleasure: Women, Fashionable Dress and Visual Culture in the Mid-Nineteenth Century." *Nineteenth-Century Contexts: An Interdisciplinary Journal* 35 (2013): 489–509. doi: 10/1080/08905495.2013.854978.

Richmond, Vivienne. *Clothing the Poor in Nineteenth-Century England*. Cambridge, UK: Cambridge University Press, 2013.

Weber, Caroline. *Queen of Fashion: What Marie Antoinette Wore to the Revolution*. New York: Picador, 2006.

3
INSPIRATION IN THE PAST: DATABASE SEARCHES TO BUILD FASHION HISTORY KNOWLEDGE

Sara Marcketti, Jennifer Farley Gordon, and Charity Calvin Armstead, Iowa State University

Contextualization

Contemporary designers and fashion industry professionals often draw inspiration for new fashion collections or marketing campaigns from historical sources. Deirdre Murphy notes that "Surviving historic garments and images which record what people have worn in the past provide an invaluable research resource for many fashion designers" (2011: para. 2). Many museums and collections offer research access to industry members and students, allowing them to study construction and stylistic details of vintage garments. However, it is rare for designers or students to have access to extant garments earlier than the eighteenth century. Surviving garments from the earliest periods of fashion history—that is, Ancient Egypt, Rome, and Greece—are nonexistent. Professors explain and illustrate these periods through other sources, such as artworks and written descriptions, but students may have difficulty in understanding the relevance of these seemingly distant periods to twentieth- and twenty-first-century fashion.

Fashion history courses, which often begin with the ancient periods, are a mainstay of most undergraduate textiles and apparel curricula (Frazier and Fulton, 2014). While many fashion history courses present the "facts" of the various periods including the technological, political, and artistic backgrounds of the different cultures and regions they consider, many instructors also seek to make the content more meaningful to their students (Marcketti, 2011). The students enrolled in fashion history courses often graduate to pursue merchandising and design-related careers, and the understanding of a wide variety of fashion history periods is paramount to their future success. As fashion professionals, they may be asked to translate, or at least to recognize, historical influences in contemporary fashion. Hae Jin Gam and Jennifer Banning (2012) note that, despite the mutual relevance of the two subjects, apparel design and fashion history are not always taught in an integrative manner. The following assignment allows students, within the context of a fashion history classroom, to engage with considerations of design adaptations.

Students are asked to locate and evaluate database articles about reinterpretations of the fashions of Ancient Egypt, Rome, and Greece for several reasons. Importantly, the assignment introduces students to a method of fashion history research. It also demonstrates the cyclical nature of fashion, and the ways in which even periods remote in time can influence the design and decoration of clothing. As future professionals in the apparel field, the assignment encourages students to think critically about the historical design influences of contemporary apparel.

Appropriate courses and course levels for the assignment: Survey of historic dress and costume, from freshman to senior level; cultural perspectives, from freshman to senior level; fashion design, from freshman to senior level.

Appropriate class size: Any course size is appropriate, as well as in-class or online formats.

Estimated time required: The assignment is best completed out of class and can be assigned and explained during one class meeting and then due in the next session. The assignment should take students no more than one hour to complete.

Required materials: Computer, Internet connection, and selected database access (often facilitated by the university library or other institution).

Learning goals

- Familiarize students with databases that are useful to historians and apparel-related professionals.
- Expand students' knowledge of and exposure to multiple periods in fashion history.
- Encourage students to think critically about how designers reinterpret previous fashion styles.

Assessment

Facility with database use will be demonstrated by the students' successful acquisition and uploading of relevant articles. Students' written reflections are crucial in evaluating learning. The instructor should review the selected articles in conjunction with the students' statements for evidence of critical thought about the styles and fashions observed. For deeper learning, instructors may wish to use the student reflections for further class discussion.

Guidelines for instructors

This exercise can be completed following specific lessons or modules, such as Classical Rome, or can be assigned as an end-of-class review of the periods discussed. Instructors may wish to create a sample of the exercise, including step-by-step screenshots detailing how students can access the databases. This can be composed on a Word document, a PowerPoint document, or through the creation of a video in which the instructor demonstrates the steps of the assignment.

Discussion questions: Instructors may wish to ask students to reflect on what they found most interesting about undertaking this assignment, what was most difficult about the database search, or how they could use this information in their future careers.

Cautionary advice for instructors

- Students who are working off-campus may need a special password to access certain databases. Not all universities may subscribe to the selected databases, all of which are part of the ProQuest database collection. Thus, not all instructors and students will have access to each of the databases, and the assignment may need to be adapted based on university resources. Institutions without access to the digital versions of the databases likely will have microfiche or hard-copy versions that students can access and search.
- The assignment encompasses a degree of subjectivity in analyzing how a previous-style influence has been translated (whether faithfully copied or derivative), so the instructor may want to provide guidelines or examples for the students (see, for example, Murphy, 2011).
- This exercise focuses on a particular region and eras, but could be adapted by instructors to focus on different regions/eras, at their discretion.

Copy of the assignment

Options for databases, fashion influences, and years

- 1. *New York Times* Historical Database; Egyptian fashions; 1923–1929
- 2. *Vogue* Database; Greek influence in fashion; 1910–1919
- 3. *Women's Wear Daily* Database; medieval influence on fashion; 1930–1939

1. Using the *New York Times* Historical Edition Database, type "Egyptian fashions" into the search box and select the years 1923–1929. Skim the articles that appear and select

an article of interest. Upload it to the course learning management system, and then write about one element of dress that was faithfully inspired by Ancient Egypt (cite your textbook), and one element of dress (including hair or makeup) that seems to have derived, yet was not exactly reproduced, from Egyptian influences. Include a statement about what you learned about Egypt and the 1923–1929 period by completing this assignment.

2. Using the *Vogue* database, type "Greek influence on fashion" into the search box and select the years 1910–1919. Skim the articles that appear and select an article of interest. Upload it to the course learning management system, and then write about one element of dress that was faithfully inspired by classical Greece (cite your textbook), and one element of dress (including hair or makeup) that seems to have derived, yet not exactly reproduced from Greece. Include a statement about what you learned about Classical Greece and the 1910–1919 period by completing this assignment.

3. Using the *Women's Wear Daily* database, type "Medieval influence on fashion" into the search box and select the years 1930–1939. Skim the articles that appear and find an article of interest. Upload it to the course learning management system, and then write about one element of dress that was faithfully inspired by the medieval period (cite your textbook), and one element of dress (including hair or makeup) that seems to have derived, yet was not exactly reproduced from medieval Europe. Include a statement about what you learned about the medieval period and the 1930–1939 period by completing this assignment.

Typical results and reflections on the assignment

- Students expressed great interest in seeing how modern periods of fashion history have been inspired by the more distant historical past. Students gained exposure to how current fashion trends are appropriated or translated from different eras or cultures. Depending on the course goals, instructors may wish to engage students in further conversations about the possibility of design originality and the ethics of inspiration and direct copying of past fashions.
- The exercises have expanded students' knowledge and use of various fashion history-oriented databases.
- These exercises help students acquire familiarity with early twentieth-century fashion resources, which may be useful for historic dress and costume, cultural perspectives, and fashion design courses.

Bibliography

Frazier, B., and K. Fulton. "Profiling Apparel and Textile Programs at 4-Year Public Universities in the U.S.: A Preliminary Report." *Proceedings of the International Textile and Apparel Association, Inc*. 71 (2014): 1–2.

Gam, H.J., and J. Banning. "A Collaboration to Teach Students to Utilize Dress as Inspiration for Apparel Design." *Family & Consumer Sciences Research Journal* 41, no. 1 (2012): 56–68.

Marcketti, S.B. "Effective Learning Strategies in the History of Dress." *The History Teacher* 44, no. 4 (2011): 547–568.

Murphy, D. "Dialogues between Past and Present: Historic Garments as Source Material for Contemporary Fashion Design." *V&A Online Journal* 3 (2011). Available online: http://www.vam.ac.uk/content/journals/research-journal/issue-03/dialogues-between-past-and-present-historic-garments-as-source-material-for-contemporary-fashion-design/.

PART THREE

FASHION FORECASTING AND TREND PREDICTION

Introduction

This section offers examples of how instructors can help their students connect theories about fashion forecasting and trend prediction and practice, thinking critically about how trends develop and get disseminated, and about how a range of national and global factors shape this development and dissemination. In their chapter, Lili Golmohammadi and Jay McCauley Bowstead draw on experiential, interactive pedagogies to help students consider the challenges involved in seeking to forecast trends. Having students analyze a range of fashion media and generate mood boards about prospective future trends, Golmohammadi and McCauley Bowstead's exercise enables students to think about the intersections between personal taste and trend prediction. This assignment also helps students to better understand how cultural, sociological, ecological, and economic factors impact trend formation, and the roles of producers, consumers, and cultural intermediaries in this complex process. Alyssa Dana Adomaitis' chapter also focuses on sharpening students' skills in fashion forecasting, discussing how to help students to build critical thinking skills through scaffolded assignments, keeping a journal analyzing current and discussing prospective future trends in the fashion market. Her exercise enables students to reflect on the evolution of fashion trends over time, the fashion industry's waves, swings, and cycles, and how national and global current events and the contemporary environmental, social, and political climate impacts fashion trends.

And finally, Katherine Schaefer's chapter has students analyze trade publications and trend forecasting sites to consider contemporary trends in accessories and apparel for men's, women's, and children's markets, having students reflect on which trends seem the most likely to endure, and how students can seek to assess trends' durability. Each of these section's chapters provide insight into large questions of how trends emerge, spread, and fade, and how students can analyze the complicated national and global forces which shape trends' growth and evolution.

4
TREND FORECASTING, TASTE AND FASHION PRODUCTION

Jay McCauley Bowstead, London College of Fashion and Lili Golmohammadi, Goldsmiths, University of London

Contextualization

This proposed workshop explores the various processes by which trends and taste are formed—including in the field of trend prediction—and situates notions of taste and trend in the context of the production of fashion. In addition to shedding light on trend forecasting as an area within the "culture industries" (Horkheimer and Adorno, 1972: 94–136), our program also offers a conceptual framework through which to understand and interrogate cultural production more generally. This theoretical context will include the theories of Pierre Bourdieu as outlined by Celia Lury in *Consumer Culture* (2014) and Joanne Entwistle as described in *The Aesthetic Economy of Fashion* (2009), as well as the more recent work of Mathilda Tham (2015) with its emphasis on creativity, sustainability, and ethics. Students are introduced to a broad range of theories of taste, consumption, and emulation derived from Simmel (1957), Blumer (1969), McRobbie (1988, 1998), Hebdige (1988), and Veblen (1994 [1899]) (see suggested reading list). Students will gain a vocabulary with which to describe and analyze the formation of taste in relation to class, cultural production and mediation, personal expression, issues surrounding diversity, group identity, and subcultural membership. They will consider a variety of models of fashion transmission, including trickle down (Simmel, 1957; Laver, 1969; Veblen, 1994 [1899]), collective selection (Blumer, 1969), and bubble up (Polhemus, 1994; Thornton, 1997; Church Gibson, 2006). Bourdieu's notion of cultural capital elaborated and updated by Entwistle will be compared to Sarah Thornton's concept of subcultural capital (1997). Students may benefit from considering the ways in which trends have emanated from marginalized and economically disadvantaged groups (as well as from elites)—for example, from within African American culture; from subcultural groups, such as punk, grunge, and hippies; and from within queer culture. Indeed, the history of popular culture demonstrates frequent examples of this "bubble up" phenomenon.

Trend prediction has been chosen as the central focus of this series of exercises because of the ways in which it encourages students to consider how taste and desire are generated within the fashion system while exploring the reciprocal, complex set of relationships between producers, consumers, and cultural intermediaries. The exercises provide tools for students to consider and generate ideas around the immaterial production of fashion. The session should help situate concepts from Joanne Entwistle (tacit aesthetic knowledge and the aesthetic economy) and Pierre Bourdieu (cultural intermediaries, cultural capital, and habitus) in the context of fashion practice.

Trends and taste are implicated in a set of processes and discourses whose study illuminates fashion as a design practice and as an industry more generally. Mathilda Tham has stated, "The true power of forecasting […] comes from participating in imagining our shared futures" (2015: 287). By integrating sociological and economic accounts with concerns around sustainability—using Tham's frames of reference—students are able to consider both the potentialities and the problematics of this form of cultural production. According to Tham, by reimagining forecasting we can conceptualize alternative futures *outside* dominant commercial frames. In this sense, these exercises are about demonstrating to students the agency they have to question and reimagine social, cultural, and fashion trends: not only to consider what is "likely to happen," but also what they would "like to happen" (Tham, 2015: 287).

The assignments described below draw upon contemporary best practices in learning and teaching by combining experiential and interactive pedagogical approaches. In this way, the exercises engage students in theory through a more experiential way of learning and knowing (Kolb, 2015). The participative, reflexive, and questioning approaches of critical pedagogy (Giroux, 2008) are central to the design of these exercises that aim not only to explore existing knowledge, but also to generate new insights.

As educators whose teaching ranges across theoretical and studio-based modes of delivery, our proposed program is designed to cater for both social science and cultural studies students, and students of fashion and fashion studies. As such, it deliberately combines approaches and materials that will be more familiar and less familiar to each. Recent discussions of fashion pedagogy have questioned and problematized the boundaries between practice and theory (Fashion Praxis Collective, 2014: 77–80). While fashion studies exists as an increasingly well-established academic field, its inherent multidisciplinary qualities are reflected in this approach.

Our philosophy of learning and teaching is one that prizes creativity; these exercises aim to combine the rigor and criticality that characterize the academic study of fashion with the sense of freedom and imagination found in studio practice. Rather than presenting a "ready-made" body of knowledge—that is, a "how-to" of trend forecasting—it instead asks students to occupy the role of cultural intermediaries on their own terms.

One of our aims in developing these exercises is to encourage students to consider their agency: by reimagining forecasting they can conceive of alternative futures outside dominant commercial frames. The key concepts that students encounter in the course of these assignments—including cultural capital, habitus, tacit aesthetic knowledge, and the aesthetic economy—are seen as tools with which to interrogate cultural production. While it is crucial to situate trend prediction in a broader social and cultural context, we are not trying to present students with an orthodox cannon: they must be free to combine notions from their readings with their own research and insights drawn from their experiences.

Appropriate courses and course levels for the assignment: These exercises are applicable to both second- and third-year undergraduate students, as well as students of masters' programs within the fields of cultural studies, sociology, fashion design, fashion media, fashion studies, design history, curation, and critical and historical studies.

Appropriate class size: Twelve to twenty students.

Estimated time required: The assignment for this session has been broken down into a series of four exercises; three that take place during class, followed by a fourth that is designed to be completed over the course of a week.

Exercise 1:	Forty-five minutes
Exercise 2:	Forty-five minutes
Suggested break:	Fifteen minutes
Exercise 3:	Seventy-five minutes
Exercise 4	(Independent study): One week

Required materials: The exercises here require each student to bring the following materials:

- Between five and ten image sources such as magazines, free newspaper supplements, online material, fliers, and leaflets/catalogues from exhibitions. Magazines may include men's or women's fashion publications, as well as topical special interest journals such as *Frieze, Nature, The Economist*, and *New Scientist*. It is advisable for instructors to clarify that these materials should be available to cut; that is, students may wish to photocopy images from magazines and other publications that they prefer to keep intact.

- Between two and three articles written within the past year. These may come from papers or journals such as *Time, The Economist*, and *The New Statesman*; from scholarly journals such as *The International Journal of Cultural Studies* (often accessible to students for free through university libraries); and from magazines such as *Britain In* from the Economic and Social Research Council. Information can also be sourced from free online platforms by social research agencies such as www.natcen.ac.uk and www.pewresearch.org. Students should look for both articles and images relating to technological or scientific breakthroughs, as well as economic, environmental, political, and social/demographic trends or shifts.

Instructors will need to provide:

- Post-Its and large sheets of paper (such as newsprint), approximately of size A1.
- Marker pens, scissors, glue sticks, and masking tape.
- Examples of recent notable economic, environmental, political, and social/demographic trends or shifts, either as a list or in the form of articles and printed material.
- Presentation slides (e.g., with exercise information and examples of different trend forecasting models, including pages from trend reports and screenshots from forecasting websites—see Exercise 2).
- A large screen or projector on which to display presentation slides.
- A list of key concepts that will be discussed during the session, including cultural capital, cultural mediation and habitus (Bourdieu), fashion capital (Entwistle), and fashion habitus and tacit aesthetic knowledge (Entwistle). This list should be sent along with the prereadings, but it is also advisable to write up the terms on a whiteboard or large sheets of paper, placed visibly in the room for students to refer to.

Learning goals

- Demonstrate a critical awareness of the cultural, sociological, ecological, and economic factors that impact on how trends are formed and forecast.
- Be able to understand and critique trend forecasting practices, defining and analyzing the meaning of "trend."
- Analyze the role of trend forecasters in the production of fashion particularly in relation to taste, cultural capital, and cultural mediation.
- Be able to propose alternative visions of the future and fashion's place within them.

Assessment

This series of assignments makes considerable demands of students as it asks them to speculate imaginatively on the future, to analyze and critique fashion and trend prediction practices, and to make sense of material from a wide range of sources (demographic, cultural, and theoretical). It is to be expected that some students will struggle to convincingly master all of this information, but all students should be able to "propose alternative visions of the future" with a degree of thought and imagination. Of course, markers will assess student work according to the conventions of their universities: our intention is for this work to be marked holistically. Contributions by students in the workshop can also be assessed formatively. Both the materials produced in groups in the session and those produced independently thereafter can be used to assess students' achievement of the learning goals. The mind maps, mood boards, and presentations should provide evidence of engagement with broader social, economic, and environmental questions. In imagining future trends and scenarios, students will attempt to apply ideas and key concepts such as taste, cultural capital, and cultural mediation that they have encountered in the suggested readings. More sophisticated students will be able to synthesize conclusions drawn from primary research materials and secondary literature.

Guidelines for instructors

This series of assignments focuses upon fashion production as a set of predominantly (though not exclusively) "immaterial" processes of communication, emulation, and mediation. As such, it would be ideally paired with a more materially based account of the production of fashion, and we have typically run it after exercises in which students undertook object analysis or physically unpicked garments.

We are aware that the readings cover a number of potentially new and complex concepts for students and therefore have recommended the inclusion of a key concepts list. We have also found that it is helpful for students to see the learning goals for the session alongside their reading so that they understand how to contextualize the information.

Prior to the session, students are asked to read:

- Entwistle, J. (2009), "Tacit Aesthetic Knowledge: The Fashion Sense and Sensibility of Fashion Buyers," *The Aesthetic Economy of Fashion: Markets and Values in Clothing and Modelling*, 129–148, Oxford: Berg.
- Lury, C. (2014), *Consumer Culture*, 89–96, Cambridge: Polity Press.
- Lynch, A., and Strauss, M. (2007), "Fashion as Collective Behaviour," *Changing Fashion: A Critical Introduction to Trend Analysis and Cultural Meaning*, 75–76, Oxford: Berg.

Discussion questions

- Where do trends come from, and how are they transmitted?
- Is it possible to have innovation without trend?
- What are the connections between the curator and the trend forecaster, and how can both be considered "cultural intermediaries"?
- What are the connections between taste and trends, and to what extent are they the same or different?
- What role do "tacit aesthetic knowledges," "cultural capital," and cultural mediation have in the formation and transmission of trends?
- What are the possibilities and what are the problems presented by trends in fashion?

- What does it mean to forecast trends today? How might we use tools of trend forecasting differently, as Tham argues, as a way of "participating in imagining our shared futures?" (2015: 287).

Cautionary advice for instructors
Specific guidelines about the exercise for instructors are as follows:

Exercise 1: Questions (forty-five minutes). Some questions are deliberately ambiguous, and encourage students to provide multiple and even contrasting or contradictory responses.

Exercise 2: Presentation and discussion (forty-five minutes). Your presentation should be designed to introduce students to current models of trend forecasting and to encourage them to think critically about these models. Begin with a brief overview of the historical and commercial context of trend forecasting, discussing, in particular, the role of trend forecasters in the production of fashion and taste. Slides should introduce students to forecasting companies such as WGSN, The Future Laboratory, and K-Hole and forecasters such as Li Edelkoort. Also include images from forecasting website homepages, and a few examples of pages from their recent reports (some universities have access to WGSN, while K-Hole's reports are downloadable for free).

As well as giving contextual background, encourage students to consider what is being conveyed in these trend reports: what trends are being identified and why? What language is being used and how? Can we think of trend forecasting as an epistemology? Who is using this information and why? How do the sites' home pages and overall aesthetics differ in approach, and how are they similar? Are there any "trends" between the focus of the home pages' and reports of the agencies themselves? (e.g., at the time of the writing of this chapter, both The Future Laboratory and K-Hole express postmodern concerns, depthlessness, meaninglessness, and brands as simulacra (Baudrillard, 1988). What is the impact of some forecasters (or cultural intermediaries) such as Li Edelkoort, questioning the relevance of trends in the production of fashion in her 2014 Anti-Fashion Manifesto? What cultural capital does she hold in this role? What do the students think of her characterization of fashion?

Facilitate connections between these questions and the key concepts from the prereadings; for example while analyzing a forecasting agency such as *WGSN*, discuss Entwistle's case study of buyers working in high fashion. Ask students to consider why some buyers or companies purposefully *don't* use trend prediction companies. How do the "fashion habitus" and "tacit aesthetic knowledge" play into this? How does trend prediction act like anthropology or sociology (Bourdieu)? Encourage students to connect shifts in technology, demography, and culture to changes in consumer habits. Does this process represent the formation of a new "fashion habitus"?

Exercise 3: Forecasting a trend, occupying the role of cultural producer, cultural mediator (seventy-five minutes).

Part A (55 minutes): Instructors may need to monitor timings when students are introducing their materials so that this part does not overrun. Overall guidelines for instructors about the exercise:

- The in-class exercises rely quite heavily on group work. Lecturers may need to circulate to aid group interaction and to draw out less confident students.
- Exercise 3 asks students to engage with theories through approaches that are traditionally practice based (i.e., making a trend board). Students from non-practice programs may feel less confident working in this way and may therefore require additional encouragement from lecturers.

Copy of the assignment

Exercise 1: Questions (forty-five minutes). This exercise is designed to generate ideas and engage you in critical thinking around trends, taste, and cultural production. You are encouraged to draw upon the key ideas from the prereading in undertaking this task. You will be presented with more information later on in the class, but at this initial stage try to keep your mind open. In groups of three to four, using different colored Post-It notes to answer each question, you will be asked to mind-map around the following questions (it is fine to provide multiple and even contrasting or contradictory responses):

Part A (five minutes): What do we mean by a fashion "trend"? (Define). What other words might we use for "trend?" What are trends for?

Part B (five minutes): Who defines trends? How are trends generated?

Part C (five minutes): Where do trends occur, and how do they travel?

Part D (ten minutes): Draw basic diagrams that this time illustrate your ideas of how, where, and by whom trends are generated and communicated. These drawings can be made up of basic lines, arrows, and abstract shapes.

Part E: Class discussion (twenty minutes): Place your work on the wall and feedback to class, discussing key points that have particularly interested you. How did you define "trend"? What other words did you come up with?

Exercise 2: Presentation and discussion (forty-five minutes). This presentation from your lecturer is designed to introduce you to current models of trend forecasting and to help you to think critically about them.

Suggested Break (fifteen minutes)

Exercise 3: Forecasting a trend, occupying the role of cultural producer, cultural mediator (seventy-five minutes). This exercise helps you to consider how the theoretical propositions discussed in the presentation and prereading are linked to the *practice* of trend prediction, while also giving you further insight into the role of trend predictors, designers, buyers, and creative directors as cultural intermediaries. A key question to be answered through this exercise is "what are the links between fashion and social trends?" As explored in the previous exercises, "trend" is a somewhat contested term, and "trend prediction" a contested practice. You should aim to generate ideas that, as Tham proposes, offer imaginative alternatives to the "dominant narratives deriving from the commercial framework" (2015: 287). Consider what sort of trend forecaster you are:

for whom are you forecasting? You can combine what is likely to happen, with what you would *like* to happen.

> **Part A (fifty-five minutes):** Again in groups of three to four, predict a trend for five years ahead; make reference to social, cultural, economic, and environmental factors. Consult the magazines, newspapers, journals, fliers, and any other materials you have brought in and identify relevant demographic information and information about social and cultural shifts.
>
> Spend two to three minutes each introducing your materials to the rest of your group, highlighting two or three things that have particularly interested you and stating why. Begin to assemble mood boards, grouping and identifying themes, and considering how fashion trends are linked to broader cultural changes. Predict where and among whom these trends will take hold. You may wish to write some key words to accompany the visual material. Reflect critically on your decision-making process as you do this.
>
> **Part B (twenty minutes):** Group discussion: Having assembled your mood boards, explain to the class the trends you have identified and how they have been identified. What are the limitations and possibilities of these trends? Reflect on your group's selection process: what role does trend prediction play in the formation of taste at various levels of the market, and how does it relate to various demographic segments?

Exercise 4: *Post-class* **assignment (independent study, one week).** Drawing on what you have learned from these exercises, you are asked to undertake a one-week project, individually researching and identifying a trend for fifteen years ahead. As with the in-class exercises, you will need to consider sociological, environmental, technological, and cultural factors. Assemble one mood board and write 300 words explaining your thinking. How radically might the world have changed? What might this mean for fashion trends? This exercise calls for speculation and imagination; don't discount responses that may initially seem far-fetched. This is an opportunity for you to consider your hopes for the future, as well as probable sociocultural developments.

> Postclass reading:
> - Tham, M. (2015), "The Futures of Future Studies in Fashion," in K. Fletcher and M. Tham (eds.), *Routledge Handbook of Sustainability and Fashion*, 283–292, Abingdon, Oxon: Routledge.

Typical results and reflections on the assignment

> - In the workshop, students interrogate their existing understandings of taste and trend formation. Using a vocabulary drawn from their readings, they apply concepts of cultural mediation, "tacit aesthetic knowledge," and "cultural capital" to their analysis of trend prediction practices.

- During the process of predicting a trend (Exercise 3), students are often able to synthesize demographic, statistical, and qualitative research with visual materials, as well as situating taste and trend in the context of economic, social, ecological, and political forces.
- The dialogic nature of the exercise leads students to identify both the potential problems of this mode of cultural production and mediation and its liberating and creative possibilities in "imagining alternative futures" (Tham, 2015).
- The workshop provides an opportunity for student to consider the ways in which taste and trends may emerge from marginalized groups, and also to think through the shifting nature of identities founded upon gender, ethnicity, age, and nationality. MA students will typically approach this exercise in a more critical manner, whereas BA students are more likely to initially reach for more simple (often economically determined) explanations of taste and trend. In this case, draw attention to examples of trend formation that happen more organically and in noncommercial contexts (such as among subcultural and subaltern groups). Nevertheless, these exercises provide a useful space in which to present students of both levels of study with a variety of models of taste formation and fashion production.

Bibliography

Baudrillard, J. *Simulacra and Simulation*. Stanford: Stanford University Press, 1988.

Blumer, H. "Fashion: From Class Differentiation to Collective Selection." *The Sociological Quarterly* 10, no. 3 (1969): 275–291.

Church Gibson, P. "Analysing Fashion." In *The Fashion Handbook*, edited by T. Jackson and D. Shaw, 20–28. Oxford: Routledge, 2006.

Edelkoort, L. *Anti_Fashion Manifesto | Lidewij Edelkoort*, 2017. Available online: http://www.edelkoort.com/2015/09/anti_fashion-manifesto/ (accessed March 14, 2017).

Entwistle, J. "Tacit Aesthetic Knowledge: The Fashion Sense and Sensibility of Fashion Buyers." In *The Aesthetic Economy of Fashion: Markets and Values in Clothing and Modelling*, 129–148. Oxford: Berg, 2009.

Fashion Praxis Collective. *The Fashion Condition*. New York: SelfPassage, 2014, 77–80.

Fong, G., S. Monahan, E. Segal, and D. Yago. *A Report on Doubt,* 2015. Available online: http://khole.net/issues/05/ (accessed March 14, 2017).

Giroux, H. *Pedagogy and the Politics of Hope*. New York: Westview Press, 2008.

Hebdige, D. *Hiding in the Light*. London: Routledge, 1988.

Horkheimer, M., and T. Adorno. *Dialectic of Enlightenment*. New York: Herder and Herder, 1972.

Kolb, D. *Experiential Learning*. Upper Saddle River, NJ: Pearson Education, 2015.

Laver, J. *The Concise History of Costume and Fashion*. New York: Harry N. Abrams, 1969.

Lury, C. *Consumer Culture*. Cambridge: Polity Press, 2014.

Lynch, A., and M. Strauss. "Fashion as Collective Behaviour." In *Changing Fashion: A Critical Introduction to Trend Analysis and Cultural Meaning*. Oxford: Berg, 2007.

McRobbie, A. *British Fashion Design*. London: Routledge, 1998.

McRobbie, A. *Zoot Suits and Second-Hand Dresses*. Boston: Unwin Hyman, 1988.

Polhemus, T. *Streetstyle*. New York: Thames and Hudson, 1994.

Simmel, G. "Fashion." *American Journal of Sociology* 62, no. 6 (1957 [1904]): 541–558.

Tham, M. "The Futures of Future Studies in Fashion." In *Routledge Handbook of Sustainability and Fashion*, edited by K. Fletcher and M. Tham, 283–292. Abingdon, Oxon: Routledge, 2015.
Thefuturelaboratory.com. *The Future Laboratory*, 2017. Available online: http://thefuturelaboratory.com/uk/ (accessed March 14, 2017).
Thornton, S. "The Social Logic of Subcultural Capital." In *The Subcultures Reader*, edited by K. Gelder and S. Thornton, 200–209. Abingdon: Routledge, 1997.
Veblen, T. *The Theory of the Leisure Class*. London: Routledge/Thoemmes Press, 1994.
WGSN. *WGSN | Create Tomorrow | Trend Forecasting & Analytics*, 2017. Available online: https://www.wgsn.com/en/ (accessed March 14, 2017).

5
FASHION FORECASTING: CRITICAL THINKING AND ANALYSES FOR TRENDS

Alyssa Dana Adomaitis, The New York City College of Technology, City University of New York

Contextualization

With the competitive nature of the fashion industry, professors strive to prepare their students for successful career paths. It is important that an undergraduate curriculum be designed so that students' work reflects high standards and incorporates critical thinking skills. Critical thinking analyses are often difficult for students who are stressed, short on time, and may be utilizing the Internet as their primary source of information. An unprecedented study that followed several thousand undergraduates through four years of college found that large numbers did not learn critical thinking, complex reasoning, and written communication skills that are widely assumed to be at the core of a college education (Rimer, 2001).

The best teaching practice shared is the application of John Dewey's *Reflection as a Meaning Process* (1933) in a fashion forecasting course. Dewey's ideas concerning reflective thinking provide a method to move students beyond rote memorization, a summation of information, or a simple rewording of an author's ideas. Fashion forecasting is an ideal context to develop critical thinking as it requires students to think beyond a tangible time and predict future fashion in a systematic way based on environmental, social, and political criteria. Critical thinking, as defined by Scriven and Paul (1987), is the "intellectually disciplined process of actively and skillfully conceptualizing, applying, analyzing, synthesizing, and/or evaluating information gathered from, or generated by, observation, experience, reflection, reasoning, or communication."

Rogers (2002) indicated that his critical thinking steps were an application and an update of Dewey's (1933) critical thinking and reflection ideas, by which Rogers provides four criteria that were integrated with Brannon's (2010) *Steps in predicting fashion trends* to produce a learning experience that developed students' critical thinking.

Table 5.1 *Fashion forecasting steps*

Rogers' (2002) criteria	Brannon's steps in fashion forecasting	Adomaitis' (2013) mini lessons
1. Reflection is a meaning-like process that moves a learner from one experience into the next with deeper understanding of relationships and connections to other experiences and ideas.	1. Identify basic facts about past trends.	1. Identify causal relationships between fashion and society.
	2. Determine the causes of change in the past.	2. Research historical continuity among fashion trends using forecasting jargon.
	3. Determine differences between past forecasts and actual behavior.	3. Consider fashion in the global stage.
2. Reflection is systematic, rigorous, disciplined way of thinking with its roots in scientific inquiry.	4. Apply forecasting tools and techniques.	4. Reflect critically upon the forecast.
	5. Determine the factors likely to affect trends in the future.	
3. Reflection needs to happen in a community in interaction with others.	6. Follow the forecast and look for deviations.	
4. Reflection requires an attitude that values the personal and intellectual growth of oneself and of others.	7. Revise forecast when necessary.	

In this assignment, students are assigned to make a forecast in a specific category (e.g., dresses, suits) projecting two years (short term) into the future. A minimum of three types of forecasts are needed per style category. For example, students can forecast silhouette, color, fabric, or texture trends for dresses for a season. Students begin the forecast by searching for current fashion trends at different levels of the market, such as high fashion or mass fashion. Students at this stage learn that fashion forecasting is a causal relationship between the specific style and the social realms of a society. Recognizing this relationship moves the student through the first two forecasting steps in Table 5.1, Adomaitis' (2013) mini lesson (1) or Rogers' step (1) and Brannon's steps (1) and (2), as it entails the identification of trends and their relationship to economic, social, political, and cultural events. For example, students recalled the dominating colors of red, white, and blue evident in fashion during the Obama–Romney US presidential election campaign of 2012.

The second step in Adomaitis' (2013) outline coincides with Rogers' second step in critical thinking and Brannon's third and fifth steps in conducting a forecast. There is historical information about past trends and actual events that shape both fashion fads and flops. By searching fashion history, researching timelines of fashion change, and studying designer interpretations of fashion trends, students are guided through a step-by-step research approach about fashion and how to forecast fashion trends for upcoming seasons by identifying repeating waves, pendulum swings, and cycles that reoccur in fashion. In this way, students can understand that fashion evolves and that trends repeat themselves throughout the decades. For example, bellbottoms in the twenty-first century (2014) were previously in style in the 1970s disco era.

The third step, continuing with Adomaitis' (2013) mini lessons, places fashion in a global context. Fashion is group behavior, a form of social copying (Stone, 2011). Thus, fashion exists in a social context. Students begin to think beyond their personal experience with fashion and reflect on how fashion is interpreted by different people, cultures, and regions of the world. For example, students begin to look at fashion trends beyond cities such as New York. By using the fashion forecasting databases *Fashionsnoops* or WGSN/Stylesight, students research urban street fashions in cities such as Tokyo, New York, England, and Milan. In more advanced courses, it may be important to add a comparison of European, Asian, and American trends. For example, in past collections, John Galliano and Tom Ford designed evening gowns inspired by intricately embroidered imperial yellow robes used during China's Qing Dynasty, circa 1644–1911 (Cotter, 2015). Trends can be also shaped by elements such as music (i.e., the style of artists such as Beyoncé) or film (i.e., garments from popular movies such as *The Hunger Games*). This will allow students to think about fashion beyond themselves and in different contexts.

The fourth step in Adomaitis' (2013) mini lesson fosters the practice of critical thinking and reflection in an actual forecast, by having students keep a journal of fashion predictions and having them write twice a week. The journal is a way to activate critical thinking, reflection, and research skills while tracking with the actual assignment of predicting fashion trends. Students' journals can log research that is currently moving forward in time revealing how trends move. Trends do not happen in isolation. The journal is used also as a reminder to note upcoming events, such as the Olympics, political events, or scientific discoveries that will once again impact and change fashion trends. Students will add this assignment to their respective portfolio or e-portfolio.

Appropriate courses and course levels for this assignment: Sophomore or junior level introductory courses in fashion forecasting, trend analysis, product development, or fashion merchandising.

Appropriate class size: Twenty-five to forty students

Estimated time required: A full semester preferable, as each mini-lesson assignment of the forecast trend book took approximately two to three weeks accumulating a full semester (fifteen weeks) worth of work, in addition to finding correct illustrations, grammatical checks, and APA citation and referencing. Lecturing on the forecast topics so that they coincide with the forecast assignment (Adomaitis' mini lesson, 2013) provided a context for each step of the forecast and critical thinking. Breaking down the assignment into smaller modules or scaffolding ensures that students were able to master course material and gradually build their skills. Each semester, having critical thinking as a guideline (Adomaitis' mini assignments, 2013) along with the Brannon's *Fashion Forecasting* text, students of varied academic abilities were able to complete a forecast trend book of their own. They were able to more deeply and thoroughly comprehend how trends move through stages that ultimately lead to acceptance by the masses (Adomaitis, 2013).

Required materials

- Brannon, E. (2010). *Fashion Forecasting* (2nd edition). New York: Fairchild Books, Inc. This text will be valuable for students as background reading in fashion forecasting, as they are working on this assignment.

Learning goals

- Analyze the direction of the fashion change. Which way is the pendulum swinging? (e.g., more conservative or risqué).
- Recognize the breadth and depth of the fashion forecasting process.
- Illustrate the "diffusion of innovation" as a framework for understanding and predicting fashion change.
- Compare and contrast the methodologies used for short-term (two years) and long-term (five years) forecasting.
- Recognize color forecasting as a coordinating factor in the apparel supply chain from fiber producer to retailer.
- Examine the methods for conducting consumer research for new fashion products and marketing initiatives.
- Prepare a color, fiber, and merchandise forecast for a future season.
- Use appropriate controlled vocabulary to navigate subject/discipline-specific databases, identify gaps in information gathered, and employ alternative search tools, including bibliographies and citations to find additional materials.

Assessment

1. *Initiative*—Students must prove resourcefulness through research and evidence, in presenting meaningful information in a well-structured report, including the trend forecasts, fabric swatches, color, etc. They must demonstrate inclusion of supporting information from course materials, such as the textbook, class readings, databases, and trade publications. They must show evidence of adequate preparation of trend reports in the presentation.
2. *Thoroughness*—Students must have covered all topic areas. They must include changes, the causes of changes, cultural factors that may have caused such changes, and if the trend is new or repetitive. They should use forecasting techniques that create a narrative that is descriptive and evocative. They should provide adequate coverage within each topic area with proper evidence and proper format.

3. *Accuracy*—Students must have reached appropriate conclusions from the information they received. The package must also include the importance of each trend and the direction it is taking. It must reflect how and why the trend will change in the future. Their trends must reflect the appropriate target market and market segmentation. Students must have applied course material accurately, reflecting knowledge and understanding of the material.

4. *Professionalism and creativity*—The promotional package and presentation should reflect professionalism in preparation and clarity, and creativity. The package should include professional jargon and terminology. They should be attractive and eye-catching. The promotional package and presentation should show evidence of advanced work and planning. The presentation should be well-organized and cohesive with the promotional report, using proper formatting.

Guidelines for instructors

Forecasting mini lessons should be taught and the corresponding part assigned for homework to ensure comprehension. Assigning the work in segments throughout the semester will prevent issues with final projects (the pace of this course is determined by your students' ability to complete the work). Please note that knowledge of the fashion cycle is necessary for this assignment. Students are required to provide supporting social, economic, and political reasoning for their trend forecasts. It would also be helpful to make your students aware that the Values and Lifestyles (VALS) survey is to be taken objectively (as a customer/target audience), not with their personal views or research target markets that are continually changing.

Used cumulatively, the processes above will prepare you for any difficulties that arise throughout the duration of this assignment. Plan to have students work with the librarian for research optimization and with members of the university writing center. This will ensure that students are building strong research and writing skills gradually and successfully over the course of the semester.

Cautionary advice for instructors

- Design students will be better at drawing sketches, but retail students can sketch or trace fashion figures to express their artistic views. They may even have someone else illustrate their respective ideas as long as that person is acknowledged for that part of the work.

- Research into and comprehension of current trends provide important information objectively for understanding important a target audience not satisfying a personal fashion view.

- Forecasting means adjusting a current garment because of certain social, economic, and political trends requiring that the garment sketches be innovative

but have a supportive education reason with citations showing that the deviations are not a whimsical guessing game.
- Because forecasting assignments build upon one another, students who are dragging behind will be lost. Therefore, the pace of the course can be adjusted to the students who are worthy but are slowest to turn in their assigned work.

Copy of the assignment

Fashion forecasting project

Part 1: Trend reports

Assume you are employed by a major fashion forecasting company (e.g., Tobé Report, Fashion Scoops, and WGSN/*Stylesight*). Your responsibility is to develop a fashion trend report for two years from now: the forecast will be *Fall/Winter of that year or Spring/Summer of that year*.

The trend report can focus on women's wear, menswear, or children's. Once you select the category, choose five trend areas (e.g., color, silhouette, fabric, prints, patterns, and textures) to analyze for the report. The category must be one type of fashion product—day dresses, sunglasses, trench coats, shoes (pumps), etc.

Developing a forecast
Identify the basic facts about each trend by using information from past forecasts. Your research should include the following:

1. Research fashion trends in the category you selected. You will need to review information from *Stylesight, New York Times, Wall Street Journal* and trade publications such as *Daily News Record* (*DNR*) and *Women's Wear Daily* (*WWD*). Look at trends in several categories (e.g., apparel, footwear, coats, and accessories). Decide if a trend new or is a repeating trend.

2. Explain the trend's appeal to the specific target market, for example, misses luxury, men's contemporary, and the junior streetwear market. You will complete a VALS survey for a research methodology used for market segmentation. Market segmentation is designed to guide companies in tailoring their products and services to appeal to the people most likely to purchase them. One needs to identify geographics, demographics, psychographics, and behavioristics as defined in the lecture to understand your target market.

    In the case of a new trend, what appears to be the cause of the trend? Are causes of the change societal? Look at past styles and look at current styles for information. What are the changes in style that are seen? What are the cultural factors they may have caused these changes (economy, war, royalty, death, rise of a celebrity)? For example, a celebrity (i.e., Rihanna) might appear at a public event wearing a style or it was a hit on a designer runway show.

3. Determine the differences in fabric, styling, color, fit, and silhouette. You will need to discuss the changes from the past to the present using additional research into fashion timelines of a style and how it has changed through the decades.
4. Determine the factors likely to affect trends in the future (i.e., is it designer? Will it trickle down?) Why will this trend change in the future? How will the trend be present in the fashion marketplace two years from now? What are the differences in the style?
5. Apply forecasting techniques. Make sure you apply forecasting terminology taught in class in this section to explain the techniques used to create your forecast (e.g., pendulum swing, cycles, waves to establish movement).

You will research three to five trends using the above steps. Reading trade and consumer publications, one can accomplish the forecast. Popular culture and fashion websites will also be helpful. In addition, you will undertake observations are useful by visiting retail locations to see how each trend is being merchandised. It will be important to observe how consumers are interpreting the trend. You may want to have a camera/phone ready to snap photos of street fashion to include and personalize your respective forecasts.

Format

Each trend will have its own report in a book format. It will include the following:

- Current trend research
- Trend report (five pages, one for each trend forecast): Write a descriptive page outlining the importance of the trend and the direction it is taking.
- Sketch of trend for two years from now. You can use outside assistance for this (the individual must be acknowledged).
- Proposed colors for the season. (Use paint swatches, but create color names.)
- Proposed fabrications (types of fabrics) for the season. (Use fabric swatches.)
- Forecast trend book will be bound like a book.

The trend report should be at least five pages and typed using Times New Roman twelve-point font. APA is to be used for citations and the reference page. The typed trend story should sound exciting. Create a name for the trend (e.g., "Bohemian Chic") and use the name as a basis for telling the story. The following website (www.fashiontrendsetter.com) is an excellent source that demonstrates how a trend story is written. The proposed sketch/illustrations and trend story should be on the same page. You could also consider doing a foldout whereby the story, sketch, color, and swatches are shown as a grouping.

Part 2: Final presentation

The project will be presented to the class. Visuals such as PowerPoint and trend boards must be included in your presentation.

Fashion forecasting is a process of visualization and intuition. One should begin by reading the trade publications such as *WWD, DNR*, and *Accessories*. This should be followed by reading consumer publications, such as *Vogue, In Style, Lucky,* and *People* magazines. *The London Times* (www.thelondontimes.com) is an excellent source for global fashion. You might also try www.parismatch.com, www.internationalheraldtribune.com, www.instyle.com, and www.style.com. Once you have done this, it is now time to visit stores and "people watch."

Typical results and reflections on the assignment

- When outlining forecasting using these steps for guidance, students began to engage in actual forecasting, rather than simply searching for forecasts by others.

- Students used critical thinking skills to move through a forecast with an understanding that fashion connects with the recent past (i.e., movies, music, celebrities), reflects current events such as economic downturns, cultural impacts (i.e., immigration reform), and political influences (i.e., a presidential race) that continually shape trends, as well as the fact that trends are adapted and modified by all types of consumers.

- In addition, using this approach, students have an easier time forecasting global trends in addition to trends for non-Western cultures. Students were able to forecast future trends, not just state what current trends were at the time.

Bibliography

Adomaitis, A. *A Fashion Paradox: Reflective Thinking for Fashion Forecasting*. International Textile and Apparel Association (ITAA) Proceedings #67. Monument, CO. 2013. http://www.itaaonline.org (also a presentation).

Brannon, E. *Fashion Forecasting*. 2nd edn. New York: Fairchild Books, Inc., 2010.

Cotter, H. "Review: In 'China: Through the Looking Glass,' Eastern Culture Meets Western Fashion." *New York Times*, May 7, 2015. Available online: https://www.nytimes.com/2015/05/08/arts/design/review-in-china-through-the-looking-glass-eastern-culture-meets-western-fashion.html?_r=0

Dewey, J. *How We Think: A Restatement of the Relation of Reflective Thinking*. Boston: Heath and Company, 1933.

Kegan, R. *In over Our Heads: The Mental Demands of Modern Life*. Cambridge, MA: Harvard University Press, 1994.

Rimer, S. "Study: Many College Students Not Learning to Think Critically." *The Hechinger Report*, 2001. Available online: http://www.mcclatchydc.com/news/nation-world/national/article24608056.html

Rogers, C.. "Defining Reflection: Another Look at John Dewey and Reflective Thinking." *Teachers College Record* 104, no. 4 (2002): 842–866.

Scriven, M., and R. Paul. "Critical Thinking as Defined by the National Council for Excellence in Critical Thinking." A Statement by Michael Scriven & Richard Paul, presented at The 8th Annual International Conference on Critical Thinking and Education Reform, summer 1987.

Shulman, L. "The Dangers of Dichotomous Thinking in Education." In *Reflection in Teacher Education*, edited by P. Grimmet and G. Erikson, 31–39. New York: Teacher College Press, 1988.

Stone, E. *Dynamics of Fashion*. 3rd edn. NewYork: Fairchild Books, 2011.

6
IDENTIFYING APPAREL AND ACCESSORY TRENDS

Katherine Schaefer, Columbia College Chicago

Contextualization

Trends in the fashion industry play an important role in men's, women's, and children's apparel and accessories, housewares, and a variety of other industries. As a result, designers and retailers are carrying products that reflect seasonal trends to fit into all aspects of their customers' lives.

Silhouette, color, pattern, textures, and embellishment are some ways that seasonal trends influence hardlines and softlines. Hardlines are products with a hard exterior such as appliances, cars, electronics, and furniture; they typically have a long span. Softlines are products like apparel and shoes that tend to be soft; they are smaller in size and allow for more flexibility in merchandising.

When students think of fashion trends, they often focus on softlines, or apparel, and more specifically, women's apparel. However, *Mintel* predicts that men's clothing sales are expected to outpace women's clothing sales over the next five years, as it has become more acceptable for men to express an interest in their personal appearance.

Children's apparel sales are also expected to increase as parents seek out fashionable attire for their children as it is a reflection of their own personal style. In fact, *Mintel* research found that 42 percent of parents want their children to be stylish and trendy.

Fashion is also used as an expression of one's overall lifestyle: consumers incorporate fashion trends into all aspects of their lives, cars to dinnerware to home furnishings. Home décor is updated seasonally; just as consumers switch out warm weather apparel for heavy-duty fall and winter apparel and accessories, linen pillows and gauzy throws are replaced by flannel pillows and wool cashmere blankets.

This chapter illustrates how apparel, accessory, and home products are influenced by seasonal trends. Through trend forecasting, students will identify recurring themes in both softlines and hardlines. In addition, students will discover that there is a direct correlation between apparel and accessory products in regards to how trends in the apparel industry influence trends found in complementary accessory products. Students are required to use industry trade publications to research seasonal trend predictions and then apply this research to existing merchandise offerings in the marketplace. By completing research and applying research to the marketplace, students are able to see not only the correlation between trend forecasting and merchandise offerings, but also the relationship between apparel silhouettes and accessories. Applying research to the marketplace allows students to see the application of trends in their local marketplace.

Appropriate courses for the assignment: Introductory fashion studies course; fashion business courses such as trend forecasting, marketing, merchandising, product development.

Appropriate class size: In-class would be twenty to twenty-five students, and could be an individual or group assignment. If working in groups, I would recommend groups of two to three students. This assignment can also be used as an out-of-class assignment.

Estimated time required: The assignment can be completed during a class period, overnight, or extended up to a week for out-of-class assignments. If it is an in-class assignment, I would recommend forty-five minutes to allow students to do appropriate research for trends in the marketplace using *Women's Wear Daily*, World Global Style Network, Fashion Snoops, or other trend forecasting sites. They can then spend approximately twenty minutes shopping online to find the identified trend in the marketplace. If it is completed as an out-of-class assignment, students can work individually or in small groups (two to three students per group) to research trends online before visiting department stores where there are extensive merchandise offerings, including both hardlines and softlines.

Required materials: Web access, as well as access to trend forecasting sites, would be ideal. If that is not possible, consumer and industry publications and sites like *Women's Wear Daily* or *Vogue* would be appropriate. Trend boards can be put together using sites such as Polyvore or Pinterest for digital boards or a physical board using images from magazines.

Learning goals

- Utilize trend forecasting sites to do trend research.
- Identify seasonal trends.
- Apply research to the current marketplace.
- Relate trends to different markets and different products.
- Present finding in visually appealing manner using Photoshop, Illustrator, Polyvore, Pinterest, or PowerPoint.

Assessment

Assignments should be evaluated based on the use of industry trade publications to complete trend forecasting and the application of the researched trend as seen in the local

IDENTIFYING APPAREL AND ACCESSORY TRENDS

marketplace. It is imperative that the evaluation component also includes the identification of trends across different categories (men's, women's, children's, accessories, and home fashions) to ensure that students understand the correlation and influence of trends in the marketplace. I also believe that by reviewing the visual boards, it becomes apparent whether or not students understood the assignment requirements.

Guidelines for instructors

This exercise is best used at the middle or end of the semester. It is important to have already covered course content focusing on men's, women's, children's, and teens' apparel, as well as the accessories market. This exercise allows students to draw parallels between each of these areas. It is also crucial to have already introduced the concept of trend forecasting and how it is utilized.

In order to get students thinking about trends, the instructor can begin class by dividing students into small groups based on trends worn to class; students work together to determine how the groups were configured. This would foster discussions among students focusing on colors, textures, and patterns as they relate to apparel and accessories.

Cautionary advice for instructors

- Students sometimes have difficulty classifying different types of trends that exist (color, pattern, texture, silhouette, theme, etc.). The majority of students are most familiar with women's apparel and accessories, so identifying the correlation across categories pushes them outside their comfort zone. I have found that giving different examples of completed assignments (preferably from different seasons to alleviate the desire to simply regurgitate the same trend, color, etc.) addresses majority of students' questions.
- Also, students are not always comfortable differentiating between hardlines and softlines, so defining the terms and showing them the different products prove to be beneficial.

Copy of assignment

Assignment overview

For this assignment, you will be using WGSN to research trends for the current season; identify a trend (color, texture, pattern, detail, or silhouette) for the contemporary fashion season that is of interest to you. You will use this trend as the foundation of the assignment to demonstrate how trends cross over to apparel and accessory categories.

Log into WGSN and access "Catwalk Analysis"; scroll down to view the reports for the current season. Consider the following questions: what is the title of the trend board? What does this mean?

Now it is time to go shopping! Visit a retailer or e-tailer to demonstrate how this trend is visible in the marketplace. Show us the trend in men's, women's, and children's apparel. Include an image of at least one men's, women's, and children's apparel item that supports the identified trend. Include your research from WGSN as well.

Using this same research, "shop" the various accessories and home fashions categories. Was this same trend visible in accessories as well? Find an example of the identified trend in at least four different categories:

- Handbags
- Hosiery
- Jewelry
- Shoes
- Men's furnishings
- Home fashions

Next, use your research to create a theme board that provides a visual representation of this trend, featuring apparel, accessories, and home fashions using Polyvore, Photoshop, or PPT. Include at least one image of apparel found in men's, women's, and children's wear, as well as at least four accessory/home fashions products that support the identified trend.

Lastly, revisit WGSN to research silhouettes that are on-trend for the current fashion moment. Choose one silhouette to focus on; explain how this silhouette trend influences at least two categories of accessories. For example, what pant length is currently on trend for the current fashion season? How does this length influence the style of shoe and type of hosiery that are found in the marketplace to complement this trend?

You will be presenting your research to your classmates, so proofread for spelling and grammatical errors. Does your theme board effectively bring your trend to life? Create a visually appealing visual representation, taking into account balance, proportion, and choice of imagery.

Typical results and reflections on the assignment

- This assignment creates a strong foundation for students to understand how interconnected the fashion industry is as they are able to see common themes and trends in a wide array of products targeting different customers.
- This assignment allows the students to act as the experts by introducing their classmates to trends that exist in the marketplace for the current or upcoming season.
- Providing a visual representation of different trends that cross over into various categories.

- This assignment allows students to gain familiarity of various resources used by industry professionals for research purposes.
- This assignment requires students to visit retailers and/or departments they may be unfamiliar with as are targeting different customers, thus exposing students to the different needs of different target markets.
- This assignment introduces students to two merchandise categories in the retail industry, allowing them to better differentiate between hardlines and softlines.

Bibliography

An, Tiffany. "How Fashion Brands Are Celebrating the Year of the Rooster, without the Rooster." *Women's Wear Daily*, January 25, 2017. Available online: http://wwd.com.colum.idm.oclc.org/fashion-news/fashion-trends/year-of-the-rooster-chinese-new-year-10763028/ (accessed March 1, 2017).

"Children's Clothing-US-February 2017." *Mintel*. Available online: http://academic.mintel.com.colum.idm.oclc.org/display/793079/ (accessed March 1, 2017).

"Encyclopedia." *Shopify*. Available online: https://www.shopify.com/encyclopedia/retail (accessed January 30, 2017).

Holt, Emily. "Accessories Report: Accessories Mimic Fall Trends in Apparel." *Women's Wear Daily*, March 14, 2005. Available online: http://wwd.com.colum.idm.oclc.org/fashion-news/fashion-features/accessories-mimic-fall-trends-in-apparel-580385/ (accessed March 1, 2017).

"Men's Clothing-US-March 2016." *Mintel*. Available online: http://academic.mintel.com.colum.idm.oclc.org/display/747672/ (accessed January 30, 2017).

"Retail Analysis." *WGSN.com*. Available online: https://www-wgsn-com.colum.idm.oclc.org/content/reports/#/Retail+&+Buying/w (accessed January 30, 2017).

Robinson, Roxanne. "Accessories Briefs: Under the Influence." *Women's Wear Daily*, May 6, 2015, 36.

PART FOUR

FASHION MERCHANDISING, MANAGEMENT, AND MARKETING

Introduction

Among many other things, fashion is a business, and it greatly benefits students and educators working in all areas of fashion studies to consider the merchandising, marketing, and managerial aspects of the industry. This section's chapters offer insight into best practices in teaching the business of fashion, providing exercises focused on identifying and addressing consumer needs, developing marketing plans, and working effectively with clients. Students come into fashion studies classrooms with varying degrees of exposure, comfort, and familiarity with consumer research, marketing principles, and mathematical skills. The following chapters offer guidance about how students can gain proficiency in all of these areas.

Michele Granger's "The Fashion Formula" provides insight into how students can identify existing consumer needs, create innovative fashion collections that serve an underserved clientele, and market these collections effectively. Focusing on women's fashion, Granger offers a model of how students can create clothing designed for women of a range of different body types, providing female consumers of all sizes with access to stylish, fashion-forward clothing.

Patricia Dillon's chapter reflects on the material value of historic costume. Often prized for its aesthetic and historical value, Dillon also encourages students to learn how garments' construction, condition, and degree of rarity help to determine their material value for prospective purchasers and insurers. Her chapter guides students through the complex processes of gauging collector demand for historic costume, assessing the market price of garments and accessories, and navigating the process of insuring and seeking funding for historic costume collections at museums and other institutions.

Shipra Gupta's chapter discusses her hands-on retail anthropology assignment, in which students have the opportunity to visit a range of different stores to consider the complex variables which impact consumer behavior. Gupta's exercise enables students to critically analyze how factors such as store layout and design, appearance and décor, and the types and marketing of different types of fashion goods shape consumers' decisions. The final chapter in this section, Michele Granger's "Fashioning a Successful Business," similarly offers students the chance to build concrete skills in the world of fashion business. Having students work with real-world clients to conduct a feasibility study, students help clients to identify new markets, differentiate themselves from their competitors, think through issues of expenses, pricing, and merchandising, and map out a plan for the expansion of their business. Undertaking these projects helps students to develop their skills in oral and written communication, problem solving, and working collaboratively as part of a larger team. Each of the chapters in this section helps educators in multiple disciplines to increase students' knowledge of and facility with the complexities of the business of fashion.

7

THE FASHION FORMULA: A PRODUCT DEVELOPMENT PROJECT

Michele Granger, Missouri State University

Contextualization

In fashion apparel, two gatekeepers regulate the apparel choices provided to ultimate consumers: the fashion designer and the fashion buyer. Graduates with fashion degrees, particularly those in design, product development, and merchandising, will very likely be responsible for recognizing and responding to target markets' desires. Customers want to know how to look their best, and many are expecting the designers, manufacturers, and retailers to educate them on how to accomplish this. Consumers are asking for products that feel customized to them, and are expecting answers in the form of the right products developed by the designer and curated by the retail buyer. Many consumers' questions pertain to body shape, trends, and image.

In "Body Shape and Its Influence on Apparel Size and Consumer Choices," E.A. Gribbin states, "Apparel fit remains a major consumer frustration and barrier to online sales growth, not because of sizes and measurements, but because few brands and retailers properly understand and address body shape. Fit, proper fit, is not about size or measurements; it's all about shape" (2014). Why do so many female consumers complain that clothing off the rack or online does not fit their body shapes? The core female body shape many brands start with represents a very small percentage of women. Some of this evolves from the women's apparel industry's use of professional fit models who have proportions more similar to those of runway models than the majority of women. The reality is very different, as evidenced in the SizeUSA study by North Carolina State University. Of the 6,000 American women's body shapes analyzed, 46 percent were rectangular, 20 percent of women were triangles, and 14 percent were inverted triangles (McCormack, 2005).

Some major retailers and designers are recognizing the female customer's interest in body shapes. Nordstrom's website, for example, provides a customer link, "Your Body

Type," and illustrates straight, pear, hourglass, apple, and full-bust body shapes (2015). Macy's website also features a "Shop by Body Type" link in which three body shapes of hourglass, apple, and pear are supplemented with full- and small-bust classifications (2015).

In addition to body shape, consumers are also asking for assistance with interpreting fashion trends. Fashion trends are impacting product development at an increasing speed. Kate Abnett of *The Business of Fashion* reports, "Today, trends are born and die within an infinitely faster and more turbulent environment, in which brands, celebrities, magazines, bloggers, and end consumers on social media all jostle for influence over what's 'in' and 'out' of fashion" (2015). Shannon Whitehead of *The Huffington Post* reports, "Once upon a time, there were two fashion seasons: Spring/Summer and Fall/Winter. Fast forward to 2014, and the fashion industry is churning out 52 'micro-seasons' per year" (2014). In *Overdressed: The Shockingly High Cost of Cheap Fashion*, Elizabeth Cline credits Spanish retailer Zara for pioneering the fast-fashion concept, with new deliveries to its stores twice per week at minimum. She stated that H&M and Forever 21 receive daily shipments of new styles, while Topshop introduces 400 styles weekly on its website (2013). This rapid acceleration of the fast-fashion market results in trends changing too quickly for consumers to react. A new silhouette trend may dominate store inventories, and the consumer asks, "How long will the trend last, and how will it look on me?" Before she can decide, a new trend arrives. Purchasing decisions are further muddied when image is added to the mix. Many fashion consumers are influenced by the image of a retailer and the fashion lines it carries.

There are two images the fashion consumer observes, those of the fashion producer (the designer and manufacturer) and of the fashion provider (the retailer). The customer selects products from lines that portray the image he or she wants to present. Image often coordinates with target market demographics. For example, "in Ralph Lauren's management's own words, the company's Lauren brand serves a customer who is essentially in the over thirty-five age group. Its other popular brand, Denim & Supply, is defined under the millennial umbrella. The new Polo women's business targets younger customers" (Team, 2014). Image, body shape, and trends impact consumer purchases. For starting professionals in the fashion industry, an understanding of how these three variables impact product development and subsequent fashion sales can positively impact career success.

Throughout the semester, students will conduct activities that result in approximately six assignments. The assignments are sequential and move from a broad view of the women's fashion industry to a more narrow view of a specific company, its target market, and its product lines. Most important, the assignments become parts of the team's final report. The report facilitates application of skills needed to identify and dress various body types for women, identify fashion trends for a specific season and year, determine the target market and articulate the image of a particular fashion firm, develop a collection for this fashion firm, and present findings through a team written report and oral presentation. The skills acquired through this project/course are critical to the success of a fashion designer and fashion buyer in providing the products and knowledge that today's consumer wants and needs from the fashion industry.

Appropriate courses and course levels for the assignment: Lower-level undergraduate courses in fashion design, fashion merchandising, marketing, product development, and related programs.

Appropriate class size: Approximately twenty to twenty-five students.

Estimated time required: It is planned for twelve weeks of student teamwork, but can be scheduled for shorter or longer semesters or quarters.

Required materials: Access to a computer, magazines, recommended readings as noted in the bibliography, and trend forecasting reports.

Learning goals

- To identify various female body types and understand how they can be modified through apparel styling
- To recognize where and how fashion trends can be identified and incorporated into product styling
- To comprehend what target market and company image are and how they relate to a brand, its product line, seasonal collections, and its consumers
- To understand the purpose and characteristics of a fashion collection and how to develop an on-trend collection
- To encourage critical thinking and application of theory in such areas as apparel design, consumer behavior, target market appeal, and merchandising
- To participate effectively as part of a team on a group project that culminates with a written report, images, and an oral presentation

Assessment

The learning goals listed above are intended to be achieved through successful completion of the assignments that are parts of the final report and presentation. The assignments are individually based on the following activities: (1) identifying and dressing a range of body types, (2) categorizing fashion trends, (3) pinpointing a specific company's target market and image, (4) developing and designing a fashion collection for a specific season and year for the company, and (5) presenting the collection and other components of the final report to peers and the instructor. The assignment sheet for students provided in this chapter can be easily adjusted to become an assessment rubric to use for grading. The instructor can determine weights for each assignment (e.g., 10 or 20 percent of the total project), the final report, and the presentation to reflect the instructor's preference and emphasis during class sessions. In addition to assessing the outcomes of the individual assignments and the final project as a whole, the instructor has the opportunity to evaluate performance of students as individual team members, performance of groups, and group and individual presentation skills—visual, oral, and written.

Guidelines for instructors

It is recommended that this exercise be introduced at the beginning of the semester. This exercise is formatted here for a twelve-week semester. In Week 1, students ought to begin undertaking readings about female body types and how they can be classified. Providing images of female celebrities and asking students to identify which body type each woman represents, this week engages the students and provides application of the principles. An interesting article that challenges current sizing standards is "It's time we stop comparing women's body shapes to fruit" at www.quartz.com. Additional resources are listed in the bibliography.

Week 2 challenges students to find trend information for a future season designated by the instructor, such as the fall or spring of a given year. Searching for future information can be daunting for students who may not be used to undertaking this type of research. The instructor can direct them to the readings provided in the bibliography at the end of this chapter, such as Li Edelkoort's Trend Union. One of the objectives of this part of the exercise is to help the students understand that designers, product developers, and buyers are working well ahead of the current season that students see in stores and on websites as consumers.

Weeks 3 and 4 are a time to examine varied fashion lines, their images, and the customers they are targeting. BCBG, Ralph Lauren, and Kate Spade are a few examples of fashion lines with target market descriptives available on the Internet. Discussion about the differences between retailers carrying their own private label lines and manufacturers/designers producing lines that retail buyers purchase for their stores is essential. For this project, the instructor will want to focus on fashion lines manufacturers produce and retail buyers purchase for their stores, as this will encourage students to view perspectives of both the designer and the buyer. At the end of this week, students will be divided into teams, each representing a different manufacturer.

Weeks 5 and 6 are scheduled for teams to organize the information they have gathered to develop a collection for their selected fashion lines. It is helpful for the instructor to show examples of collections from the Internet. Many students do not understand what a collection is, until they are presented with actual groupings, and common elements among collection pieces are pointed out to them. In Weeks 7 and 8, student teams will prepare and revise their projects. During Week 9, a final critique given by peers and the instructor for each team will be scheduled. During Weeks 10 and 11, presentations to the class by each team will help students solidify the concepts they have studied, view the work of their peers, and gain verbal and visual skills through their presentations. Week 12 is set aside for final examination period and return of projects and assessments.

Discussion questions

- Can you identify the range of different types of female body shapes, as defined in this assignment?
- Where can you locate fashion trend information? How do you sift through the breadth of information and different points of view available about fashion trends?
- What are the image and target customer for the specific fashion line you have identified?
- What is a collection? Define and provide visual examples.

Cautionary advice for instructors

- If fashion drawing, illustration, or a program like Illustrator is not a prerequisite for this course, students who do not draw may feel at a disadvantage. One solution is ensuring that each team has at least one student who is comfortable drawing in the group. The instructor may want to reassure students that they can use images from the Internet or magazines, or can trace over a croquis (an outline sketch of a figure model used as a template for drawing apparel design ideas).
- Aesthetics, culture, environment, family, personal experiences, and a myriad of other factors can affect what a student believes is appealing or not in body shape and dress, and which parts of the body women wish to highlight, deemphasize, reveal, or conceal. While discussions about women, their bodies, and choices about dress are certainly sensitive topics, this exercise nonetheless has led to exceptionally positive discussions about diversity, awareness, acceptance, self-expression, and marketing imagery. Instructor preparation should include recognizing and planning for the course's potential to raise difficult issues among students with different viewpoints. In the first week, for instance, a student may make a derogatory comment about a specific female celebrity's body, and the instructor will need to diffuse the comment and the assumptions that underlie it. Issues of the body and body image can be difficult and painful for women. Laura Bates writes about women's body image anxiety in the United Kingdom, citing that 37 percent of women aged eighteen to twenty-four and 43 percent of women aged thirty-five to forty-nine are not satisfied with their appearance (2014).
- One of the first rules of classroom conversation is that a negative approach is unacceptable. Students are advised that these conversations must be respectful and positive. If a student makes a negative comment, the instructor can reframe it, either by restating it or by asking questions that result in positive answers. In Week 1, students will be asked to write about their views of body types in a reflection paper that explores personal feelings and experiences about women's bodies and aesthetic preferences, cultural backgrounds, the media, and the fashion industry. This self-assessment helps the students gain understanding

about themselves and others. Information about body types and apparel manufacturers follows in Part A and is suggested as another topic of discussion during Week 1.

Copy of the assignment

Guidelines to the fashion formula: A product development project

Body shape + trend + image = Knowledge needed to design or buy a balanced, fashion-forward, and target market–focused collection

Stages of the product development project (A through G)

At each stage of the project (corresponding to letters A to G as follows), there will be an in-class critique (for points) in which your instructor and classmates will participate. This will help you to stay on schedule and to make revisions, if needed, before moving on to the next step.

A. Identifying and dressing body types

Study each of the five women's body types, or shapes: circle, rectangle, inverted triangle, triangle, and hourglass. We will use these terms for our discussions so that we are speaking the same language in class. During your research, you will find other names for the body types, such as "spoon" or "pear" for the triangle, or "straight" for rectangle. You may make note of these next to the given terms in your project. Locate a croquis online to represent each body type and incorporate these into the chart discussed below. Next, research to discover which silhouettes, patterns or prints, styling, and garment details are said to best flatter each body type. Locate a minimum of three references for each body shape. Compile a chart of recommendations of "what to wear" for each body shape. The focus should be on "X is flattering for Y body type," rather than "Z body type should not wear X" as the latter emphasizes avoiding supposedly negative parts of a specific body type, rather than celebrating positive parts.

It is important to note that this activity broadly assumes that the majority of consumers want to conform to existing, dominant ideals of beauty, which are about emphasizing some body parts while de-emphasizing others. The intent of this part of the assignment is to provide guidance for consumers about body types and traditional aesthetic preferences in dress. Such an approach allows manufacturers to provide apparel products for a mass market. Alternately, to accommodate the individual customer who disagrees with these traditional ideals of beauty, personal measurements and preferences are needed—resulting in custom apparel, rather than products for a large target market.

B. Knowing the trends

Identify the trend forecasts for a future season of an upcoming year as assigned by your instructor. Use websites such as WGSN, *Women's Wear Daily*, Trend Union, and Cotton, Inc., to create a summary of the season's trends, including colors, silhouettes, theme, fabrics, and styling details. Remember to include the sources as references and to keep track of them as you collect content for your team's report.

C. Pinpointing the company target market and image

Select an apparel designer/manufacturer's line that your team is interested in exploring, to be approved by the instructor to avoid repetition. Research its target market: what are their ages, interests, income ranges; which competitive lines do they buy; where do they live; and what do they do. After defining the target market, research the image, or personality, of your company. The line's image should be visible in your collection designs. It is important to *blend* into your collection: the line's image, the trends you have identified, *and* all body shapes. The collection should reflect your target market. Include a summary of who your line's customer is (the target market) and what the company's image is in the team's report.

D. Preparing to develop the collection

Start pulling photos of inspiration, ideas, and examples of each body shape from the Internet and magazines. Use removable tape to organize your drawings and clippings in a journal or folders with divider tabs, or create an online file of this information; bring this information to class for the critique session.

E. Creating your collection

Develop a collection that (1) represents the trend forecast for the assigned season, (2) is reflective of the line your team selected, and (3) includes an ensemble for each body type. Your collection should be fashion forward and complement the full range of body shapes. Most important, it should reflect your line's image and its target market. Polyvore, Prezi, Pinterest, or PowerPoint may be used for the presentation. If you prefer to draw, you may use your croquis to sketch designs or locate images that represent your choices.

F. The finishing touches

Create an eye-catching and informative cover, a title page, and a table of contents. Add the appendices and include these in the table of contents. All pages, except the cover page and table of contents, should be numbered (printed, not handwritten).

G. Due date

When it is the due date for this project, it will be turned at the start of class in two formats: as a hard copy and as a digital copy.

Typical results and reflections on the assignment

- The student will use research tools for identifying future seasonal trends.
- The student will be able to distinguish the image and target market of a fashion producer.
- The student will have the knowledge and skills to identify companies for potential future employment.
- The knowledge and skills provided by the course will support upper-level fashion courses.

- Knowing the tasks of each stage of product development enables the student to select the part of the process he, she, or they prefer, potentially leading to a career path.
- The student will learn how to differentiate the range of body shapes and apply the knowledge to a personal wardrobe and professional work.

Bibliography

Abnett, K. "Do Fashion Trends Still Exist?" *The Business of Fashion*, January 9, 2015. Available online: www.businessoffashion.com

Bates, Laura. "Why Is Women's Body Image Anxiety at Such Devastating Levels?" *The Guardian*, October 14, 2014. Available online: www.theguardian.com/lifeandstyle/2014/oct/14/women-body-image-anxiety-improve-body-confidence

Cline, Elizabeth. *Overdressed: The Shockingly High Cost of Cheap Fashion*. New York: Penguin Random House, 2013.

Granger, Michele. *The Fashion Industry and Its Careers: An Introduction*. 3rd edn. New York: Bloomsbury, Inc., 2015.

Gribbin, E.A. *Body Shape and Its Influence on Apparel Size and Consumer Choices*. Oxford: The Textile Institute and Woodhead Publishing, 2014.

Hirsch, Gretchen. *Gertie's New Fashion Sketchbook: Indispensable Figure Templates for Body-Positive Design*. New York: Harry N. Abrams, Inc., 2015.

McCormack, Helen. "The Shape of Things to Wear: Scientists Identify How Women's Figures Have Changed in 50 Years." *Independent*, November 21, 2005.

Pauper, Peter. *Essentials Fashion Sketchbook: A Designer's Companion (366 Figure Templates)*. New York: Peter Pauper Press, Inc., 2013.

Team, Trefis. "Ralph Lauren's New Polo for Women Shows That It Is Now Moving with the Times." *Forbes*, December 26, 2014. Available online: www.forbes.com/sites/greatspeculations/2014/12/26/ralph-laurens-new-polo-for-women-shows-that-it-is-now-moving-with-the-times/

Whitehead, Shannon, "5 Truths the Fast Fashion Industry Doesn't Want You to Know." *The Huffington Post*, October 19, 2014. Available online: www.huffingtonpost.com/shannon-whitehead/5-truths-the-fast-fashion_b_5690575 .html

8
THE IMPORTANCE OF UNDERSTANDING THE MARKET VALUE OF HISTORICAL COSTUME

Patricia Dillon, New York University and Putnam Art Advisors & Consultants

Contextualization

There is no greater satisfaction for historical costume faculty than seeing students go forward and make significant contributions to the field. Whether students make their mark in academia, curating, or retail, each of their contributions preserves the appreciation of these valuable historical artifacts for generations to come. Given the possibilities of what can be contributed, it is imperative that students have a full and complete understanding of costume.

It is not difficult for faculty to educate and inspire students with their enthusiasm and love of historical costume. We value costumes for a number of different reasons, and, ultimately, they are priceless to us. We cherish the costumes for their historical connection to another time: a link to those who were fortunate enough to own and wear them. We appreciate the garments for the aesthetic achievement and remarkable craft in their design and manufacture. We value them for the vibrant richness and luxury of fabrics from a time when these extravagances were not available to all. We treasure them for the innovation of generations of skilled dressmakers who made and remade the garments to fit new figures in more modern fashions. Each of these qualities is essential to understanding the full significance of a costume.

Accurate evaluation of historical costume is based on two different but related premises: *worth* based on assessment in terms of money and *value* based on aesthetic excellence or historical significance, as well as other desirable qualities such as rarity or condition. Monetary worth is objective, concrete, and measurable. Abstract value is subjective, hypothetical, and idiosyncratic. Financial valuation and pricing, though influenced by the economic law of supply and demand, and fluctuations in the national and international economy, are directly a function of competing collector demands for similar objects. These factors are also influenced by trends, avarice, and acquisitiveness. Market price is ultimately established by a consensus: a collective judgment and general agreement of opinion based upon information that is generally known and widely shared. Of course, connoisseurship plays a significant role in arriving at monetary worth, but it does not always dominate.[1] Estimates for lots at auction reflect the assemblage of this information.[2] Monetary worth is a decisive event arrived at through the evolution of all these factors.

It is often counterintuitive to academics to consider the marketplace as a material element of the value assigned to costume. Many find the "business" of anything to be misguided, trend dependent, and not at all reflective of what essentially matters. Most academics and curators rightfully want to preserve the nonmonetary value of these historical artifacts, and they may not care to have their valuation influenced by currency. Market value is the monetary value at which a garment is exchanged between willing buyers and willing sellers. It is established from auction sales, retail stores, shows or fairs, and private sales.

Understanding the monetary value accorded to a piece allows one to better curate a collection and responsibly protect that collection. One cannot responsibly insure a collection without having an understanding of its market value. For insurance purposes, for example, collections should be appraised by a competent appraiser every three to five years, depending on market conditions. Fully understanding monetary value also provides curators with fodder to whet the appetite of the museum-going public, who in turn support collections and academic studies.

Having a reasonable understanding of collection value also informs grant applications and conversations with prospective donors who can underwrite conservation or improved storage facilities. Being able to show prospective donors that a museum or university is fully aware of the value of its holdings and is taking every precaution to protect these assets conveys confidence to the public. It encourages anyone considering donating their personal collections that the costumes will be well cared for and preserved.

As with any other asset or commodity, the market value of costume can be skewed by outliers such as a single auction doing very well or clothes with celebrity provenance that command unusually high prices.[3] This is to be expected in any asset class, but is more disruptive to the market when an asset such as historical costume is in its nascent stage of its investment potential.

Including market value in the education of costume history professionals does not supplant any traditional academic training. It is an additional element that contributes to the understanding of the discipline and realistically prepares students for success in the twenty-first century. It is meant to ensure confidence and ease the burdens on today's professionals.

While worth is not a new aspect of fashion, an understanding of the elements that create worth has broader implications today than ever before. Unfortunate or not, market worth will determine what will endure in collections and history. Costume history professionals acknowledging this paradigm and familiar with the required polymath skills that define it are able to better contribute expertise in connoisseurship and cultural value to those market forces resulting in a better integration of value and worth.

Looking for employment in the academy or museums, a costume historian with an understanding of the current or potential worth of a collection can more responsibly enhance or deaccession collections, acquire proper insurance, and provide for appropriate conservation. Moreover, they can educate student populations, the public, and the ever-elusive donor to the value of their collections using worth as an enticement. By engaging in this exercise, students will be able to identify, distinguish, and contribute to different market elements.

Appropriate courses and course levels: Market valuation of historical costume can be included in any course at any level but has the most impact at the postgraduate level as a required course, as lower-level courses often are focused on the primary orientation of style, design, and construction. One course in a multiyear graduate program will enrich the student without depreciating the historical, aesthetic, and construction requirements of advanced study. Alternately, undergraduate or shorter-term programs could at least incorporate basic market principles into foundational courses. The exercise below is one that is easily adaptable to a number of different classes, including courses in fashion business studies, economics, marketing, or material culture.

Appropriate class size: To fully utilize and conceptualize the research done by students, class discussion is imperative. It reinforces the formal lesson and is illuminating to hear the observations of each student, particularly if the class is diverse in geographical or cultural representation. Accordingly, an ideal-sized class is eight to twelve students. Larger classes can be accommodated by breaking students into smaller groups for discussion. For example, those who followed certain types of garments could be grouped together and present a unified report to the class. Those working with garments from other countries or inspired by other cultures could make up a second group. Those working with accessories could constitute a third group.

Estimated time required: The exercise can be made simple: a brief research assignment followed by discussion in the next class, or more extensive research conducted over a week or longer.

Required materials: Access to dedicated auctions and/or retail stores. While it is often more enjoyable for students to attend an auction preview or the auction itself, this is not always practical. Internet access is sufficient to access these resources. Most colleges and university libraries have free access to private sources that report a variety of auction and retail transactions. For example, students can access sites such as artnet.com, and most major auction houses feature live auctions via their websites. Students can therefore experience auctions live, regardless of their location.

Learning goals

- To facilitate students' development as fully functioning professionals who are at ease working in academics, curatorial capacities, and/or retail and corporate positions.

- To promote understanding of the market, by removing the mystery that often surrounds the concept of market value and providing practical skills for analyzing market value
- To provide the marketplace with knowledgeable experts whose expertise will educate those in sales, stabilize the marketplace, and promote the importance of historical costume

Assessment

Assessing a student's progress in this class is a measure of the identification of factors affecting market value and the ongoing development of analytical skills to understand those factors. Defining the goals of the class from the start will provide a baseline for that assessment. These goals should include the identification of important market players—auction houses, dealers, fairs, and private sales—as well as the differences among them. Students need to recognize and identify factors that should but do not always contribute to market worth, such as rarity, authentication, condition, artistic achievement, and technical construction. Trends making particular periods or styles popular should be recognized and analyzed as to importance.

By including assignments that incorporate students into the commercial sphere, students have a better understanding of the market and can utilize appropriate *lingua franca*. An exercise that encourages students to fictitiously place a garment for sale in various market venues, for example, auction house, dealer, fair, or private sale, identifying and resolving various issues arising in each can measure a student's understanding of the mechanics of the market.

Guidelines for instructors

Sometimes persons involved in connoisseurship are inherently cautious and uninterested in financial or economic concepts. It is important to emphasize the benefits of a basic understanding of market value over any discomfort students might have in working this material. Going to auction or seeing a live auction via the Internet is often a very exciting experience for students.

Discussion questions

- What is the marketplace for historical costume?
- What is high value? What is low?
- What makes a garment valuable in the marketplace: condition, rarity, aesthetic value, construction, or styling?
- How varied are the garments offered at auction or retail in terms of class, ethnicity, or culture?

- What styles, period, and qualities are not available in the market?
- What factors affect change in market values?
- What is the effect of fabric on the market value of a garment?
- How does ornament affect value?
- Pick a costume, style, or period of origin, and discuss your findings from multiple sources. Which kinds of costumes have been most popular in the marketplace, and why do you think this is the case?
- How much accuracy is there in market descriptions?
- Who is buying at auction: the public, serious collectors, museums, or retailers? How are they buying: multiple lots or investing as a group?
- How soon before a recently sold costume is available again in the market are buyers retaining these garments, or "flipping" them?

Copy of the assignment

Finding the market for historical costume

Option 1. Attend an auction

Attend an auction, including both the preview and the auction itself. Auction previews allow liberal examination of lots, giving a much better sense of the quality of lots offered. As an alternative, you may peruse a catalog and then watch an auction live online, at the website of an auction house.

Task: Observe/analyze/write

1. In the preview or via the catalog (please note: catalogs can almost always be found online), pick two garments.
2. Before the auction is held, estimate the price you expect the garments to fetch and report that to the instructor.
3. In a brief essay, report trends observed in the sale or the impact of the overall auction result.
4. Prepare a brief written analysis of the lots you chose and the factors that affected the sale, and why or why not your earlier predictions held true.

Option 2. Exploring the national market

Peruse prior auction results and/or current auctions being held in other regions by examining online catalogs and price archives or observing an auction in real time via webcast.

Task: Research and write a brief essay on the following

1. Compare and contrast overall market value in different garments sold in varied regions, at different-sized auction houses.
2. Do different types of garments sell better in certain regions?
3. How many examples of garments from a variety of cultures are available?
4. Do you observe any cultural appropriation in the garments for sale?
5. Pick a type of garment from a distinct period and see how many similar examples you can find in the various regions. How much does value vary? What factors affect that?

Option 3. Values and availability in the retail market

Retail value is the price asked for by a retail establishment. While sometimes a buyer can bargain with retailers and/or there may be sales, garments generally have a fixed price determined by the seller and paid by the buyer.

Peruse local dealers, fairs or shows, or online websites of retailers. Visit the stores or booths at fairs and carefully observe the garment(s).

Task: Observe and report your findings in a brief essay

1. What types of garments are available in retail sales? Do dealers specialize in certain types of garments? How many dealers of the number you investigated sold only costume?
2. Was there a trend in pricing? Do retailers tend to be expensive or less expensive?
2. Why?
3. Was there a typical condition found in costume available in retail?
4. How many dealers could you find that specialized in multicultural or ethnic clothing?
5. Pick a costume, style, or period of origin, and track it through multiple sources. Which kinds of costumes have been most popular in the marketplace, and why do you think this is the case?

Typical results and reflections on the assignment

- Once the exercise is commenced, students find it exciting and illuminating. After the exercise has been completed, students who typically avoid studying math, finance, and economics feel more secure in the purchase and sale of costume, negotiating a deal and promoting a collection.

Notes

1. Often simplified to what the late Albert Sack termed "good, better, best, superior and masterpiece"; See Albert Sack, *The New Fine Points of American Furniture: Early American* (New York: Crown Publishers, 1993).
2. Together with some strategic analysis by the Auction House to establish the estimate range that both invites prospective buyers and ultimately enhances the overall value of the sale. It is not unknown for auction houses to lower expectations, creating a wider pool of bidders and allowing the house to rightfully claim that the lot exceeds estimates.
3. For example, in the early summer of 2015, Kerry Taylor Auctions had a very successful offering, which included a Balenciaga gown (1965–1966) estimated at $6,784.00–$9,000 that sold for $63,620.00, a 1962 Pierre Cardin gown estimated to sell for $2,000.00–$3,000.00 that actually sold for $41,250.00, and a 1962 Balenciaga dinner dress estimated to sell in the range of $5,000–$6,000 that actually sold for $42,413.00. Note: the numbers appear to be odd values as they represent the currency exchange between the British Pound and the US dollar and may include buyer's premiums.

Bibliography

Garrett, Wendell et al. *Appraising Art: The Definitive Guide to Appraising the Fine and Decorative Arts*. New York: Appraisers Association of America, 2013.

McAndrew, Clare. *Tefaf Art Market Report*. Helvoirt, The Netherlands: The European Fine Art Fair, 2015.

McNulty, Tom. *Art Market Research: A Guide to Sources and Research*. 2nd edn. Jefferson, NC: McFarland, 2013.

Velthuis, Olav. *Symbolic Meanings of Prices on the Market for Contemporary Art*. Princeton, NJ: Princeton University Press, 2007.

Winkleman, Edward. *Selling Contemporary Art: How to Navigate the Evolving Market*. New York: Allworth Press, 2015.

Legal

Internal Revenue Code Section170 (f) (11)
Internal Revenue Code Rev. Proc. 96–15

9
RETAIL ANTHROPOLOGY

Shipra Gupta, University of Illinois-Springfield

Contextualization

Shopping has now come to be an established form of social science. It is essential for retailers to understand that their choices and decisions about their store design, presentation, and services have a direct impact on consumers' traffic patterns and buying decisions. In retailing, the shopping environment is as important as a product's price and construction, as it is a proven fact that an increase in a shopper's "browsing time" boosts the chances that she/he will make a purchase.

To understand the consumer's browsing time, a new field of study, retail anthropology, has emerged in recent times. Retail anthropology is the study of consumers' shopping habits that not only help retailers strategize the best retail designs but also help them efficiently maximize the shelf and store space with each store. Many retailers like Levi Strauss, Zara, and Victoria's Secret study their customer's browsing and buying habits. Retail anthropologists spend hours analyzing consumer' shopping behavior: what they touch, how long they spend reading packages, how they move in stores (e.g., narrow aisles mean "butt brush," a major turnoff for many female consumers), their responses to signage, how they negotiate the heights at which products of interest are placed, etc. Based on the findings, they advise retailers on how these and other factors can affect the sales and profits of the company.

The purpose of this assignment is to help students understand the concept and process of retail anthropology and how they can help retailers improve their retail strategies.

Appropriate courses and course levels for the assignment: This assignment is appropriate for upper-division courses in retail management, merchandise management, and visual merchandising that are offered in business schools or in consumer sciences departments.

Appropriate class size: There is no limit for the number of students. Depending on the class size, it can be a group project or an individual assignment.

Estimated time required: Students should be given at least one week to conduct retail investigation in the field. The instructor might need an hour to explain the exercise. Also, instructor can use all the six attributes listed above or can pick and choose attributes depending on the objective of the class.

Required materials: Students may need computers to work on presentations and reports. If they are choosing to take pictures of the stores they visit, they will also need a camera or camera phone.

Learning goals

Retailers often hire consulting firms and retail anthropologists to conduct studies that analyze how consumers act and move in store settings. This activity is extremely beneficial for students who are trying to make their careers in the field of retailing or visual merchandising. Through this assignment, students will learn the art of observing the retail stores and how different attributes like store layout, customer traffic flow, crowdedness, appearance, promotion, and merchandising influence consumer buying behavior.

Guidelines for instructors preparing this assignment

This exercise can be implemented at any point in a course, but is ideally suited toward the end of a semester when the students have learned the concept of store layout and merchandise. No advance reading is required, but suggested reading would include chapters 12 ("Managing the Merchandise Planning Process") and 17 ("Store Layout, Design and Visual Merchandising") of *Retailing Management* by Levy, Weitz, and Grewal.

Given that students have to visit three stores, the biggest obstacle in conducting this exercise will be time commitment. Students may not have time to visit the stores and do the assignment. One effective strategy to avoid the time conflict is to give students a class period off, and ask them to utilize that class time to visit the required three stores.

Cautionary advice

One of the biggest challenges in this assignment is when students visit stores; in addition to observing, they may also want to take pictures and make videos. If store employees or customers see students taking pictures or videos of them without their consent, students may also be asked to leave the store. Hence, instructors should caution students, advising them to diplomatically observe the store, and to only take pictures or videos of store employees or customers with their informed consent about the purpose and use of these images and videos.

Copy of the assignment

There are several issues that can help retailers make sure that their store design is optimized for their customers.

RETAIL ANTHROPOLOGY

This assignment requires you to conduct some retail investigation in the field. You will choose three retailers in the same category. (For example, if you pick Macy's, then you will have to pick J.C. Penney and Sears, as all three are departmental stores.) You will compare these three retailers on the following six attributes: store layout, customer traffic flow, crowdedness, appearance, promotion, and merchandising (see Table 9.1).

  a. Visit three retail stores in a part of the clothing industry that interests you, such as department stores, discount clothing stores, specialty boutiques, etc.
  b. Observe these retailers on the following attributes: store layout, customer traffic flow, crowdedness, appearance, promotion, and merchandising.
  c. Store layout:

- What type of layout is used? Would another type of layout be better? Why or why not?
- Does the store layout help draw consumers throughout the store? Why or why not?
- How does the layout facilitate purchase among the consumers?

  d. Customer traffic flow:

- In each store, first watch how consumers move through the store.
- Do they follow similar paths?
- Are they attracted by certain displays or areas of the stores?
- Is the traffic flow efficient?

  e. Crowdedness:

- Compare how crowded each store is. When reporting the crowd density, do mention the days you visited (as the amount of traffic is different on weekdays as compared to weekends).
- Are the aisles wider in one store versus the other?
- Do customers get in each other's way?

  f. Appearance:

- Are the store layout, design, and visual merchandising techniques used consistent with the image of the store and the location?
- What does it say about the type of the store and the market it is trying to attract?
- Is the store's ambience consistent with the merchandise presented and your expectation as a consumer?
- Does the store need a face-lift, update, remodel, or renovation? What improvements would you suggest?

g. Promotion:

- Evaluate the store's signage. Does it effectively sell merchandise?
- Has the retailer used any effective promotions to help sell merchandise?
- Does the store make creative use of wall space to sell products?
- Is the sales staff friendly and helpful?
- Is the image of the staff consistent with the image of the store?

h. Merchandising:

- Has the retailer employed any techniques for achieving greater space productivity, such as downsizing gondolas and racks, minimizing no-selling space, etc.?
- Are there any displays that increase interest in the products being offered? If not, would you recommend any?
- How did the retailer organize merchandise (category management)? What improvements can be made?

i. Discuss your findings. Furthermore, summarize your findings in the chart (posted below):

- Were there patterns in the ways that customers behaved?
- Were certain stores better than others?
- What would you recommend if you were a consultant?
- Summarize your suggestions on how this retailer can improve the shopping experience for its customers, increase sales, and improve its image.

Table 9.1 *Retail anthropology*

Stores	Store Layout	Traffic Flow	Crowd-ness	Appearance	Promotion	Merchandise	Overall Score
Store 1, name and address							
Store 2, name and address							
Store 3, name and address							

Compare the retailers on the above attributes and then assign an overall score. For this exercise, use simple rating scales from 1 to 10, where 10 is best and 1 is worst.

(Note for instructors: Based on their observations, students can prepare either a PowerPoint presentation, written report, or both. In their presentations and written report, students across different attributes can incorporate visuals of the different stores and compare stores accordingly.)

Typical results and reflections on the exercise or assignment

This exercise will help the students taking retail management/visual merchandising classes. It will help them understand the concept of retail anthropology and how it helps the retailers in strategizing their retail plans. Students will learn to analyze consumers' shopping habits based the attributes of store layout, customer traffic flow, crowdedness, appearance, promotion, and merchandising. This experiential exercise will also help them apply theoretical concepts that they have learned from their readings in the field of retailing management. Besides enhancing their analytical skills, students will also be able to enhance their observation and presentation skills.

Bibliography

Fuentes, C., and J. Hagberg. "Socio-Cultural Retailing: What Can Retail Marketing Learn from This Interdisciplinary Field?" *International Journal of Quality and Service Sciences* 5, no. 3 (2013): 290–308.
Gladwell, M. "The Science of Shopping." *The New Yorker* 4, no. 11 (1996): 66–75.
Levy, Michael, Barton A. Weitz, and Dhruv Grewal. *Retailing Management*. New York: McGraw Hills, 2014.
Underhill, P. *Call of the Mall: The Geography of Shopping by the Author of Why We Buy*. New York: Simon and Schuster, 2005.
Underhill, P. *Why We Buy: The Science of Shopping*. New York: Simon and Schuster, 2000.

10
FASHIONING A SUCCESSFUL BUSINESS

Michele Granger, Missouri State University

Contextualization

A feasibility study is a planning tool completed prior to constructing a business plan. The feasibility study explores the possibilities in an initial business idea, or business concept. It is prepared primarily for the entrepreneur's benefit and projects the success or failure of a potential business concept. If the business concept is affirmed by the feasibility study, the business plan is then constructed to fully explain how the business will work along with its financial projections to investors, lenders, and future executives. Evangeline Marzec describes the difference, "Feasibility studies answer the question, 'Will this work?' A business plan answers the question, 'How will this work?'" (2015). More specifically, it responds to the queries "Will anyone buy the product or service?" and "Can the business make a profit?" (Moyes and Lawrence, 2003).

The feasibility study focuses on defining of the proposed business, the size of the potential market, estimated income and expenses, availability and pricing of merchandise, location options, abilities and experiences of the entrepreneur, and expansion opportunities. If the feasibility study shows a likely failure, the fashion entrepreneur can look for a better opportunity instead of developing a business that has no or little chance for success. This preliminary planning is worth its weight in gold. In the United States, entrepreneurs hold an impressive amount of wealth. While about one in ten Americans, or thirteen million people, is self-employed, they hold 37 percent of all wealth in the United States (Fetch, 2016).

A diverse group of future entrepreneurs are attaining college degrees and entering the entrepreneurial sector. The Kauffman Foundation reports that the national entrepreneurial Startup Activity Index in the United States reversed a five-year downward trend in 2015, the largest year-over-year increase over the past two decades. While the 2015 rate of new entrepreneurs in the United States increased by 10 percent (Kauffman Foundation, 2015), inequities in demographics of start-up business owners prevail. According to the Small Business Administration, as of 2013, African-American-owned firms represented 7 percent of all US businesses, Asian-American-owned firms represented about 4 percent, and Latinx-owned firms' share was only 10.5 percent (Kauffman Foundation, 2016).

Although research shows that women and people of color are underrepresented in entrepreneurship, the US Census Bureau's recent Survey of Business Owners (SBO) highlights the growth of women of color as business owners (Fetch, 2015). Thirty-six percent of all non-farm and non-publicly held businesses are owned by women. When broken down by race, the SBO reports women of color are more likely to own businesses than women overall (Fetch, 2015). The number of African American women-owned businesses has increased over three times the rate of African American men-owned businesses, while Latinx women-owned businesses doubled the rate of Latinx men-owned businesses (Kauffman Foundation, 2015). While Asian American women-owned businesses have increased by 44 percent since 2007, Asian American men-owned businesses have only increased by 25 percent (Fetch, 2015).

New entrepreneurs in the United States are also gaining ground in education: those with college degrees increased from 24 percent in 1997 to 33 percent in 2015 (Kauffman Foundation, 2015). With their connections to higher education, these entrepreneurs are reaching out to their universities and community resources for assistance with their visions of future businesses. With Small Business and Technology Development Centers and the Small Business Administration to fashion and business colleges with their classrooms and students, future entrepreneurs are collaborating on the development of successful business start-ups.

"The Feasibility Study: Fashioning a Successful Business" exercise was created as a result of this growing collaboration and increased student interest in fashion entrepreneurship. Students who have completed entrepreneurship courses are paired with entrepreneurs, or entrepreneurs-to-be, who have new business concepts. The student teams develop feasibility studies for their "clients." In this chapter, the student has the opportunity to assess that risk and success potential of an entrepreneur's proposed business concept through activities that apply business theory in such areas as business ownership, management, merchandising, marketing, and finance. The outcomes of this course/project have proven to be mutually beneficial as students (and future entrepreneurs) learn to assess the potential of a business concept and prospective entrepreneurs in the community become partners (and future employers) in this learning activity.

Appropriate courses and course levels for the assignment: Upper-level undergraduate courses in entrepreneurship, fashion, fashion design, or fashion merchandising.

Appropriate class size for in-class exercise: Approximately thirty to thirty-five students.

Estimated time required: In a twelve-week semester, approximately six weeks would be allocated for in-class instruction and guest lecturer presentations, and six weeks would focus on client meetings and out-of-class student work. (These times can be adjusted according to instructor's semester lengths and classroom needs.)

Required materials: Access to a computer; required books (an entrepreneurship text of the instructor's choice and a secondary book); a feasibility study or start-up book of the instructor's choice. Suggestions of books and websites to potentially use are presented at the end of this chapter.

Learning goals

- Understanding the challenges and opportunities of entrepreneurship
- Demonstrating knowledge of feasibility study components, and how to assess the risk of a start-up business
- Understanding the roles and requirements of management, marketing, merchandising, operations, and finance in a start-up business
- Performing effectively on a team in a consulting role for an assigned entrepreneurial client
- Developing learning skills: sharpening critical thinking abilities through creative problem solving, applying theory to real-world scenarios, and strengthening communication skills (oral, written, and visual)

Assessment

The learning goals of "Fashioning a Successful Business" are initially facilitated through interviews, question–and-answer sessions, and other meetings with the entrepreneurial "clients" assigned to each team. The student learns to work as a member of a team. The student also learns how and where to collect information needed to complete the various sections of the feasibility study report, whether from the entrepreneur, online research, or business resource centers. The results of this research are compiled into the final feasibility study report, using the feasibility study framework that follows. This framework can also be used as a rubric for scoring the team reports, one in which the instructor can determine grading weights for the various sections to reflect course prerequisite work, course lectures (to include guest speakers), and assigned readings. Assessment can also include evaluations of the student's skills and efforts in the areas of professional conduct, such as reviews of the student as an individual team member, of the team presentations scheduled at the end of the semester, and of the client's feedback on meetings with the students.

Guidelines for instructors

During Weeks 1 through 3 of a twelve-week semester, background and foundational information is presented on the purpose and process of building a feasibility study during the rest of the semester. During Week 4, students meet with clients. From Weeks 5 through 11, students work on the different parts of the feasibility study, to include business overview, market assessment, financial assessment, operations and management assessment, and feasibility decision. During the last week of semester, students present their projects to clients.

Discussion questions

- What is a feasibility study, and how does it differ from a business plan?
- Where can we find research data on consumers, types of business, physical locations, and Internet trends?
- Where can we find statistics on fashion retail sales, stock turn, and markup?
- How will the client differentiate the business from the mass of competitors (e.g., specialty store chains, Internet retailers, and discount stores)?
- How can entrepreneurs reach new customers and promote their businesses on a budget?
- What are the factors that determine whether a business is feasible or not? If a business is not initially feasible, can changes be made to make the concept feasible?

Cautionary advice for instructors

- Fashion products are perishable. They age and "spoil" as trends and seasons change. It is critical to recognize the need to turn inventory (and, perhaps, take markdowns) to generate funds for purchasing new goods seasonally.
- Clients may change their minds about how, where, and what they want to do with the prospective business midway in the feasibility study process. They may become very confident, and want to include more and more in the opening business. Others may become disillusioned about their concepts when being presented information they did not know or do not want to hear. As the instructor, guiding the client is a significant part of the course. Clients may need to be reminded that the students are working on the concept initially selected for the course, although it will evolve throughout the process.
- Students may feel they are not getting enough information from the client. While that certainly can happen, it is rare. More often, the students may be expecting the client to find and/or give them the information needed in the feasibility study. At the start of the semester, the instructor may want to explain the role of a paid consultant in this type of business situation. The successful consultant takes care not to insult or disparage a client. Hard work and honesty are important, as are tact and effective communication.
- Teams can be challenging for students and instructors. Attendance, effort, and work ethic can vastly differ among student team members. Detailed individual student assignments for all team members help foster accountability and aid

the instructor in assessing who has done what. Regularly scheduled (and well-attended) meetings between the instructor, clients, and students keep communication lines open and deadlines met.

Copy of the assignment

The following information is sent by the Small Business and Technology Development Center, Small Business Administration, or Entrepreneurial Center (whichever organization partners with the class) to potential clients.

The *Feasibility Study* is a partnership between _____ and the university's Fashion Entrepreneurship Program. It is a semester-long project in which students conduct research and evaluate all aspects of a client's business concept to determine whether or not it is feasible. We are seeking individuals who have a valid idea for a new business, a clear passion for their business concept, the ability to invest in it, and availability to meet and communicate with the students throughout the semester.

At the study's conclusion, the client receives a written report that includes the following:

- **Business overview:** Discussion of the purpose of this study, industry trends and benchmarks significant to your business, business concept, products and services offered by your business, and consumer appeal.
- **Market assessment:** Discussion of the size and characteristics of your primary target audience, number of competitors as well as their strengths and weaknesses, competitive advantage, marketing mix strategy, suggested price strategy, suggested promotional strategy, and recommended customer loyalty techniques
- **Financial assessment:** Discussion of the financial opportunity of the proposed business, estimated start-up costs, sales projections and calculations, pro-forma income statement, and annual break-even analysis.
- **Operations and management assessment:** Discussion of the proposed location, possible building layout, possible legal issues, labor availability, equipment needs, recommended operating hours and procedures, and experience and skills of owner and key personnel.
- **Feasibility decision:** Recommendation of whether or not your business idea is feasible, including detailed reasoning for the decision, possible alternative strategies, and additional suggestions. When applicable, expansion opportunities are discussed.
- **Research sources:** All sources of quantitative/qualitative research will be documented.
- **Presentation/findings/outcome:** Oral presentation and detailed report of your study's findings.

Next, the following spreadsheet is given to students as a framework for the feasibility study report.

	Estimated Page #s in Study	Subtopics (Follow Cover Page and TOC)	Instructor's Suggestions/ Student Resources	SBTDC Suggestions and Resources
Part 1. Business Overview:	p. 1	Purpose of this study	Draft this section; plan to go back and revise.	What is the client asking for?
	p. 2	Business concept		Bizminer Reports are available and will provide: # of businesses in industry locally and nationally, number of start-ups, number of failures, average sales (growing or declining), and other trends
	pp. 3–4	Industry trends significant to the business	Research industry trends for your business: international or national, state, and city.	Help the client focus the concept to a specific target market, or niche
	p. 5	Products and services offered by the business	Description and proportion of products/services.	
	p.6	Consumer appeal	How does business fill consumer needs and market niche?	
Part 2. Market Assessment:	p. 7	Size and characteristics of the primary target audience	Research statistics for business target market	Research data available. Age, income, gender, education, interests, etc. of target market; where do they live?
	p. 8	Benchmark(s)	Examples of aspirational business(es)	Preferably out of competitive area
	pp. 9–10	Number of competitors and their strengths/weaknesses	Eegin competitor analysis at start of semester.	Identify direct competitors; further analyze based on prices, location, customer service, experience, etc. Research resources available.

FASHIONING A SUCCESSFUL BUSINESS

	p. 11	Competitive advantage	Analyze competitors as they relate to all segments of the feasibility study. Build a competitors' matrix comparing variables.	What sets client apart? Why would target market buy from client over competitors?
	p. 12	Suggested price strategy	Refer to text.	May come from client; compare to competitors and make new suggestions if necessary
	pp. 13–14	Suggested promotional strategy	See text and research guerilla marketing strategies.	How will you market to target consumers? How will you reach them? What strategies appeal to market?
	p. 15	Recommended customer loyalty techniques	Discounts, previews of new mdse., free gift with multiple purchases, and much more. Be creative.	Are repeat customers important? How will you encourage them to return?
Part 3. Operations and Management Assessment:	p. 16	Proposed location	Find actual location from listings online, realtor, or in person. Rent or buy or build? Where should client locate and why? What does client need in a building/land/location? Leasehold improvements? Analyze pros and cons of three or more locations; choose one for financial statements.	Research data available for locations, especially demographics of location.
	p. 17	Possible building layout	As above	What should building look like? Include floor plan and images. What costs will be incurred?

Estimated Page #s in Study	Subtopics (Follow Cover Page and TOC)	Instructor's Suggestions/ Student Resources	SBTDC Suggestions and Resources
p. 18	Possible legal issues	See text for Forms of Business Ownership.	LLC, corporation, etc. Process of becoming a business locally, nationally. Pros and cons of type of incorporation. Use government websites here.
p. 19	Labor availability	Research employment statistics, classified advertisements, etc.	Where should client look to find employees? Licenses needed? Employees or subcontractors? What should employees be paid? Research salaries of employees in industry. Will employees be difficult or easy to find? Ways to market to employees.
p. 20	Equipment needs	May be included in start-up costs if need to be purchased.	What does client need to purchase before opening day? Furniture, machinery, equipment, etc.
p. 21	Recommended operating hours and procedures	Competitor comparison can help here.	When should client open and close each day? How many/which days per week? How much will owner work? How many employees needed? What are employees' tasks? Look at competitors.
pp. 22–23	Experience and skills of owner(s) and key personnel	Refer to text chapter.	Does client need management positions? Is experience necessary to hire? What are qualifications of owner that will add value to business?

Part 4. Financial Assessment:	p. 24	Estimated start-up costs	Start this chart with location costs. Include equipment needs and other costs before opening business: marketing materials, training employees, costs of incorporation, etc.
	pp. 25–26	Sales projections and calculations	Industry analysis needed, as well as monthly projections. How much of target market will you capture based on your marketing strategies? Break into different lines of revenue.
	pp. 27–28	Pro-forma income statement	Required meetings on financials with instructor and SBTDC. Analyze COGS and all relevant expenses; document EVERY assumption.
	p. 29	Annual break-even analysis	As above. Determine if expenses are variable or fixed; calculate sales break-even as a unit break-even.
	p. 30	Financial plan for client to open business	
Part 5. Feasibility Decision:	p. 31	Is the business concept feasible or not? Why or why not	Are there changes that can be implemented to make it feasible?
	p. 32	Possible alternative strategies	
	p. 33	Additional suggestions	Maintain a list of alternatives throughout project to review later. Long-term goals? Future plans?
References Appendices	p. 34, etc.		

Typical results and reflections on the assignment

- The student gains experience in using the research tools introduced in class and provided by the SBTDC and other college resources (e.g., library and Entrepreneurship Center) to identify risk and potential for future analysis of business concepts, whether their own or the concepts of others.
- The student has experience in assessing the size and potential of a target market and recognizing how to narrow market data into niche markets.
- The student has the knowledge and skills to identify the steps needed to acquire funding to start a fashion business.
- Knowing the tasks of each stage of the feasibility study enables students to select the part of the process they prefer and excel in to help identify preferred career paths, whether entrepreneurship, finance, operations, marketing, etc.

Bibliography

Fetch, Emily. *Including People of Color in the Promise of Entrepreneurship*. MO: Kauffman.org, December 5, 2016. Available online: www.kauffman.org/what-we-do/resources/entrepreneurship-policy-digest/including-people-of-color-in-the-promise-of-entrepreneurship

Fetch, Emily. *Women of Color in Entrepreneurship: New SBO Data and What It Means for the Economy*. Kansas City, MO: Kauffman.org, September 17, 2015. Available online: www.kauffman.org/entrepreneurship-new-sbo-data-and-what-it-means-for-the-economy

Granger, Michele, and Tina Sterling. *Fashion Entrepreneurship: Retail Business Planning*. 2nd edn. New York: Fairchild Publications, Inc., 2011.

Harder, Frances. *Fashion for Profit: From Design Concept to Apparel Manufacturing and Retailing-a Professional's Complete Guide*. 10th edn. CA: Harder Publishing, 2015.

Kauffman Foundation. *Small Businesses in the US on the Rise, Reversing Six-Year Downward Trend*. MO: Kauffman.org, December 3, 2015. Available online: www.kauffman.org/newsroom/2015/12/small-businesses-in-the-us-on-the-rise-in-2015-reversing-six-year-downward-trend

Kauffman Foundation. *State of the Field: Distilling the Universe of Entrepreneurship Research*. MO: Kauffman.org, September 6, 2016. Available online: www.kauffman.org/microsites/state-of-the-field/topics/background-of-entrepreneurs/demographics/race

Kidder, David. *The Startup Playbook: Secrets of the Fastest Growing Startups from the Founding Entrepreneurs*. CA: Chronicle Books, 2013.

Marzec, Evangeline. "Business Plan vs. Feasibility Study." Houston, TX: Small Business Chron, 2015. Available online: smallbusiness.chron.com/business-plan-vs-feasibility-study-43382.html

Moyes, Frank, and Stephen Lawrence. *Feasibility Plan Framework*. Colorado: Deming Center for Entrepreneurship of University of Colorado-Boulder, 2003.

Scarborough, Norman, and Jeffrey Cornwall. *Essentials of Entrepreneurship and Small Business Management*. 8th edn. Upper Saddle River, NJ: Pearson Education, Inc., 2016.

Thiel, Peter. *Zero to One: Notes on Startups, or How to Build the Future*. New York: Crown Business, 2014.

PART FIVE

CONSTRUCTION-, DESIGN-, AND OBJECT-BASED PROJECTS

Introduction

Significant as fashion is on a symbolic level, it is also inherently material, visual, and tactile. Garments are all (to one degree or other) made by human hands and worn on human bodies. The chapters in this section bring students into the material realities of fashion, drawing on kinesthetic learning styles, and transforming students into makers who draw, analyze, and create fashion objects. Ingrid Mida's chapter on her "slow approach to seeing" method encourages students to cultivate a careful, patient mode of examining fashion objects. Offering a model of how students can engage in thorough, deliberate observations of garments, Mida emphasizes the need for students to meticulously consider what small details reveal about daily fashion practices, and to both physically draw and engage in written thick description of fashion objects, to enrich student understandings of materiality of fashion.

Diane Maglio's chapter gives another perspective on the objects of fashion culture, emphasizing the significance of students' unique reactions to the material aspects of fashion. Encouraging students to engage with historic costume in museums and with contemporary fashions in their own closets, Maglio's chapter helps students develop confidence in their personal responses to fashion, as a vital part of learning to trust their distinctive perspectives and taste, and fostering their personal creativity. In her chapter, Alexandra van den Berg Christensen helps students to think in more nuanced ways about an object of perennial interest in fashion studies: the corset. Christensen's exercise encourages students to learn about the history and evolution of corsets during different eras, by crafting paper models of corsets from diverse time periods. Through engaging in this hands-on exercise, students both learn more about garment construction and engage in valuable reflections on the complex intersections between body modification and notions of class and gender in different time periods and cultures.

Patricia Dillon's chapter helps bridge the virtual and physical fashion worlds, discussing exercises in which online students engage in a range of different types of field work in their on-ground communities. Dillon discusses how to have students collect and analyze a diverse assortment of textiles, visit local history museums and examine their costume collections, and join in acts of clothing creation by participating in sewing projects and classes. These assignments thus bring the tactile aspects of the (fundamentally digital) world of online learning. In her chapter, Anna Green similarly offers a useful model of how to have students engage with the "real world" of material fashion, beyond the classroom. In her exercise, students go into thrift stores in their community, buying items to repurpose into new, innovative looks. This assignment helps students not just think creatively about construction and build their skills in working collaboratively, but also engages them in discussions of fashion, sustainability, and income inequality, in access to clothing.

Chapters by Jody Aultman and Sara Marcketti, and Alice Payne and Kiara Bulley, also enable students to think about fashion design and clothing construction from innovative new perspectives. Aultman and Marcketti's exercise brings together fashion design and the science, technology, engineering, and mathematics (STEM) field, helping students to apply principles from STEM disciplines to their design work, in terms of shape, texture, space, and form. Payne and Bulley's exercise helps design students to use classic fashion forms as inspiration for their own original designs, drawing on old fashion forms as productive jumping-off places for the creation of fashion-forward new designs. All of the chapters in this section provide students with opportunities to think about and work in physical, tactile worlds of design, construction, and objects, and to consider issues of fashion and materiality in complex, inventive ways.

11
THE SLOW APPROACH TO SEEING

Ingrid Mida, Ryerson University

Contextualization

In describing the role of objects in our lives, museologist Susan Pearce wrote: "Objects hang before the eyes of the imagination, continuously representing ourselves to ourselves and telling the stories of our lives in ways which would be impossible otherwise."[1] Engagement with objects is a long-established pedagogy that allows students to directly engage with the past.[2] Objects can be used for inspiration and design research as well as serve as active teaching tools in a range of courses in the fashion curriculum, including illustration, construction methods, fashion history, curation, and material culture. However, in an era where photography is ubiquitous, students may lack the close observational skills and the patience required to make a careful study of an unfamiliar object.

In my book, *The Dress Detective: A Practical Guide to Object-Based Research in Fashion*, I advocate an approach to looking that I call *The Slow Approach to Seeing*. Like other slow movements, this entails taking the time to be fully present, to really look at the object under consideration to see the subtle details that are not readily apparent from a cursory glance or in taking a photo. When drawing an object, not as a quick sketch, but as a careful exercise that records each contour and subtle variation, there is a greater chance for students to really see those minute details of texture, construction, or wear that could reveal a hidden story within the garment or object itself. For example, there might be a subtle patch of wear on a shoulder of a coat or jacket, suggesting that a purse or bag was carried on that shoulder; or there might be signs that a dress was let out for the early stages of pregnancy. The stories of a garment are often revealed in these details.

The purpose of these exercises is to encourage and develop the skills of close observation through slow looking. Such skills serve both design and theory students, and are especially useful for courses in which careful observation is critical in the research process such as material culture studies and ethnography.

Appropriate courses and course levels: Undergraduate courses in art history, fashion history, fashion illustration, research methods, reproducing historic dress, and the sociology of fashion; graduate courses in fashion theory, museum studies, oral history and ethnography, and research methods.

Appropriate class size: Ten to twenty-five students.

Estimated time required: Sixty to seventy-five minutes in class. This exercise can be adjusted to suit shorter or longer intervals. Generally, the time allotted will depend on the level of engagement of the students. As the exercises progress, students often become so engaged in the exercise that they do not wish to stop.

Required materials

- Pencils, pens, or markers.
- Paper (ideally drawing paper at least 8.5 × 11 but printer paper is adequate).
- Objects (one for each student is ideal; alternatively, one for two students). Examples of preferred objects include garments or accessories with complex textures, patterns, embellishments, or methods of construction such as tailored bodices and jackets, corsets, bonnets, and dresses with lace or flounces.
- Note: The objects used in this exercise do not have to be fashion artifacts per se, and the exercise can be done with any object, including paintings, sculptures, tools, or housewares. Any object with a lot of detail and/or texture can be used for these exercises.

Learning goals

- To practice the close observation of dress artifacts, objects, or artworks.
- To develop and improve skills of observation in general, and for dress artifacts in particular to notice subtle aspects of construction, textile patterns, as well as signs of wear, use, or condition.
- To develop the ability to write "thick description" that fully describes an object or artwork. For dress artifacts in particular, this would include details of construction, possible alterations or changes due to use or wear, as well as their current condition.

Assessment

Assessment of students should be based on evidence of participation and engagement. The goal of these exercises is not to produce pretty drawings or accurate representations of the artifact or artwork. Engaged students will produce messy drawings and a richly textured and lengthy description of the artifact or artwork. Students should submit their drawings and descriptions at the end of class for review by the instructor to encourage active participation in the exercises.

Guidelines for instructors

This exercise can be implemented at any point in a course, but is ideally suited toward the beginning of a semester to encourage students to slow down and be fully engaged when looking at objects. No advance reading is required, but suggested reading would include Chapters 2 and 3 of *The Dress Detective: A Practical Guide to Object-Based Research in Fashion*.

There may be certain artifacts, such as bustles or crinolines, that may be unfamiliar to students depending on their cultural background, especially if they have not yet taken a fashion history course.

The biggest obstacle to conducting this exercise will be that some students may be reluctant to disengage from their mobile devices and be fully present. Students may also protest that they cannot draw. However, the exercises are specifically designed for nonartists and are not intended to produce an image, but are focused on the act of close observation. Instructors should be vigilant in monitoring the level of engagement and intervene if necessary. One effective strategy is to have the students change the orientation of the object: turning it upside down or orienting it another way to present a novel viewpoint at any stage in these exercises. It is also helpful to show "messy" examples of drawings.

Discussion questions

- Can you see a difference in the description you wrote about the artifact before the exercise and the description you wrote after the drawing exercises?
- What happened to your perception of time when you were engaged with the object?
- What circumstances enhance or encourage "slow looking"?

Cautionary advice for instructors

- Students who have artistic training may ignore instructions and want to draw in their usual manner, while others may protest that they cannot draw and therefore cannot participate. These exercises are appropriate for all learners and are supposed to end up looking messy and incomplete. The idea is not to focus on the drawing, but on the looking. It can also be helpful if the instructor does the exercises prior to the class and shows the students an imperfect drawing to emphasize that the point of the exercise is the process and not the product.

- Ask students to put away their mobile devices.

Copy of the assignment

There are four parts to this exercise. Before beginning the exercise, I recommend that you close your eyes briefly and take several deep breaths. Commit to being fully present and to letting go of expectations and judgment.

Figure 11.1 Pink and gold changeable silk cape with black satin and chiffon ties. Ryerson Fashion Research Collection FRC2014.07.158, gift of the Suddon-Cleaver Collection.

THE SLOW APPROACH TO SEEING

- 1. Observe your object closely and write as full and complete description of the object as you can. Upon completion of this part, set that aside. Time: five to ten minutes.[3]

- 2. Using a pencil and blank piece of paper, draw the object using one continuous line and without looking at the paper. The idea is to record the movement of your eyes and not make a pretty picture. Stay focused on the object, and do not look down at the paper. (See Figures 11.1 and 11.2.) Time for students drawing: fifteen minutes. Class discussion of student drawing: ten to fifteen minutes.[4]

- 3. Take a second piece of blank paper (or turn paper over). This time, turn the object over or around to see it from a different perspective, and then draw the object with the nondominant hand. Time: fifteen minutes.[5] (See Figure 11.3.)

- 4. Lastly, write a second description of your object. Aim to write a thick description, fully describing the object so that a person without sight might read the description and be able to visualize the object. Time: fifteen minutes.

Once you have completed all four parts of the exercise, be prepared to compare your first description to your final description. What changed? What did you add in the final description of your object? Time: five minutes.

Figure 11.2 Pencil drawing of cape (Ryerson FRC2014.07.158) with continuous line by Ingrid Mida, 2017.

Figure 11.3 Pencil drawing of cape (Ryerson FRC2014.07.158) with nondominant hand by Ingrid Mida, 2017.

Typical results and reflections on the assignment

- This exercise is usually met with some initial resistance, especially from students who do not think they can draw. The instructor should remind students that they need not to be artists—that the point is not to create a realistic drawing of the object but to engage with the object through drawing.

- Those students who draw may need to be encouraged to do the exercise as asked and follow instructions instead of drawing as they normally would. Remind them that this is not about the end product but rather about learning to see.
- Over the series of exercises, there will often be a shift in the mood and tone of the class with students becoming more focused and serious as they become engaged and reflective.
- Students are often surprised by what they notice about an object or artwork with focused and attentive looking. This is the goal.

Notes

1. Susan Pearce, *Museums, Objects and Collections: A Cultural Study* (London: Leicester University Press, 1992), 47.
2. See Helen J. Chatterjee, "Object-Based Learning in Higher Education: The Pedagogical Power of Museums," *University Museums and Collections Journal* 3 (2010): 179–191.
3. Instructors may wish to collect each stage of the exercise from the students so that they do not revise. In that case, ask students to write their names on each part of the exercise.
4. Remind students that the goal is not what is on the paper but focusing on what is in front of them. At this point, the instructor should walk around and observe what the students have done. Encourage them to celebrate drawings that are not perfect and that show careful observation and attention to detail. The drawings may be fragmentary with overlaps. If the drawing closely resembles the object, the student has been looking at their paper and not the object.
5. Students may look at their paper but should be encouraged to do so only as necessary. Again the focus is on the object and not on the results. Lines should be fragile and fragmentary. Remind students that perfection is not the goal.

Bibliography

Chatterjee, Helen J. "Object-Based Learning in Higher Education: The Pedagogical Power of Museums." *University Museums and Collections Journal* 3 (2010): 179–191.
Mida, Ingrid. "The Curator's Sketchbook: Reflections on Learning to See." *Drawing Research Theory and Practice Journal* 2, no. 2 (2017): 283–254.
Mida, Ingrid. "'Drawing as an Antidote to Technology' in 'Scholars' Roundtable 2017.'" *Dress* 43, no. 2 (2017): 121–125.
Mida, Ingrid, and Alexandra Kim. *The Dress Detective: A Practical Guide to Object-Based Research in Fashion*. London: Bloomsbury, 2015.
Palmer, Alexandra. "Untouchable: Creating Desire and Knowledge in Museum Costume and Textile Exhibitions." *Fashion Theory: The Journal of Dress, Body & Culture* 12, no. 1 (2008): 31–64.
Pearce, Susan. *Museums, Objects and Collections: A Cultural Study*. London: Leicester University Press, 1992.

Simpson, Andrew, and Gina Hammond. "University Collections and Object-Based Pedagogies." *University Museums and Collections Journal* 3 (2012): 75–81.
Steele, Valerie. "A Museum of Fashion Is More than a Clothes-Bag." *Fashion Theory: The Journal of Dress, Body & Culture* 2, no. 4 (1998): 327–336.
Taylor, Lou. "Doing the Laundry? A Reassessment of Object-Based Dress History." *Fashion Theory: The Journal of Dress, Body & Culture* 2, no. 4 (1998): 337–358.

12
OBJECT ANALYSIS AND ADAPTATION FOR THE CURRENT FASHION MARKET

Diane Maglio, Berkeley College

Contextualization

Students in fashion merchandising and management are trained, in part, to study, evaluate, and criticize objects: clothing and accessories for men, women, children, and the home. During their business careers, they will be handling volumes of stockkeeping units (SKUs). The business of fashion begins with looking at objects and the environment in which they were made and used. Two critical considerations for success in the fashion business are determining customers' wants and needs and assessing the spirit of the times, which gives structure to those needs.

To historian Jules Prown, material culture, which includes fashion merchandise, is "the study of [objects] to understand … [and] discover the beliefs-the values, ideas, attitudes, and assumptions-of a particular … society at a given time."[1] Objects produced for consumption are primary sources of study, offering students a personal experience in analysis and interpretation. Primary objects, viewed in their physicality, can also engender an immediate emotional response. Fashion studies in this digital era rely heavily on images and sources examined through the filter of a screen and an electronic device. In the object analysis method, students will not only develop their observation skills, but also learn to listen and record their inner voice in response to the multidimensional object seen in its authentic materials and colors. This assignment has been directed to clothing analysis but can easily be adapted for other fashion objects such as home products and automobiles.

The primary issues to address are materials (textiles, metals, or other), methods of construction, and standing in the period in which they were used. For contemporary commercial applications, the student must then integrate the past with the future. This requires an examination of the zeitgeist in past eras and now. Not to say all garments studied are from the distant past, as fashion business is about the "newness" of tomorrow. Accordingly, an early twenty-first-century garment seen in an exhibition or a study collection is "old news" for the wholesale and retail worlds. Preparing students to be leaders in the fashion industry includes the ability to bring an original perspective to their jobs that can be nurtured through a combination of sensory and intellectual assessments.

This assignment considers object study as the "perfect analytic tool for … student centered learning."[2] Scholarly works that inform this assignment include the methods of Jules Prown, E. McClung Fleming, Charles F. Montgomery, and Ivan Kopytoff that have been adapted to the particular subject being taught within the fashion curriculum. *The Dress Detective: A Practical Guide to Object-Based Research in Fashion* by Ingrid Mida and Alexandra Kim also details case studies of objects analyzed and provides checklists to assist researchers.

Drawing from Prownian analysis, the assignment begins with detailed descriptions, then deduction, followed by speculation. At this point, research is begun leading to interpretive analysis. Students are trained to observe and analyze with the ability to clearly document conclusions. They will then research and determine if and how they can integrate the object from the past with the needs of the market in the future. A study by Cho and Lee has studied consumer emotions as "a kind of macroscopic model of recent fashion trends."[3] As consumers are emotionally stimulated by garments and products they find attractive, they respond to those objects based on their positive sensory responses.[4] So, too, must fashion students cultivate their own emotional responses, in order that they may better empathize with the emotional drive that propels future consumers to choose one garment rather than another.

While big cities have many museums, colleges, libraries, and historic houses to study material culture, local communities also often maintain collections in libraries and regional historic houses. A blue-velvet smoking chair belonging to General Philip Kearny, who fought in the US Civil War, for example, can be seen in the Kearny Museum at the Kearny Public Library in New Jersey. The description of this object simply reads "a hinged cigar box on the chair's back upholstered armrest." Questions may arise when seeing a box attached to an opulent chair dedicated to cigar smokers. Research may lead to examinations of the culture of smoking in mid-nineteenth century, and the specific informal wardrobes worn by men in the domestic sphere. The roles of women in this society could also be examined. The investigation of one chair in a local museum may thus lead to an understanding of the organization of a home, occasion-specific clothing, and the division of gender roles during the era in which this chair was created and used.

A common thread gleaned from conversations with employers in the fashion business was "passion" for the work. The aim of this assignment is to teach students how to recognize their personal emotional connections with objects and to integrate emotions with factual research to provide products for their customers that will stimulate market enthusiasm and generate sales. Valerie Strauss of *The Washington Post* reported: "There is a large and growing body of research that suggests that the skills of emotional intelligence-the ability to reason with and about emotions to achieve goals-are correlated with positive outcomes … Emotions affect learning, decision-making, creativity, … and people with more developed emotion skills do better."[5] Fashion students who foster their emotional responses to objects may also see more creativity and better decision making in their trend analysis. The blending of emotion and intellect and the ability to clearly document and present their findings with visual images and rational writing will make students more readily employable and have successful careers.

Appropriate courses and course levels for assignment: Undergraduate courses in fashion design, fashion marketing, and fashion merchandising. The basic assignment can be modified as students improve and perfect the process and learn to listen to their own emotional responses.

Appropriate class size: This assignment is appropriate for any size class. For a class fewer than twenty students, the findings can be presented with images to the class. Students can photograph or sketch the object they have analyzed, and other images related to the findings of their research. They can then discuss their interpretation and their emotional engagement to the object as catalyst to the final products in a PowerPoint presentation.

Estimated time required: The time required to research and write the paper can take multiple hours depending on the skill and familiarity students have with resources. Subject to location, travel time must be considered to visit a museum or study collection. When a visit to a collection is not possible, the alternative would be to gather personal objects from students or faculty that can be used as a study collection. Examining online collections would not be an alternative for this exercise, since the goals are to have students consider their emotional engagement with an actual three-dimensional object.

Required materials

- Pencil
- Paper (to sketch and document the object)
- Camera for images when permitted
- Access to Internet and libraries for research

Learning goals

- Identify and foster students' feelings engendered by viewing material, three-dimensional objects.
- Integrate personal emotions with object engagement to identify with consumers' desires.
- Probe and discover the surrounding reasons for shifting erogenous zones and silhouette modifications through garment construction or surgical body modifications.

- Analyze and identify direction of fashion change and trends, including developments and degrees of quality in fiber technology, smart textiles, and shifting moods of color.
- Forecast appropriate adaptations of past styles to future retail merchandise with consideration from past to future zeitgeist.
- Articulate and communicate enthusiastically, through both writing and verbally, changes in fashion clothing, textiles, and color trends.
- Think critically about clothing and consumers' preferences.

Assessment

This assignment is worth 100 points. Distribution of points over the assigned components will be as follows:

1. Examination of objects to find the one object that inspires a surge of emotion in the student. The image of the object must be included and a cogent essay describing the allure and excitement generated by the object. (Ten points)

2. Description-Observation. This evaluation will be assessed on comprehensive detailing of all visible elements of the object supported by written and visual documentation. (Fifteen points)

3. Deduction. The student must demonstrate ability to interpret the object and the customer who wore or used the object. The writing must be clear and properly composed according to the assigned academic style. (Fifteen points)

4. Speculation. Creativity and imagination are evaluated in this section as the student compares the spirit of past and present times to modify the object and make it suitable for the marketplace of tomorrow. (Fifteen points)

5. Research. The designer or maker should be studied in the context of the era in which the object was made or used. Documentation must follow the assigned academic style. Consideration will be given for the quality of the primary and secondary sources referenced. (Fifteen points)

6. Interpretive Analysis. In this section, thoroughly answer all the questions posed. The student will be rated on the ability to concisely integrate sensory and analytical interpretation of the object. The student will make clear and specific connections between the original object and the research. The writing must conform to required academic style and proper grammar. (Fifteen points)

7. Presentation. The final presentation should demonstrate enthusiasm for the object and professional demeanor in delivery. Images must be included to support the research and the interpretation for future fashion. These points

will be given for the quality and content of the presentation and the ability to communicate with the audience. (Fifteen points)

Guidelines for instructors

In preparation for this assignment, instructors need to manage related objectives: encourage students to identify their emotions, locate objects for study, and assign readings related to object analysis and material culture to establish the process. The readings can include *The Dress Detective* (the full reference for which is available in this chapter's bibliography), with case studies that demonstrate object analysis for fashion. After a discussion about the methods of object analysis, students can establish a checklist to guide them in their observation and determining objectives.

Students then need to locate actual objects. The readings and personal garment analysis can be part of the first third of the semester. The second third of the assignment integrates each student's detailed appraisal and research of the object in historical context, with contemporary forecasting services that can be found online or through college library services. The written and oral report based on actual object analysis and forecasting should be developed in the last third of the semester. Students may approach the writing assignment with varying levels of proficiency. Instructors may allocate the project in smaller segments that can be written and evaluated as a precursor to the final work.

Cautionary advice for instructors

- Instructors will need to work with students to evaluate their ability to use research materials and ensure that they can clearly understand the distinction between primary sources and secondary sources (i.e., that the object itself and other firsthand historical materials found in research from the same period are among primary sources, while interpretations or commentary by others regarding the object would be secondary sources). Having students accumulate documents and sort them as primary or secondary would be a valuable process in advance of the assignment.
- Invite the library staff to give a tour of library resources for research and forecasting as a means of helping students develop their research skills. Instructors along with library staff should also distinguish credible sources from art and historical institutions that have been properly documented and to verify content from other sources.
- Students, depending on the college level, may struggle with organizing their assignment. The use of a template and a rubric can establish a guide to organizing the exercise. Offering an evaluation of the work as it progresses will continue to focus students in the proper direction.

- In addition, students may have difficulty in expressing the emotions that a particular object inspires in them. Exercises in thinking about how they feel when they view objects can be initiated in class by first using a study collection. Students can be trained to integrate their feelings for specific objects with clear communication skills in the context of a business environment.

- Instructors should always insist on respectful interaction among classmates and audience. Gender, sexual orientation, status, or cultural differences are complex issues within the spirit of the times. Clothing and fashion have advanced beyond the classic gender binary to include the LGBTQ sectors and multicultural segments of the market. Study objects cannot be censored by personal prejudice but evaluated and presented in an unbiased professional manner. Teachers can foster a model of objectivity to expose any overt or covert obstacles that may impede the examination of the current complex fashion market. The instructor can begin with the broad spectrum of fashion consumers and the role of forecaster to satisfy consumers with no judgment on their gender and/or sexual identity. Potentially controversial material can have a "spoiler alert," advising that something is about to be shown that may be offensive to someone in the audience. Students will take the lead from an instructor who consistently maintains objectivity in the classroom and respect for all students.

- Anxiety about making presentations is often a concern among students. An instructor can demonstrate the "square breathing" method of overcoming anxiety as a simple and effective way of quieting nerves. ("Square Breathing" is to inhale breath for approximately four seconds, exhale four seconds, hold four seconds, and repeat until anxiety lessens. The process may be up to ten minutes.) The process may be done in the class, and the group practice may, of itself, lessen concerns. In addition, an introductory assignment may have students make short presentations to get comfortable in front of an audience to dispel qualms about public speaking.

- College students often have a visceral understanding of emotional engagement with objects through their personal shopping consumption. The instructor must move the student beyond personal taste in this method to incorporate the universal consumer for a particular business. A study of demographic and psychographic traits for a group of consumers can be assigned, and this consumer segment can be the target for the balance of the object analysis.

Copy of the assignment

"WOW! The object that make my heart sing": Object analysis and adaptation for the current fashion market

Visit an exhibition, and store or arrange to bring objects into the classroom.

Explore the exhibition space or examine other available objects.

a. Select one garment that "sings to you," that is, a garment with which you have an emotional connection—something you really like.
b. Take notes and sketch or photograph your garment.
c. What specific elements make this garment "sing to you"? Why?

Write a report using this guideline and answering all parts.
Use headings for each part of the assignment.

1. Description

Take detailed notes describing the garment and include all of the following: color, textile, silhouette, and specifications (sizing, length of skirts, and width, at the bottom or shoulders).

2. Deduction

What does the garment say to you about:
The person who wore or bought it.
The place where it was made.
The environment in which it was worn.

3. Speculation

How would you interpret your garment for today's market?
What would you change to make it suitable for today's market?
What similarities or differences do you see in today's zeitgeist from the spirit of the times in which the garment was made?
Answer all the above questions as you look at the garment before you do the research.

4. Research

Using the library's electronic resources and other credible sources, report on the reviews and criticisms about the designer or how the garment silhouette was accepted in its time.

5. Interpretive analysis

Write a report describing the assignment according to these questions: Why did you select the garment?
How does the research relate to your first impression?
How did your first or initial impression of the garment compare to the actual material or facts you discovered after you did the research?

6. Present findings to class

You will begin with the object and your reactions, proceed to the research about the object, share your conclusions, and offer your interpretation of the product for tomorrow's market. The trend product should also include a profile of tomorrow's consumer and any similarities to the person using the original object.

Fashion is a business of looks, and so your presentation should have images with identification and minimal text. You can offer discussions of your procedure and results with an appropriate number of images to include the original object, the supporting images found in research, and the final product. If available, you will use PowerPoint or

AirTime to present to your classmates. When electronic presentations are not possible, you can prepare a foam core board using images that would have been used in a digital presentation. In this presentation method, no more than two boards need to be utilized. Your presentation should be approximately ten minutes in length.

Typical results and reflections on the assignment

- When students look inside themselves for their feelings about objects, they learn to become empathetic with the person wearing or using the object. This enables them to form a closer bond with the consumer making a similar purchase in the future. For example, one student observed a Thom Browne suit with protruding spikes at the shoulders and around the crotch and knees from Fall 2012. The student concluded that the garment was a product of the times, noting: "This item tells us that we are in a more carefree era where expressing you[r] sexuality and being raunchy is very in the norm." Through this assignment, the instructor learned that the student made a clearer connection between the physical details of an object and the consumer's attitudes toward gender, sexuality, and personal bravado. Looking at the garment, the student inferred something about the sexual freedom and boldness of the early twenty-first century. After researching and scanning the market for future menswear, the student made appropriate adjustments from the cutting-edge styling of Thom Browne for a more commercial market by simply relocating the spikes as a pocket outline.

- On completing the exercise, students are often better able to analyze and identify the direction of developments and degrees of quality in fiber technology, smart textiles, and shifting moods of color. They are often not able to detect methods of construction by observing an image. Inspecting a patchwork men's coat from menswear retailer Chipp by Corbin Limited, 1973, for example, a student puzzled the construction and asked: "Did the designer first put together patchworks from the long fabric and from there he cut the pieces and created the garment? Or perhaps he made the pattern for the jacket and then he cut the small pieces of the different fabrics and put them together directly on the pattern? Did he use leftover fabrics or did he intentionally cut the small pieces to make this garment?" As students cultivate a better understanding of the relationship between textiles and garment construction with consumers' preferences, instructors also have opportunities to understand what a student has yet to learn about textile weaving and clothing construction.

Notes

1   Prown, Jules David, "The Truth of Material Culture: History or Fiction?" in *American Artifacts: Essays in Material Culture*, ed. Jules Prown and Kenneth Haltman (Lansing, MI: Michigan State University Press, 2000), p. 11.

2   Amy Werbel, quoted in "The Truth of Material Culture: History or Fiction?" in *American Artifacts: Essays in Material Culture*, ed. Jules Prown and Kenneth Haltman (Lansing, MI: Michigan State University Press, 2000), p. 9.
3   Hyun-Seung Cho and J. Lee, "Development of a macroscopic model on recent fashion trends on the basis of consumer emotion," *International Journal of Consumer Studies* 29, no. 1 (2005): 17–33. doi:http://dx.doi.org.ezproxy.library.berkeley.org/10.1111/j.1470-6431.2005.00370.x accessed January 19, 2017.
4   Ibid.
5   Valerie Strauss. "Why College Freshmen Need to Take Emotions 101." *The Washington Post*, September 28, 2014, https://www.washingtonpost.com/news/answer-sheet/wp/2014/09/28/why-college-freshmen-need-to-take-emotions-101/?utm_term=.898df4da7ad3 (accessed January 20, 2017).

Bibliography

Cho, Hyun-Seung, and J. Lee. "Development of a Macroscopic Model on Recent Fashion Trends on the Basis of Consumer Emotion." *International Journal of Consumer Studies* 29, no. 1 (2005): 17–33. doi:http://dx.doi.org.ezproxy.library.berkeley.org/10.1111/j.1470-6431.2005.00370.x (accessed January 19, 2017).

Kopytoff, Igor. "The Cultural Biography of Things." *W*, July 2002, http://blog.metmuseum.org/alexandermcqueen/corset-dante/ (accessed February 8, 2013).

Mida, Ingrid, and Alexandra Kim. *The Dress Detective: A Practical Guide to Object-Based Research in Fashion*. New York: Bloomsbury Press, 2015.

Prown, Jules. "The Truth of Material Culture: History or Fiction?" In *American Artifacts: Essays in Material Culture*, edited by Jules Prown and Kenneth Hartman, 11–27. Lansing, Michigan: State University Press, 2000.

Strauss, Valerie. "Why College Freshmen Need to Take Emotions 101." *The Washington Post*, September 28, 2014, https://www.washingtonpost.com/news/answer-sheet/wp/2014/09/28/why-college-freshmen-need-to-take-emotions-101/?utm_term=.898df4da7ad3 (accessed January 20, 2017).

13
UNDERSTANDING FASHIONABLE FIGURES VIA PAPER CORSET MODELS

Alexandra van den Berg Christensen,
Independent Scholar

Contextualization

Corsetry is complicated. Up until a few decades ago, most women in Western society wore a corset in one form or another every day. Sometimes they were used to support the body, at other times to transform it. Some corsets could be worn while performing a day's hard labor; other versions were uncomfortable to wear even when sitting still. Some women rejected the corset because they felt it impeded their natural growth and vitality, while others felt empowered with the ability to sculpt their own image and thereby gain social capital that could be maintained even as they aged. It seems impossible to make a universal statement about the use or meaning of the corset. Its impact varied from woman to woman, and each era debated its value vis-à-vis ever-evolving ideas of sexuality, femininity, self-image, control, power, feminism, and more. Although in today's society corsets are no longer the focus of these debates, the same issues are still intimately familiar to consumers and scholars of modern fashion. Perhaps this is why the corset's allure survives to this day.

In courses focused on costume studies, corsetry is often the star of the show. Even dress history newbies usually have been exposed to sensational corset stories. Corseted characters in movies regularly faint from the supposed effects of the garment. Vintage graphics show internal organs violently displaced in the name of fashion, and students have gawked at the photographs of wasplike women with waists the circumference of mayonnaise jars. Shocking stories of Victorian women surgically removing ribs in order to achieve tinier measurements still circulate, along with other urban legends on the Internet. The logical assumption to make is that corsets were and are uncomplicatedly harmful—

physically, socially, and emotionally. While many aspects of these anecdotes are founded in fact, there is more to the story than meets the eye.

Valerie Steele addresses the dangers of oversimplifying the issue of corsetry in her book *The Corset: A Cultural History*:

> By patronizing the women of the past as the passive 'victims' of fashion, historians have ignored the reasons why so many women were willing to wear corsets for so long. Explanations that demonize patriarchy also ignore the complex gender politics surrounding the corset controversies of the past, since opponents of the corset included not only feminist women but also many men. Conversely, many women defended corsetry, and women were intimately involved in the production and sale of corsets. (Steele, 2003: 2)

In other words, when discussing the corset's influence on women, it is necessary to remember that women have been "proactive consumers" throughout the garment's history (Sorge-English, 2011: 195). Historians must strive to understand the desires and motivations of these women on their own terms, rather than through a modern cultural lens.

This exercise will introduce students to the most basic aspect of the history of corsets: the evolution of form and the physicality of the garment itself. Let us start with a few basic corset facts:

- A corset's function is to mold the body through constricting some places and not constricting others.
- Corsets create the body shape that is fashionable (or considered therapeutic) at any given time; thus, not all corsets have been the same in different cultures and in different historical eras. Even corsets from the same place and time can vary widely depending on the tailor (or the doctor) and the client involved.
- Women of all sizes wore corsets; in other words, corsets were built in every size.
- Woman of all occupations and social standings wore corsets while doing all kinds of activities. Corsets could be constructed out of many types of materials and with degrees of structure to create varying levels of restriction depending on the wearer's social and physical requirements.

The sheer variety of corset shape and construction, as well as the molding capabilities of the garment, is best understood through direct observation of extant corsets. Images are not nearly as successful at conveying the nuances of a three-dimensional (3D) figure, and the physicality of historical pieces adds an additional level of information about the wearing of these garments. Well-rounded museum collections of costume usually contain examples of corsets and clothing in different shapes, sizes, and of various materials, and a visit to such a collection is highly recommended, if available. If such variety is unavailable, or when an additional experiential component is desired, the exercise outlined in this chapter is recommended. Instruct your students in building their own corset collection out of a convenient and inexpensive material: paper. Not only will the class end up with a well-curated exhibition of mini-corset models, but the kinesthetic involvement in the assignment can help students engage more fully with the question of corsets and their varied shapes, sizes, and purposes.

Studying foundation garments is important. Aesthetically speaking, the corset has been indispensable in creating the fashionable silhouette for hundreds of years. But more important, corsets have molded notions of female identity and continue to have an effect, long after falling out of mainstream use. This assignment asks students to construct a small corset as an important step in the process of understanding its history and physicality.

Appropriate courses and course levels for the assignment: Fashion history classes; costume or fashion design and construction classes; women, gender, and sexuality studies classes (particularly those with units on body image and body shaping.)

Appropriate class size: The ideal class size for this activity is between fifteen and forty students; enough so that eight to ten corsets can be constructed (creating a comprehensive timeline ranging from the sixteenth to the twentieth centuries) with the students working in pairs or small groups of three to four.

Estimated time required: This exercise takes approximately an hour and a half of in-class time, not inclusive of discussion.

Required materials: Instructors should ensure that each pair or small group of students has the following:

- Paper printouts of corset patterns, both right and left sides, about one-fourth to one-half of life size
- Diagram to show how the pieces are supposed to go together
- Instruction handout (given later in the text)
- Scissors
- Clear tape, preferably the kind with its own disposable dispenser
- Handout with discussion questions (if desired)

Enough tape and scissors must be provided for the whole class, preferably so that each student has his or her own. In the past, I requested that students bring their own scissors from home, which seemed to work out well.

A note about the printouts: to make the pattern printouts, photocopy corset patterns onto 11×17 copy paper, resizing as necessary. I used the patterns in Norah Waugh's *Corsets and Crinolines*, enlarging them by 150 percent. Corset patterns are available in other books (see bibliography) and online, but Waugh's book collects an impressive range into one convenient resource.

In order to build whole corsets, you need a right and left side of every pattern. Usually only one-half of a corset pattern is diagramed in a book, since, for construction purposes, the other half is a mirror image. Print off the pattern twice. If you are proficient with a photocopier and have a sufficiently high-tech model available, you can reverse the image on the second printout of each page so that the outlines of the pattern will be visible on the outside of both halves. Otherwise, in order to create a left and a right side, one of the halves of the corset will need to be constructed "inside out," with the printed pattern on the inside of the corset shell. Either way works, although having to construct half of a corset inside-out may stymie some students.

For the diagram of how the pattern pieces should go together, photocopy the pattern onto 8.5×11 copy paper as a reference page. I used a photocopy of the entire pattern page from Waugh's book, which includes a sketch of the fully constructed corset as well as the order of how the pattern pieces should attach to each other.

Learning goals

- Learning more about garment construction basics; educating students about how curvy two-dimensional (2D) lines make curvy 3D shapes; improving spatial visualization.
- Recognizing that idealized female body shape has not been consistent across different time periods and cultures and that the stereotypical hourglass corset shape (with which many students will be most familiar) is only a small part of corset history.
- Critical and sensitive reflection on the politics and processes of body shaping, both historically and in modern times.

Assessment

Throughout this assignment, instructors should be engaged in informal and ongoing formative assessment of students' learning. As students construct their model corsets through trial and error, the instructor can correct mechanical misunderstandings as they occur. During discussion, the instructor will ask students to demonstrate their analytical understanding of the material history laid out in front of them. If this is the class's first exposure to the subject of corsetry, assessment should focus on logical reasoning and comparative skills, and discussion can serve as an effective introduction to a variety of topics, such as corsetry history and construction, fashionable silhouettes, reform dress, etc. If previous lectures have already addressed relevant topics, the discussion could serve as an assessment for that information and can serve as an informal review as needed. Including all learners in the discussion is important for accurate assessment. This type of assessment generates no formal grades, but provides instructors with information about student comprehension which can be applied immediately in discussion and/or in future classes.

Guidelines for instructors

An excellent reading for this assignment is Anne Hollander's chapter "Nudity" in her book *Seeing Through Clothes*. In this chapter, Hollander suggests that fashionable shapes of clothing influence the fashionable nude body in all of its depictions, even when an unbiased or "natural" vision of the body is intended. She also describes the evolution of the emphasis on and eroticizing of different body parts from the medieval period up to the modern era. This reading helps students see ideals of corporeal beauty as more fluid than usually assumed and as manufactured by the garments that clothe it.

Prepare a wide range of corset patterns from different eras, beginning with late sixteenth-century garments and finishing with a 1920s girdle or even a 1950s wasp-waist-revival corset. Also prepare patterns with differing levels of difficulty based on the number of pieces, the curvature of the seams, and the addition of gussets.

Divide the students into pairs or small groups and pass out the patterns, instructions, and supplies. So as to not unnecessarily frustrate them, I ask students to rate their own "craftiness level" while I am distributing the corset patterns. I can then give the self-identified less-crafty people the simpler-to-construct two- to six-seam corsets. Students who are excited to prove their crafty prowess can be given the sixteen-piece patterns, which they would more likely enjoy constructing. It may also help to pair a crafty person with a less-crafty person so that they can work together and reduce the amount of questions pairs or groups may have for the instructor.

Once each group has the necessary materials, take a moment to explain and demonstrate the activity. Cut out a simple corset pattern and start taping it together in front of the class, reviewing the steps and suggestions from the instruction handout as you go. As the students begin work on their own patterns, be available to assist and answer questions as needed.

Enough time should be allowed for students of all skill levels to complete their corsets. There may be a long gap between when the first pair or group and last pair or group finishes. You may want to provide an additional activity for students who finish first, such as bringing a stack of modern fashion magazines for students to look through and identify modern clothing or silhouettes influenced by the historical corsets they just built. You could also direct them to help their classmates who are still working on the project.

Once all of the corsets are completed, you may either have students hypothesize the timeline and seek to line corsets up in chronological order, or you may line them up in chronological order yourself. Present this timeline in front of the class, either on a table or taped to a wall. Use the following questions to guide students through discussion of the corsets, or develop and use your own.

Discussion questions

- What shapes do you see? How do these shapes relate to the fashions we have seen in class thus far?
- How do 2D shapes turn into 3D forms? Which corsets are the most complicated in construction? Which are the simplest? Is there an evolution in construction that you can see?

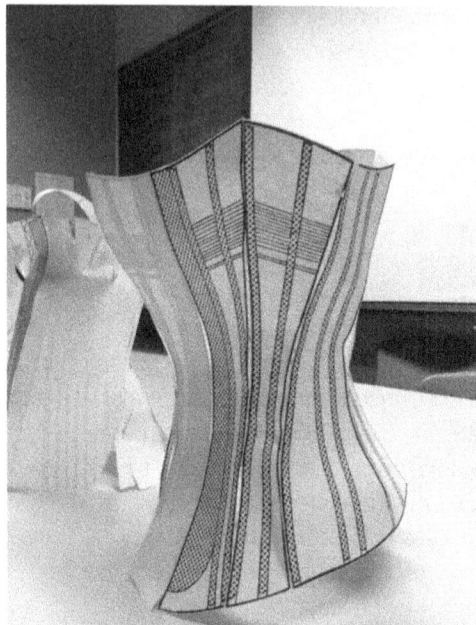

Figure 13.1 Paper model of late 1880s corset, constructed by students in the author's Fashion History class. Copyright © 2013 by Alexandra Christensen. Reproduced by permission of Taylor and Francis Group, LLC, a division of Informa plc.

Figure 13.2 Paper model of late 1820s corset, constructed by students in the author's Fashion History class. Copyright © 2013 by Alexandra Christensen. Reproduced by permission of Taylor and Francis Group, LLC, a division of Informa plc.

- Which corsets look the most comfortable? Which look the most uncomfortable? What makes you think so?
- How have idealized female body shapes changed over time? What body parts are being emphasized with each type of corset? How does the construction of the corset create that emphasis?
- The ideal of a narrow waist was often obtained through illusion rather than constriction. Do any of these corsets fall into this category? How does the corset construction create this illusion?
- Corsets do not reduce the mass of the body; they simply move it around. How do these corsets alter the body to create these idealized shapes? If one part of the corset is built to be smaller, is another part cut more generously?
- Are any of these shapes familiar? Modern? If so, which ones, and how?
- Think about how we mold, shape, or construct our bodies in modern times. What is the same as what you can see in these corsets? What is different?
- What do you think motivated women to wear these garments? How are these motivations similar or different to motivations you may feel related to your clothing choices? Would you want to try any of these corsets on? Why or why not?
- Why do you think we do not use these corsets (in mainstream fashion) anymore?

Cautionary advice for instructors

- This activity requires and develops hand–eye coordination and spatial visualization. Instructors will face a lot of questions and perhaps some frustration as students work on this exercise. Be prepared by practicing the activity yourself and being ready to provide encouraging assistance to students.
- Because of the hand–eye coordination involved, this exercise may be difficult to complete for students with dexterity limitations; arrangements should be made for supportive teamwork or additional aid.
- Body shape is the focus of this activity and can lead to broader discussions on modern body shaping practices. Because of the sensitivity of these issues, instructors should call for and model thoughtful discussion practices, such as presenting information clearly and accurately, avoiding sensationalism or flippancy, and listening respectfully. Be aware of students' personal reactions during class and, when appropriate, take the time to address these reactions, either during or after class.

Copy of assignment

Name: _____

Description and date of corset style: _____

1. Before you cut out the pattern, label the right-side pattern pieces with the letter "R" and the left-side pattern pieces with the letter "L." If your pattern includes letters or symbols to help match up corners (A to A, B to B, etc.), take the time to write these letters on the inside of each pattern piece so that you do not cut them off.

2. As you cut out the pieces, keep the left and right sides separate from each other so that they do not get mixed up.

3. If your pattern includes any gussets, insert these first. A gusset is a separate triangle-shaped pattern piece and is meant to add space in the hip or breast areas. Cut a slit where indicated on the main pattern piece. Match up the letters on each of the three corners of the triangle to the letters at the bottom and top sides of the slit. Tape the two outer corners in place first, then tape the point, and finally finish taping all the way around the "seam."

4. Use the diagram sheet to figure out which pattern piece connects to which other pattern piece. Carefully tape the edge of one pattern piece to the edge of another. Don't attach one upside down! It may be helpful to align and tape the middle of the pattern pieces (around the waistline) first, and then the top and bottom corners. Then tape along the rest of the "seam."

5. If you have difficulty matching up edges that curve away from each other, try holding the pieces in the air instead of flat on the desk. Remember that 2D curves turn into 3D curves. Paper is not the most willing material to take a curve, but once it is taped into shape, it will hold that shape well because of its lightweight stiffness.

6. Once you have the right and left halves assembled, tape them together at center front and center back.

7. If your pattern has separate hip tabs, tape them to the corset body where indicated. If your pattern has hip tabs incorporated into the pattern pieces, cut them apart on the lines provided.

Typical results and reflections on the assignment

- Although many students protested their lack of crafting skills, every pair and small group was able to produce an acceptable model corset that could be used as a teaching tool.

- Students have expressed surprise at the variety of shapes evident in the lineup of paper corsets.
- This exercise helped students understand that the noncorseted body in later eras was not less idealized (or constricted or controlled) for the lack of a structured undergarment.
- Students enjoyed having a physical project to complete in class, and the use of new senses and skills helped them engage with the material in a deeper way.
- This activity prepared students to better understand primary source texts about corset-wearing, nineteenth-century dress reform, and the gradual abandonment of the corset in the twentieth century because of their more intimate knowledge of the structure of the garments in question.

Bibliography

Arnold, Janet. *Patterns of Fashion: The Cut and Construction of Clothes for Men and Women c1560–1620*. London: Macmillan, 1985.

Hollander, Anne. "Nudity." In *Seeing Through Clothes*, California: University of California Press, 1993, 83–156.

Sorge-English, Lynn. *Stays and Body Image in London: The Staymaking Trade, 1680–1810*. London: Pickering and Chatto Ltd, 2011.

Steele, Valerie. *The Corset: A Cultural History*. New Haven: Yale University Press, 2003.

Tiramani, Jenny. *Seventeenth-century Women's Dress: 2*. London: V&A Publishing, 2012.

Waugh, Norah. *Corsets and Crinolines*. London: Routledge, 1990.

14
OVERCOMING THE CHALLENGES OF DISTANCE LEARNING IN HISTORICAL COSTUME STUDIES

Patricia Dillon, New York University and Putnam Art Advisors & Consultants

Contextualization

Once considered, at worst, a second-rate option for the disaffected and, at most, a financial enhancement and marketing tool for mid-level schools, distance learning is enjoying a multitiered surge in quality and respect from the academic and museum communities alike.[1] As technology advances, the ever-widening accessibility of newly developed academic tools and digital presentation has created an increased demand for distance learning. As Smithsonian Secretary Emeritus G. Wayne Clough notes of distance learning "We're only at the beginning of this technology and it is really going to dominate our approach to learning in the next few decades."[2] The benefits and challenges of this approach to learning are complex for educators, particularly for those creating classes in such traditionally "hands-on" fields as historical costume studies.

Distance learning is conducted via links usually grounded in a web-based course site that can be as richly endowed as instructors make it. The course site offers instructors the opportunity to post resources, create lessons and assignments, and provide tests or quizzes. Materials can be updated continually. Within distance learning classrooms, students have ample opportunity to post information, engage in discussions, and exchange ideas.

It is essential that the group dynamic of learning and exchange be framed by instructors keeping classes fully engaged and that students have an opportunity to interact frequently with one another, as well as with the instructor. Goals of a distance learning approach to historic costume include understanding basic costume styles, construction and attaining a better understanding of the influence of different global, ethnic, and socioeconomic factors by mixing students from all walks of life.

Distance learning provides unique opportunities to include diverse research reflecting different cultures or ethnicities represented in each student's home base. Gathering a diverse group of accomplished students from all over the country and the world encourages multicultural perspectives. While most universities have international students, one unique aspect to distance learning is that these students remain in their home cities, states, or countries and retain more extensive access to local primary documents, native historic examples, and regional expertise, which they can share with their classmates.[3] Scholarship for international students increases the ability to compare and contrast styles, construction, fabrics, and socioeconomic or ethnic traditions along truly global lines.

Distance learning classes also often draw a higher percentage of career-accomplished professionals. They frequently work in museums, academia, or the fashion industry and have a very clear sense of what they want to learn and what they can best contribute to the classroom environment. Bringing together successful professionals and traditional students in distance learning classrooms can offer a multitude of material contributions that greatly enrich these courses.

One of the challenges of distance learning programs is the risk of students feeling disconnected. It is incumbent upon instructors to keep the classes lively, enlightening, and intellectually engaging. Student presentations, pop-up polls or frequent quizzes to introduce or reinforce topics, and multimedia presentations should be utilized to keep the class dynamic, interesting, and worthwhile for students.

Distance learning instructors have several, specific challenges in teaching historic costume. Fabrics and garment construction cannot be fully understood without using one's physical senses. In-person examination of garments allows students to immerse themselves using touch, smell, and even hearing, each necessary to fully understand a garment.

The Internet is improving every day, and multimedia presentations can be useful in providing students with new tools to understand garment construction. However, there is still not a satisfactory level of technology to fully accomplish the goal of full sensory immersion for students. This chapter provides an example of an exercise that provides students with an opportunity to fully understand and appreciate historic costume through "field work," combining academic inquiry with off-campus activity.[4] This exercise serves to keep students engaged in the course, providing an opportunity to contribute to class discussion and group knowledge. Moreover, this exercise can be adjusted to reflect the course level or time constraints of the class.

Distance learning is an active exercise in diversity and allows the student to become a fully formed and prepared professional in the twenty-first century. This inherent diversity is more than international; it importantly includes economic class, American regionalism, and gender identification. Students may be from rural areas with their own rich history, major metropolitan sophisticates, neophytes, seasoned or emerging professionals, industry employees, or academics. Different generations exchange insights and perspectives.

Moreover, the distance learning classroom is a reenforcement of the universality of the world. Every culture has adopted coverings and transformed them into clothes evolving design into cultural fashion. Each of these choices reflects social, economic, and political developments in cultural history.

Becoming a professional in the twenty-first-century fashion or historical costume world requires polymath skills. Distance learning students are confident and conversant with new technological developments. Today's fully integrated world demands universal skills and knowledge; making lifelong diverse industry contacts allows professionals to tap any number of resources.

Sometimes forgotten, students often have had no exposure to accomplished industry professionals who confront the realities of the historical costume world on a daily basis. By working with local curators, students slowly gain a confidence and ability to effectively communicate in both a business and an academic manner.

Comfortable with technology, educated by diverse exposure, and more confident in their ability to interact with persons of all cultures, backgrounds, or level of expertise, students uniquely benefit from the broad scope of distance learning.

Appropriate course level: Distance learning is accessed by a broad cross-section of undergraduate and postgraduate students. The success of the exercise is dependent upon the dedication and seriousness of the student at all levels. Benefit and reward both for individual students and the class as a whole are directly related to the extent of each student's efforts. The exercise could be used in a wide range of courses, including art history, US history, historical economics, material culture, and museum management, among other disciplines. Previous exposure to the basics of costume history is not required.

Appropriate class size: Distance learning classes in historic costume connoisseurship are ideally small. However, this exercise can be adapted for any class size. One method to address larger class size and to keep the research meaningful is to use designated categories. Students may pick any garment or object that falls within their assigned category. Categories include but are not limited to considering the intersection of costume and different immigrant communities, individuals of different socioeconomic statuses, children, elderly, or considering objects that have evolved via clear multicultural contributions or cultural appropriation.

Estimated time required: This exercise can be as broad as a multisession internship and as narrow as a single several-hour visit.

Required materials: Access to a museum, historic site, personal collection, or perhaps a theater that has a costume collection. Students should bring pencils, a pad, a nonmetallic measuring tape, and something to photograph the garment. As an alternate approach, students could view costumes from digital collections.

Learning goals

- Discovery through primary evidence of historic style, construction, and quality of historical costume.
- Gain a better understanding of the diverse contributions of different cultures to style and fashion.

- To become better informed of local history, costume, and material culture.
- To learn proper preservation techniques and the ramifications of unsuitable storage.

Assessment

Assessing student performance in distance learning classes is unabashedly challenging. Nonetheless, student success is measured in traditional forms—acquisition of knowledge, analysis, and application and growth. Regular interaction between instructor and students is mandatory.

We are accustomed to assessing growth and validating our own communication abilities by taking inventory of student's body language, facial expressions, and visible level of interest. Technological distance can dim these important signals, making it imperative that instructors frequently check in with students, require discussion, and encourage give-and-take among students. To make it less likely that students slip through the cracks or drift off, instructors can adjust lesson plans when it is apparent that important points have been missed or misconstrued. This starts in the very first class, where an active discussion creates a baseline of ability.

Weekly homework assignments involving investigative tasks and brief class reporting bring reticent students into the discussion, providing a barometer for student growth.[5] To the extent that the students are working in their communities outside of the college or university, brief confidential follow-up surveys could be sent to curators or other professionals with whom they worked, to provide additional assessment.

Guidelines for instructors

All students should be taught the basics of the care and handling of historic costumes before engaging in this exercise. This includes handling instructions regarding the use of gloves, moving garments "palms up," and using appropriate tools such as a nonmetallic tape measures and pencils.

Students should also be cautioned to remove all jewelry including rings, bracelets, or longer necklaces. Long hair should be secured away from the garment. Instructors should teach a brief overview of proper conservation of garments, including using archival paper and boxes and laying clothes in a horizontal manner.

Students can find examples of historic costume in a wide variety of regional locations reflecting regional tastes, populations, and economies. They can choose objects from local museums and historic houses or research a garment saved by a family member or friend. Almost all museums and historic sites are very welcoming to students. Smaller museums or historic houses are less likely to have an organized costume collection that is fully researched, properly catalogued, or preserved. They are often most appreciative of any assistance in understanding and enhancement of their garments. They often present a more comprehensive and meaningful experience for the student simply due to their lack of resources.

While online costume collections are convenient, if at all possible, I recommend students visiting physical sites, as directly engaging with physical objects best serves the exercise objective of discovering costume in all its dimensions.

Cautionary advice for instructors

- Faculty should be familiar with outside institutions where students wish to research. Having a sense of the collections, the needs, and the culture of specific museums or historic sites allows both the instructor and the student to make an informed decision about pursuing a project at this particular institution.[6]
- A significant consideration in this exercise is that students be acutely aware of the limitations of their own knowledge and skills. They tend to be very enthusiastic and prone to well-meaning action, but no student should touch, deconstruct, or alter preservation techniques unless they have advanced skills and the permission and cooperation of the institution housing the garment. A great deal can be gained by basic observation or assisting a professional curator with a simple task, at the curator's discretion. If the student's placement at the museum or historic site is an extended one, a written agreement detailing the student's responsibilities and limitations should be agreed to by the student, instructor, and institution.

Copy of the assignment

Finding history in your community

Task

This exercise is an opportunity for you to explore the history of your community by examining, researching, analyzing, and writing about a piece of historical costume.

Remember that historical costume not only includes court dress and Gilded Age ball gowns, but, more importantly, also includes the wardrobes of the working people and immigrants from every age and culture.

What to do

1. Explore local resources and places where you would be likely to find an interesting piece of costume. This might include a local museum, a historic house, a retailer, or a piece from your family's heritage. If you have difficulty in locating an appropriate piece, speak with the instructor. Remember that costume includes accessories such as hats, pockets, shoes, etc. Essentially, you are "adopting" a garment for a short period of time.

2. Speak with the director or curator from the institution or current owner, explain the assignment, and ask permission to view and research your chosen piece.

Agree to provide the institution with your research when the assignment is completed.

3. Spend some time looking at the garment. With a curator's permission do the following:

   i. Identify fabrics, ornament, closures, construction, condition, and preservation techniques.

   ii. Measure every aspect of the garment.

   iii. With permission, photograph the piece.

   iv. Sketch the piece to the best of your ability including measurements.

4. Interview knowledgeable personnel and research the provenance of the piece.

   (i) What records does the museum have about this garment? Are there any supporting documents such as letters or journals?

   (ii) Can you find out anything about the original owner? Where did they live? What did they do? Use census records to research the family.

   (iii) Look at fashion plates, publications, and period advertisement to understand the cost and popularity of the garment.

5. Write an essay on your findings. Include photographs. Discuss the fabric, construction, measurements, and condition. What were you able to discern about the original owner?

6. Be prepared to discuss the following:

i. What information do the garment and its preservation impart as to the values of our society now and then? Are there unique clues that inform your knowledge about this region?

ii. How typical was this garment to the attributed time period and region?
   a. Was it unique to a particular age, gender, or ethnicity?
   b. What was the socioeconomic status of the original owner? How did you come to your conclusion?
   c. What regional characteristics are present in the garment?

iii. In examining the garment, which cultures have contributed to its style or construction?

iv. Of the information available about the garment, is there anything that you feel is mistaken or should be investigated further?

v. What challenges do museums face in the collection and preservation of garments?

Typical results and reflections on the assignment

- Whether a minimal short-term effort or a lengthier internship, students do very well. They transport to the period of the garment and tend to develop a personal affection for the specific garment or garments they have worked with, often making them lifelong enthusiasts of historical costume.
- More important, students are exposed to the diverse ethnic, socioeconomic, and gender-ordered world that prior generations negotiated.
- Students also frequently make contacts within the museum or historic site and often continue the relationship long after the class has concluded.
- Moreover, museums and historic sites appreciate any additional input that enhances the understanding and appreciation of individual garments that are not available via an (often-limited) staff.

Notes

1. Sometimes referred to as "Online or Digital Learning." Currently, all the Ivy League schools are offering distance learning degree programs. Harvard, Cornell, and Columbia offer robust programs. While Yale, Penn, and Dartmouth are adding courses on a regular basis. See also Crystal Bridges, Museum of Modern Art, and the Smithsonian.
2. See Jeff Levine, *Exploding the Four Walls: Museums Face the Prospects and Perils of Digital Learning, Museum*, American Alliance of Museums, July/August 2015, 31.
3. Although most universities tend to focus on historical American costume studies, the reality is that much of the pre Second World War fashion is directly from or highly influenced by European stylings, which in turn are periodically influenced by other regions of the world.
4. Barbara Gross Davis, *Tools for Teaching* (Hoboken, N.J.: John Wiley & Sons, 1993), 166. Davis goes on to divide field-based instruction as independent study where a student works in on their own in a different organization, field-based academic study often paired with an internship and fieldwork assignments where tasks are incorporated into lessons or lectures.
5. Such as creative invasion of closets, used clothing stores to determine different aspects of costume—compare and contrast linings, ornament, weave, closures, redesign, etc.
6. Publications such as the *National Directory of Arts Internships* by Ron Clawges and Warren Christenson 10th edition (Raleigh, North Carolina: National Society for Internships and Experimental Education, 2006–2007), or *Volunteer U.S.A.* by Andrew Carroll (Ballantine Books, 1991) are two of the many resources available.

Bibliography

Clough, G. Wayne. *Best of Both Worlds, Museums, Libraries, and Archives in a Digital Age*. Washington, DC: Smithsonian Institution, 2012.

Davis, Barbara Gross. *Tools for Teaching*. Hoboken, NJ: John Wiley & Sons, Josey—Bass Higher and Adult Education Series, 1993.

Dougherty, Alice, and Michael Russo. *Information Literacy Programs in the Digital Age: Educating College and University Students Online*. Chicago, IL: Association of College and Research Libraries, American Library Association Publishing, 2007.

Kirkland, Arden, Kathy Martin, Marlise Schoeny, Kiki Smith, and Gayle Strege. "Sharing Historic Costume Collection Online." *DRESS, the Journal of the Costume Society of America* 41, no. 2 (2015): 107–127.

Levine, Jeff. *Exploding the Four Walls: Museums Face the Prospects and Perils of Digital Learning, Museum*, American Alliance of Museums, July/August 2015.

Strayker-Banks, Allyson. *The Effect of Participation among Teachers Who Are Field Dependent or Field Independent on Their Perception of Computer Self Efficacy, Computer Anxiety and Computer Usefulness*. New York, NY: Proquest Dissertation Publishing, New York University, 2002.

15
PROJECT RUNWAY: SECOND-HAND CLOTHING CHALLENGE

Anna Green, Michigan State University

Contextualization

In developing a survey course of twentieth-century US fashion, I began with the goal of teaching students the materiality of history. Following Daniel Roche, who has described analysis of fashion as "another way of penetrating the heart of social history," I decided to construct a course that would encourage students to see fashion trends—both mainstream and subcultural—as interwoven visual stories, metonymic of broader changes in American political and cultural attitudes.[1] I also wanted my students to understand that this history cannot be safely relegated to the past; rather, the rejections and recuperations of today's fashion trends must always be placed in dialogue with the trends of the past.

Reading garments as always symbolic of ideas without engaging with garments as physical, tactile objects, however, risks disregarding fashion's important materiality and the human relationships that surround the production of that materiality. Analyzing garments on a purely symbolic level has the potential to erase the creative and physical labor that constructs the fashion's garments and accessories, and the consumerist notions of disposability that underscore fashion's changefulness, as well as its status as a cladding for physical bodies. In short, I needed course materials, activities, and assessments that fostered student understanding of twentieth-century US history while also helping students to view their own fashions with a critical eye, appreciating the dialogic relationship between fashion as both physical and ideological construction.

Ultimately, I created a course that wedded historical and materialist approaches to fashion studies, in what Amy De La Haye and others have called a "material culturist" methodology. According to De La Haye, attending to "materiality" involves simultaneously thinking of "the fabric (frequently described as material) from which garments are made and the infinite possibilities it holds as an embodiment of value and meaning," possibilities constrained or made available by particular cultural circumstances.[2] Guided by recent pedagogical imperatives to "gamify" the classroom by providing more opportunities for hands-on learning, as well as Arjun Appadurai's recent claim for the meaningful relationship between design study and the pursuit of social justice, I devised a course that paired traditional readings and seminar-style discussion with weekly creative challenges, inspired by the format of the popular television show, *Project Runway*.[3] One day of class each week was dedicated to understanding course readings and films and one to applying those concepts via the collaborative construction of an actual garment. The challenge differed each week, but always drew conceptually from the readings. Each challenge, as such, not only asked students to apply and transfer what they had learned in a creative context, but also ensured that this application be underscored by a critical inquiry into fashion as both a willing and an unwilling form of visually differentiating people.

The larger conceptual underpinnings of the course, therefore, dictated the design of the students' first challenge of the semester, which pragmatically allowed them to acquire the materials they would need to use throughout the semester, and introduced self-reflection as a key component of the course. In the challenge, students broke into groups and were tasked with acquiring the materials that they would transform, reuse, and repurpose to accomplish the design challenges of the subsequent weeks. They received a list of items and were asked to acquire as many of these items as possible without spending more than $20 total ($5 per person). The group that purchased the greatest number of items under budget "won the challenge." Although I allowed students to approach this exercise with an air of frivolity, their subsequent (and required) reflective videos emphasized that physically traveling to, moving about, and interacting with other customers of the secondhand store they visited to acquire these materials made them incredibly aware of their own positions of relative privilege.

Ultimately, the observed "results" of this activity underscore its value in the classroom—that is, it helps widen college students' views of the world around them. It helps students recognize that a seemingly innocuous item—like a T-shirt—is an ideologically charged object that personally places them into the complicated political webs of environmentalism and economic disparity. The reason for undertaking this exercise, then, should be to provide students with the tools to instigate small but vital changes in their everyday lives—whether it be a simple recalibration of awareness, more thoughtful purchasing practices, or an effort to donate rather than discard unwanted items—while also stressing that many individual changes can combine to become the makings of broader social change.

Appropriate courses and course levels: This fashion course was designed to meet the requirements of an introductory course in interdisciplinary studies in the arts and humanities, a required distribution for all students at my university. I recommend a similar venue: introductory, general humanities courses, or courses that include humanities and nonhumanities majors for instructors interested in adapting their own version of these *Project Runway*-inspired projects. Parts of the project might also be tailored meaningfully for more period-focused history courses, women, gender, and sexuality studies courses drawing from materialist methodologies, rhetoric and composition courses on multimodal writing and cultural rhetoric, and literature courses with emphasis on representations of fashion.

By devoting attention to the issue of sustainability, this activity might also be used for courses at the intersection of business and environmental studies. The purpose of these hands-on, playful activities is to encourage students to take risks in what they perceive to be a low-stakes situation, as they begin to think analytically through engaging in these processes of creativity. Empowering students to exercise and believe in their own analytical abilities is, to me, the hallmark of any introductory course.

Appropriate class size: Ideal class size is twenty to twenty-five students; ideally no more than forty students.

Estimated time required: Sixty to ninety minutes in class. The time constraint is part of what makes this in-class project challenging, competitive, and fun; it also alleviates the strain of asking students to spend large amounts of time on group work outside of class.

Required materials: The entire exercise set students up to acquire most of their materials they would use for the entire course. The list of these items appears in the following assignment sheet. The short list of remaining items that are required to complete just this challenge is as follows:

- Camera (to take pictures "proving" that class time had been used appropriately. Most students used the cameras on their phones.)
- Five dollars, to be provided by each student, as a contribution to the overall cost of the materials. (Important note: Because I asked students to spend cash on this project, I ensured that all books and reading materials were available to students free of charge, through the library or other, open sources.)
- Transportation, either private or the bus. (Student IDs at my university give students free access to the bus system, and I provided maps to secondhand stores located along bus routes.)

Learning goals

- Students will demonstrate creative thinking by choosing garments that can be reused and repurposed for the semester's design challenges.
- Students will reflect and revise on their understanding of fashion, particularly regarding issues of economic privilege and disposability.
- Students will use fashion as a means of politically engaging in a critical yet empathetic manner, treating differing viewpoints with respect and fairness.

Assessment

Because students respond and process this assignment in a variety of ways, it's important to provide them with an opportunity to reflect on how the experience of the "secondhand clothing challenge" had made them question and reconsider previous ideas. As such, my mode of assessment took the form of video diaries—"vlogs" (video-blogs)—a medium that invites students to be more casual and conversational. I asked students to film and share with their classmates a video addressing two groups of questions: (1) How did you personally contribute to the challenge, and what role did you play in your team? (2) How did the challenge cause you to think differently about your own practices of buying, sorting, and discarding clothes? How might this change your future behavior? I assigned scores for these videos based on the individual student's thoughtfulness and ability to identify opportunities for personal change.

Guidelines for instructors

To make these types of creative projects possible, you must have a group of students that is willing to engage and play along. To ensure student investment in the exercise, instructors must clarify *how* the creative work will factor into students' overall course grade.

When students are required to work collaboratively, they should be given an opportunity to exert some level of control or input. I recommend that groups create their own contract or agreement at the beginning of the project (included in the sample assignment) and then use the contract to evaluate themselves and one another throughout the semester. The instructor should honor this evaluative process by articulating a plan for how these will factor into a final grade and should plan to carefully read these evaluations and intervene to resolve frustration and conflict, if necessary.

Because students will be venturing out into the community, instructors must stress the importance of respect, reminding students that many secondhand shoppers do so out of economic necessity. Beyond reiterating the importance of general politeness to fellow patrons and storeworkers, I consider it especially important to remind my students about the ways their behavior might be perceived by others in the store or even by their own group members. Discussing possible "scenarios" like loudly criticizing the store or clothing can help students begin to think carefully about how off-handed comments can be perceived as offensive or rude. Though I am invested in getting students to think about economic privilege, I also remind them that it's inappropriate to use the exercise an excuse to "gawk" or be voyeuristic of other customers.

Discussion questions

At the end of each week, students are required to post a reflective "vlog" where they talk about the creative process. The purpose of this part of the assignment is for students to talk about their own contributions to the week's challenge. The vlogs also act as a mode of assessment for instructors, and to assess how students had furthered their understanding of the week's topic through their challenge. Questions students should address include the following:

- Briefly reflect on last week's class.
- How did visiting a secondhand store make you think about your own practices of buying, donating, and/or discarding clothing?

- Who do you think buys (and does not buy) from secondhand stores like Goodwill, and why? Who do you think donates? Why do you think people choose to donate?
- What are some of the political and/or economic reasons that someone might *choose* to shop at Goodwill as opposed to a store like Target or American Eagle? What values do people who *choose* to shop secondhand hold? How is this different from people who are economically unable to shop elsewhere?
- What have you personally learned or taken away from class this week? (This can be related to the course concepts but doesn't necessarily have to be; students could also consider what they have learned about their roles as group members, creative thinkers, competitors, etc.)

Cautionary advice for instructors

- Because this exercise deals with issues of economic privilege, it certainly has the potential to alienate or distance students used to operating under significant monetary constraints. Instructors should use discussion *prior* to the exercise to open up the various reasons that people shop at secondhand stores, allowing all students a voice to share their experiences. As a way of disarming students while also challenging assumptions, I offer a personal example: I am a graduate student, privileged to be pursuing my PhD but also restricted by a modest teaching stipend. Secondhand clothing stores offer me to purchase the garments that my job requires while also helping me stay within a budget. I use this as a jumping-off point, inviting students to share their own experiences and impressions.
- In a separate challenge, students were asked to acquire materials like markers, duct tape, thread yarn, staplers, sewing needles, and glue. I did not offer instructions on sewing; however, many students had previous experience. Some chose to self-educate by watching YouTube videos, and still others found creative means of construction that did not rely on sewing expertise.

Copy of assignment

Secondhand clothing challenge

Part 1: Designing a group contract (week 1, meeting 1)

Description
Your first task as a group is to design a rubric for group participation; this rubric will also act as a kind of contract between the four of you. Together, you'll decide what it means to get a "20/20." You'll describe this on a contract that you collaboratively create. Each student will submit his or her own electronic copy, signaling that they "agree" to the terms.

Questions to consider:

- What criteria should each group member be evaluated on each week? What do you expect from each other? Traditional rubrics often consider participation, effort, creativity, preparation, and teamwork.
- Together, you must decide what it means to receive a "20/20."
- Consider what happens if a group member is absent.
- Consider what happens if a group member doesn't complete the reading and therefore can't fully engage with the project requirements.

Evaluation
- Twenty possible participation points each week:
  - You will use the agreed-upon contract to evaluate yourself each week and will also use the contract to evaluate each of your group members.
  - Each week, four scores are averaged for your overall participation grade. For example, if you give yourself 20/20, group member 1 gives you 18/20, group member 2 gives you 14/20, and group member 3 gives you 18/20, your final score will be 17.5/20 for the week.

Part 2: Out and about (week 1, meeting 2)

Description

In place of today's class, your group's task is to schedule a group outing to a secondhand clothing store. Here, you will work together to collect the clothing supplies you'll need for this week's design challenges. We will discuss local options of secondhand stores you might possibly visit, and I will provide information to you about how to reach these stores via public transportation, as applicable. Please keep in mind that as you venture out into the community, you are representing our class and our university; although you can and should have fun with this exercise, please also be respectful to the spaces you enter and the people you encounter.

Goals

- You will demonstrate creative thinking by choosing garments that can be reused and repurposed for the semester's design challenges.
- You will reflect and revise on your understandings of fashion, particularly with reference to issues of economic privilege and disposability.
- You will use fashion as a means of politically engaging in a critical yet empathetic manner, treating differing viewpoints with respect and fairness.

Rules

- Group members must contribute EQUALLY to the cost.
- Each person will spend NO MORE than $5 ($20 together).

PROJECT RUNWAY: SECOND-HAND CLOTHING CHALLENGE

- Group will attempt to purchase as many items on the list (below) as possible, for under the $20 limit.

- Groups will choose items that can be reconfigured into new garments in interesting ways, keeping in mind that you may have to reuse garments for multiple challenges. You should also keep in mind that someone in the group must be prepared to model the garments that you will create.

- Groups will send *five* pictures to me showing that you have used class time wisely; these pictures will earn the day's participation points.

- Required pictures:

  - Most interesting garment
  - Group picture
  - Final sales receipt totally no more than $20 (with tax)
  - Two additional pictures of group members modeling chosen garments.

- Tweet or email pictures to me at e-mail address and to the Twitter account I have provided; note that if you choose to tweet pictures, these are not private. If anyone in the group prefers to remain private, this decision must be respected and your group will submit pictures to me via private email.

Supplies list

You should try to get at least one item from each category, but after you get items from each category, you may select multiples. Group with the highest number of items under budget wins this challenge. Groups that do not submit the required pictures will be disqualified. Groups that exceed the budget will also be disqualified.

_____ T-shirt
_____ Button-down shirt
_____ Sweater
_____ Jacket
_____ Dress
_____ Skirt
_____ Trousers/slacks
_____ Blue jeans
_____ Sheet/large piece of fabric

Challenges:

- Each week, for a deadline I will set, your group will assemble (and be prepared to model in class) a different type of outfit or look, outlined below. Please be prepared to briefly present your outfit in class, discuss how and why you crafted it in the ways that you did, and how your outfit ties into our course readings. The specific challenges you will be undertaking this semester are as follows:

  - A "professional" look (keeping in mind that your group will need to be prepared to discuss how you have defined "professional")

- An outfit representing youth in revolt (using pop culture such as *Rebel Without a Cause* as a possible inspiration/jumping-off-point)
- A look conveying cultural pride (using Louis Valdez' *Zoot Suit* as inspiration)
- An outfit that embodies the style of a contemporary hipster (drawing on essays by Jack Kerouac and Alan Ginsberg)

Typical results and reflections on assignment

- The students' reactions are suggestive of the power of an approach to fashion studies that centers the material and the results cluster around two main ideas: sustainability and self-reflexivity.
- Most students were startled by the simple experience of being forced to think about how much an item of clothing costs precisely because they had never been forced to purchase clothing on a budget (and such a small one, at that), touching on Katherine Appleford's notion that practices of fashion consumption and disposal can be deeply telling of class divisions.[4] Being forced to do so allowed students to consider the economic privilege attached to shopping at popular stores like Hollister or American Eagle.
- Many students had never visited a secondhand clothing store before and did not know that clothing could have a life after its first owner, and after this activity, most began to develop a plan to collect and donate (rather than simply discarding) unwanted items of clothing; every group redonated its leftover clothing items at the end of the semester.
- Students recognized that secondhand clothing stores are a good, lower-cost, and sustainable alternative resource to the mall, making them more aware of what Jennifer Farley Gordon and Colleen Hill have described as the benefits of "repurposing and recycling clothing and textiles," including the prolongation of the life of an item of clothing, the reduction of environmentally harmful production processes, and the elimination of waste.[5]
- Students saw the use of secondhand clothing as an extension of existing frameworks that value practices of recycling, DIY-ing, and upcycling. The "challenges" students encountered later in the course forced them to reuse the same starting materials to create a variety of different garments. One week they were asked to respond to *Rebel Without a Cause* by creating an outfit that, for them, represented youth in revolt. The next week they were asked, in response to Louis Valdez' play *Zoot Suit*, to imagine a fashion that represented cultural pride. These challenges forced them to repurpose and reuse.
- Courses and lessons like these help students become aware of the ideologies they support through their clothing choices. Ask them to seriously reflect on the values they have left on the rack along with rejected items of clothing and provide them with avenues for enacting small but vital changes in their own daily fashion practices.

Notes

1. Daniel Roche, *The Culture of Clothing: Dress and Fashion in the Ancien Régime* (Cambridge: Cambridge UP, 1994), 5.
2. Sandy Black, Amy De La Haye, Joanne Entwistle, Agnes Rocamora, Regina A. Root, and Helen Thomas, eds. *The Handbook of Fashion Studies* (London: Bloomsbury, 2013), 231.
3. See Morris et al. "Beyond Rigor." *Hybrid Pedagogy: A Digital Journal of Learning, Teaching, and Technology* (2013) for discussion of the benefits on learning, particularly as it pertains to the cultivation of student empathy. See Appadurai's foreword to Susan Yelavich and Barbara Adams, eds., *Design as Future-Making* (London: Bloomsbury, 2014). Appadurai's discussion of design study is an important mechanism for reflecting on the past, disrupting existing assumptions, and through these processes, imagining a better future. Appadurai asserts that design studies "reopen[s] such issues as ephemerality, artifice, and innovation to deeper scrutiny" as it opens "up a new ethics of thingness, which might make social life both more exuberant and more just" (11).
4. See Appleford's essay in Sandy Black et al., eds., *The Handbook of Fashion Studies* (London: Bloomsbury, 2013), 101.
5. Jennifer Farley Gordon and Colleen Hill, *Sustainable Fashion: Past, Present, and Future* (London: Bloomsbury, 2015), 25.

Bibliography

Black, S., A. De La Haye, J. Entwistle, A. Rocamora, R. Root, and H. Thomas, eds. *The Handbook of Fashion Studies*. London: Bloomsbury, 2013.

Gonzalez, A., and L. Bovone, eds. *Identities through Fashion*. London: Berg, 2012.

Gordon, J., and C. Hill. *Sustainable Fashion: Past, Present, and Future*, London: Bloomsbury, 2015.

Hebdige, D. *Subculture: The Meaning of Style*. London: Routledge, 2011.

Morris, S., P. Rorabaugh, and J. Stommel. "Beyond Rigor." *Hybrid Pedagogy: A Digital Journal of Learning, Teaching, and Technology*, 2013. http://www.digitalpedagogylab.com/hybridped/beyond-rigor/ (accessed January 20, 2018).

Roche, D. *The Culture of Clothing: Dress and Fashion in the Ancien Régime*. Cambridge: Cambridge University Press, 1994.

Yelavich, S., and B. Adams, eds. *Design as Future-Making*. London: Bloomsbury, 2014.

16
DEVELOPING CONSTRUCTION AND DESIGN SKILLS THROUGH APPLICATION OF SCIENCE, TECHNOLOGY, ENGINEERING, AND MATH (STEM)

Jody Aultman and Sara Marcketti,
Iowa State University

Contextualization

In the new millennium, the integration of science, technology, engineering, and mathematics (STEM) has gained momentum in education reform worldwide. The importance of STEM is undeniable, particularly given the fact that when compared to other nations, the rate of STEM-related higher education degree attainment in the United States, specifically, is inconsistent with a nation considered the world leader in scientific innovation (Kuenzi, 2008). Some contend that STEAM, or the addition of "art" to the popular acronym, will lead to knowledge, advancement, and pedagogy, which combine aesthetics and analytical modes of thinking to the betterment of both STEM and the arts (Fitzsimmons, 2011).

Fashion, both historically and contemporarily, has been influenced by and contributed to advances in STEM. Science has always played a part in the production of new materials for fashion and textiles, whether creating manufactured or synthetic fibers, reengineering natural ones, or providing finishes, treatments, or coloration. From the introduction of the first manufactured fiber rayon, to nylon, to polyester, these fibers enabled both the speed of fashion and the wash and wear aspect of consumer laundering that we cherish today (Quinn, 2002). In the next wave of innovation, companies such as Bio couture seek ways to free our petrochemical dependence, and experiment with microorganisms including bacteria, fungi, and algae to create smarter, more sustainable additions to our fashion system. Technology, or the science of the application of knowledge to practical purposes, is incredibly important in fashion. For centuries, clothing wrapped around or went on to the body. However, in the Middle Ages, the use of buttons allowed clothing to have a closer fit to the body and increased intricacy of design. This later Middle Ages period, coinciding with the introduction of buttons, patternmaking, and tailoring apprenticeship system, was not so incidentally the start of the concept of fashion or the rapid obsolesce of one style in place of another.

Today, technological innovations in fashion include those on a spectrum from expressive (i.e., Iris Van Herpen's use of 3D printing) to fully functional (astronaut suit) to somewhere in between (fitness tracking devices) (Seymour, 2008). Engineering is the work of designing and creating large structures or new products or systems by using scientific methods. It was in the sixteenth century—with its wheel farthingales, bum rolls, ruffs, and conches—that fashion literally reached new heights. It was also in the sixteenth century that we find some of the earliest published pattern books. The 1580 work *Book of the Practice of Tailoring, Measuring and Marking Out* instructed tailors on methods of cutting out patterning pieces so as to get the most garment from the least amount of fabric. The next revolution in patternmaking would coincide with the late nineteenth-century invention of the sewing machine, dress forms, and the availability of fashion periodicals, which meant increased ease of both home-sewn and factory-made clothing (Emery, 2014). In the twenty-first century, computer-aided design helps designers and retailers plan their garments, create samples, examine fit issues, and even represent the next wave of engineering innovation, in which consumers control the process of design.

Mathematics is the science of numbers, quantities, and shapes and the relations between them. The intersection of math and fashion is most clearly evident in design inspiration and fashion retailing. In the early 1900s, innovations in glass allowed for large window displays. In tandem with advertisements, consumers desired and demanded increased fashion change (Leach, 1994). Today, we no longer need department store windows, as we can shop from anywhere in the world with our fingertips and fashion bloggers take a front seat with fashion editors.

The exercise uses STEM, as students set out to create a design of their choosing. This will be accomplished with students understanding spatial value along with the creation of a mirror image. This will be done by first using paper to create a design and then recreating the piece using Adobe Illustrator. Once the layout is achieved, it can then be reflected as a mirror image horizontally and vertically. This advances the student's ability to comprehend how a design can become more complex and easier to manipulate by using the technology of Adobe Illustrator.

Appropriate courses and course levels for the assignment: Sophomore or junior-level course. This exercise would be useful in the following disciplines: design courses teaching Adobe Illustrator and Adobe Photoshop; math courses including basic math and geometry; basic engineering courses.

Appropriate class size: Fifteen to twenty students

Estimated time required: This course would require at least two hours in class lab sessions of two to three hours each, and then could be completed over a week's time out of class.

Required materials

- Rulers
- Paper
- Scissors
- Glue sticks
- Pencil
- Computer with access to Adobe Illustrator

Learning goals

- How STEM interacts with design.
- Learning more about the basics of elements of design, including color, shape, texture, space, and form.
- Learning more about the principles of design, including balance, proportion, rhythm, emphasis, and unity.
- The principles and elements of design are important when designing for fashion studies. It is very important for the student to understand the principles and elements in design by using other disciplines such as STEM to guide them in their work.

Assessment

This exercise will vary from student to student depending on the complexity of the design they choose to create, making grading somewhat subjective. To eliminate any bias, students should be evaluated on key areas using a rubric. The rubric should include points for design outcome and technical quality, evaluating students according to how STEM disciplines are intertwined in their designs. Instructors should consider how students used the basic elements of design in their creation, including color, shape, texture, space, and form. Principles of design such as balance, proportion, and unity are also important things to consider in students' creations, especially when they are reflected. After completing the assignment, students should have an understanding that the principles and elements of design, along with STEM, are very important when designing for fashion studies.

Guidelines for instructors

Instructors need a working knowledge of Adobe Illustrator and should work through the exercise on their own so they have familiarity with this program and exercise. Depending on the course that this exercise is used in, it could be a nice introduction into the use of Illustrator for design work. When using the reflective qualities in Illustrator, it can help students see how the principles and elements of design can change the perspective of the design.

Discussion questions

- How did the elements/principles of design play into your paper construction?
- How did math skills help you with your composition?
- What specific math skills were the most useful?
- How did the principles of design change when you reflected your composition?
- How did the elements of design change when you reflected your composition?
- How does using technology assist you in your design thinking?

Cautionary advice for instructors

- Instructor needs working knowledge of Adobe Illustrator.
- Students may have problems understanding the technology. They need to understand that there is not always one right way to get to the end product. They may need one-on-one time with the instructor to solve the issues that arise.
- The shapes in the designs must match up exactly when reflecting so that the pattern repeats match exactly.

Copy of the assignment

This exercise is to help you learn about the elements and principles of design, as well as to learn how STEM is useful and necessary in design work. The exercise is done in two different parts. The first part is to design a composition on a twelve-inch square piece of paper. You will cut out shapes from primary and secondary colored paper. The shapes have to fit into the twelve-inch square piece of paper. While doing this process, you will need to be mindful of the principles and elements of design. Once the composition is complete, you will glue the pieces down on the paper, making sure the pieces all fit together. You will then use basic math skills for measuring your shapes and geometry for creating your shapes.

The second step of this exercise is done using Adobe Illustrator on the computer. You will open a file in Illustrator and create a twelve-inch square. You will recreate the shapes by measuring your paper shapes and using Illustrator tools to create the shapes and fit them into the twelve-inch square. Once the shapes are created in the twelve-inch square, you will reflect the square left to right and top to bottom resulting in a twenty-four-inch square. At this point, you will again study the elements and principles of design to assess the outcome of their creation. Exercise guidelines:

- Paper pattern must be twelve-inch square.
- You must use all six colors of paper.
- You must use at least four different shapes (circle, square, rectangle, triangle, etc.).
- Illustrator file must be twenty-four-inch square.
- Illustrator file must be reflected left to right and top to bottom.
- Illustrator file must be colored.
- Illustrator file must have clean lines (no overlap of shapes).

Typical results and reflections on the assignment

- Figure 16.1 shows a typical created design.
- Figure 16.2 shows the pattern when it is reflected.
- This exercise will help the creator use STEM skills to produce the pattern. Specifically:

  - Science: Thinking about rhythm and movement of a finished piece in cloth.
  - Technology: Using the computer to recreate something that was on paper.
  - Engineering: Creating something that uses shape and proportion.
  - Math: Line assists in the creation of the overall aesthetic of the piece.

- Principles of design used include unity in making the final piece balanced and emphasis on specific shapes.
- Elements of design include line, color, and shapes chosen.
- Texture could be added to this project by using filters in Adobe Illustrator if the student is more advanced.

Figure 16.1 Jody Aultman one-fourth design of Reflected Symmetry, 2011. Photo courtesy of author's private design collection.

Figure 16.2 Jody Aultman reflected design of Reflected Symmetry, 2011. Photo courtesy of author's private design collection.

Bibliography

Emery, J. *A History of the Paper Pattern Industry*. London: Bloomsbury Academic, 2014.

Fitzsimmons, C. "How Education at the Nexus of Art and Science Can Change the World." 2011, Available online: http://www.artofscience-learning.org/conferences/san-diego/admin/108-admin.html

Kuenzi, J. "Science, Technology, Engineering, and Mathematics (STEM) Education: Background, Federal Policy, and Legislative Action." *Congressional Research Services report for Congress*. 2008, Available online: http://www.fas.org/sgp/crs/misc/RL33434.pdf

Leach, W.R. *Land of Desire: Merchants, Power, and the Rise of a New American Culture*. New York: Vintage Books, 1994.

Quinn, B. *Techno Fashion*. London: Bloomsbury Academic, 2002.

Seymour, S. *Fashionable Technology: The Intersection of Design, Fashion, Science, and Technology*. Austria: Springer, 2008.

17
EXERCISES IN CRITIQUING FASHION'S CLASSIC STYLES IN THE DESIGN STUDIO

Alice Payne and Kiara Bulley,
Queensland University of Technology

Contextualization

Central to fashion design practice is an awareness of the classic garment forms: the shirt, the tailored jacket, the pencil skirt, the denim jacket, and many more. As well as aesthetic significance, these classic styles hold rich cultural and symbolic meaning: a trench coat may be associated with hard-boiled detectives or with the film *Casablanca*; a babydoll dress may invoke Vladimir Nabokov's *Lolita*. Fashion designers can adapt, subvert, and reinvent these forms—or indeed can propose entirely new forms. They can play with the visual look and feel of these items as well as their symbolic meaning.

This exercise stemmed from a quote from fashion theorist Anne Hollander:

> The new freedom of fashion ... has been taken up as a chance not to create new forms, but to play more or less outrageously with all the tough and solid old ones, to unleash a swift stream of imagery bearing a pulsating tide of mixed references.[1]

Hollander's "tough and solid old forms" are part of the grammar of fashion design, or the classic forms or style tropes repeated and reinvented by designers. Comprehension and understanding of forms is key to development of one's design integrity as a fashion designer. As educators, we identified a number of students who were "stuck" on designing only classic forms (generic designs such as the circle skirt and the blazer) and not extending their design work. We asked ourselves: How could we help students identify these forms as "classic," and prompt them to reflect on how imitation of these forms can appear clichéd or underdesigned? As a corollary of this, how can we use these classic forms to push their design skills and encourage students to "play outrageously" with the old forms, or indeed invent new forms? Our aim was to expand student comprehension of these classic styles and present them as part of fashion's historical and contemporary material dialogue.

In this two-part task, first-year fashion design students are encouraged to examine the notion of classic forms. In Part 1, teachers prompt students to critique and subvert one of fashion's "tough old forms." In Part 2, students create "new forms." The task raises questions as to the role classic forms can play in fashion design. They may be continually referenced, reinvented, exaggerated, simplified, or deconstructed, with designers' approaches including reflection, appropriation, or imitation. Critically, fashion designers can move beyond cliché to homage, pastiche, or even subversion in which new meanings are applied to old objects, much like punks made domestic objects, such as the safety pin, into ones suggestive of violence.

In terms of resources, textbooks such as *Beyond Design: The Synergy of Apparel Development* and *Technical Sourcebook for Designers* illustrate classic garment shapes, and books such as Colin McDowell's *The Anatomy of Fashion* present the cultural and historical context for these garments.[2] The blog "An Illustrated Fashion Alphabet" is also a good starting point resource that students can check online in class.[3]

This in-class task is designed to prompt design criticality in students. By identifying the history and inherent symbolism of classic forms, a semiotic language of fashion is made available to students. From this understanding, students can approach the use of classic forms in contemporary design as a critical and playful interaction with the grammar of fashion design. Classic forms can be conceptually analyzed, unpacked, extended upon, or subverted. This goes on to provide a framework for students to imaginatively speculate on what a new form might be, and how meaning might be attributed to it.

Appropriate courses and course levels for the assignment: This is appropriate for first-year fashion design students. However, it can also be a warm-up exercise for any level in a fashion design course. An adapted version of Part 1, with its discussion of fashion style's history and symbolism, would be relevant for fashion history or fashion theory students and students studying costume and characterization.

Appropriate class size: Fifteen to twenty-five students, working in small groups of three or four.

Estimated time required: This exercise is in two parts and can be run over two sessions of one to two hours each.

Required materials

- Paper and drawing equipment (Part 1)
- Printouts of "tough old forms" examples—including illustration/technical drawing (Part 1)
- Mannequins/dress stands (Part 2)
- Muslin, calico, or Vilene (Part 2)
- Pins and scissors (Part 2)

Learning goals

- Extending understanding of fashion styles and history
- Exploring how fashion styles hold aesthetic, cultural, temporal, and symbolic meanings and how the designer can work with these
- Examining how the classic forms can be adapted, disrupted, and upended—not only aesthetically but when considering the meanings and messages behind these forms

Assessment

This task is designed to be run as an in-class design exercise. As mentioned earlier, the task can be run as a design methodology exercise for first-year students or as a warm-up exercise for more advanced students. Due to the nature of the task as instructive and generative, it will generally be assessed as part of the student's process work rather than as an assessment outcome. However, the task, if expanded, has the potential to be adapted for a full-design brief as well.

Assessable outcomes of the task would include ability to identify and critically analyze classic garment forms, evidence of research, ability to synthesize research into design ideation, evidence of design development from old forms and imaginative exploration of new forms, as well as communication skills.

Guidelines for instructors

This task could be run early or mid-semester as an in-class exercise designed to prompt creative thinking in the class, encourage students to study and research fashion history and culture, and to critique their use of the classic garment forms in their design work. No prior knowledge of either design history or designing skills are needed, but the task can be tailored to different students' existing abilities and knowledge (see the previous section). Part 1 can be viewed as an exercise for design and ideation as well as a means to discuss the historical and cultural significance of common garment styles. Part 2 promotes hands-on design and ideation through experimenting in 3D on the mannequin.

Discussion questions

Part 1: Tough old forms

- Can you identify the "classic form" you have been given?
- What does your style mean? How does it work?
- How can you "play outrageously" with it?

- How far can you push the style away from its origins, and when does it cease being a classic form?
- Are the classic forms designed? How much do you have to change them for them to be considered designed?

Part 2: New forms

- Can new forms be created?
- What are our limitations when creating new forms for fashion?
- If the tough old forms are part of fashion's language, how would a new language change fashion?

Cautionary advice for instructors

- Encourage playfulness and a "low stakes" approach: the sillier the better with upending and reinventing the tough old forms.
- Ideas for getting started are provided with the student brief, but teachers may choose to omit these, so that students approach the task without preconceptions.
- Encourage students to engage in a meaningful way with the tough old forms, not only aesthetically but also philosophically. For example, what connotations around sexuality and femininity does a babydoll dress hold when compared to a pencil skirt? Encourage students to share their experiences of wearing or viewing these forms.
- When moving into the "new forms" exercise, prompt students to invent a symbolism for their new form: again, encourage a playful response.

Copy of the assignment

Part 1: Tough old forms

For this assignment, you will be divided into groups of four. Consider this quote from Anne Hollander:

> The new freedom of fashion ... has been taken up as a chance not to create new forms, but to play more or less outrageously with all the tough and solid old ones, to unleash a swift stream of imagery bearing a pulsating tide of mixed references.

Once you have been divided into groups, each of you will be presented with one of the "Tough old forms." In your groups, discuss the following questions and then design four variations of the classic garment. Later, you will present these variations to the larger class.

- What does your style mean? Brainstorm as a group the look and meanings/symbolism of the style. (Who do you imagine wearing it? What is its history? What ideas/moods do you associate with it?)
- How does it work? Discuss the functional elements, the fastenings, the silhouette, the kinds of fabrics it would be made in and why, etc.
- How can you "play outrageously" with it? (Note for instructors: the following ideas could be omitted.)

Design *four* variations of your classic garment. Following are some ideas to get started:

- Exaggerate—take the style to the *extreme* (whatever you decide that means!).
- Play with its lines/shapes/volume/fabrics to see how radically you can reinvent it.
- How far away can you take the style, while still retaining something of its essence?
- Stretch the style conceptually—take one of your "meanings" of the style and explore how you can upturn or amplify this meaning.
- Mess with the details—how much can you play with in terms of stitching, pockets, adding a print or embellishment, color, and texture.

Present your style and your four designs to the class: tell us about your group's garment, its meanings, and the ways you decided to shake it up.

Part 2: New Forms

In Part 1, we examined the old forms, and discussed why they have proved so "tough." For Part 2, you will be again divided into groups of four, but this time challenged to invent a "new form." New forms may feel new due to their different relationship with the body, as seen in the experimental work of Rei Kawakubo and other avant-garde designers in which the body is swathed or draped or revealed in ways that depart radically from the style tropes of Western casual dress. To consider how designers may wrap and cover the body in new ways outside of the "tough old forms," you have been given a letter of the alphabet as a prompt for developing shapes or concepts to drape on the mannequin in order to propose a new form.[4]

- Develop a new form in your groups. To get started, discuss with your group how you may interpret the shape of your alphabet letter—for example, will you use one big letter as your pattern piece or many smaller ones?

- Use the provided materials and work on the stand (half scale or full size) to develop your new form.
- Consider details: develop six characteristics of your new form.
- Meaning: invent a meaning, story, or symbolism for your new style. Who wears it, and how is it worn?
- Present your new form and its meaning to the class.

Typical results and reflections on the assignment

- The "tough old forms" task encourages students to critique their subsequent designs with greater depth: Have they merely followed the classic form of a blazer and, if so, have they truly "designed" the garment? After this exercise, students approach design work with greater criticality in examining how closely they are mimicking classic styles. Rather than mimicry, the task prompts students to view fashion styles as part of a rich tradition of fashion's language that can be playfully rewritten and examined.
- The "new forms" approach inspires students to play with experimenting on the stand and taking a different starting point in their design process. With an extreme limitation such as a letter shape, they are forced to work with the shapes on the 3D form, embrace "happy accidents," and explore new ways for cloth to cover and interact with the body.
- In both tasks, students have benefited from the philosophical discussion around the meaning and symbolism of clothing styles, and how these meanings accrue and change over time.

Notes

1. Anne Hollander, *Seeing Through Clothes* (Berkeley and Los Angeles: University of California Press, 1993), 166.
2. Sandra J. Keiser and Myrna B. Garner, *Beyond Design: The Synergy of Apparel Product Development*, 2nd ed. (New York: Fairchild Publications, 2008); Jaeil Lee, *Technical Sourcebook for Designers* (New York: Fairchild, 2014); Colin McDowell, *The Anatomy of Fashion: Why We Dress the Way We Do* (London: Phaidon, 2013).
3. Illustrated Fashion Alphabet, "Index." Available online: https://illustratedfashionalphabet.wordpress.com/index/ (accessed June 15, 2015).
4. The alphabet letter idea was inspired by the final section of the book: Dennic Chunman Lo, *Patternmaking* (London: Laurence King, 2011).

Bibliography

Hollander, Anne. *Seeing Through Clothes*. Berkeley and Los Angeles: University of California Press, 1993.

Illustrated Fashion Alphabet. "Index." 2015. Available online: https://illustratedfashionalphabet.wordpress.com/index/ (accessed June 15, 2015).

Keiser, Sandra J., and Myrna B. Garner. *Beyond Design: The Synergy of Apparel Product Development*. 2nd ed. New York: Fairchild Publications, 2008.

Lee, Jaeil. *Technical Sourcebook for Designers*. New York: Fairchild, 2014.

Lo, Dennic Chunman. *Patternmaking*. London: Laurence King, 2011.

McDowell, Colin. *The Anatomy of Fashion: Why We Dress the Way We Do*. London: Phaidon, 2013.

PART SIX

DIVERSITY AND IDENTITY

Introduction

This section discusses exercises designed to enable students to analyze the intersections between race, ethnicity, class, gender, sexuality, age, region, and ability and fashion culture. These assignments consider how individuals and groups from different subject positions craft personal and collective identities through their fashion choices and clothing practices, the power which fashion has to both uphold and subvert existing social hierarchies, and how popular culture and social media inform (and shape) the connections between dress and difference. Anya Kurennaya's chapter centers on the issues of fashion and intersectionality, reflecting on an assignment in which students create a visual map of their different subject positions and daily fashion practices. This exercise enables students to consider how they use fashion as a means of negotiating the interconnections between diverse facets of their identity and their choices about dress.

Elizabeth Stigler's chapter concentrates how fashion images engage with (and shape) larger cultural discussions of women, feminism, and empowerment. Having students select a specific advertisement, this exercise asks students to evaluate whether the advertisement is feminist or antifeminist, creating their own criteria for assessment. This exercise enables students to consider issues of intersectionality (particularly how ideas about women interconnect with ideas about race, class, size, and ability), the assumptions and stereotypes that underlie visual depictions of female bodies in media, and the complicated meanings behind even the most seemingly straightforward of images. In her chapter, Mel Michelle Lewis similarly focuses on developing students' media literacy, having students critically reflect on historical and contemporary images of black glamour in popular culture. In her assignment, students analyze representations of black fashion, drawing connections between past and current depictions of black glamour and style, and analyze what these images and depictions reveal about racial identity and pride and struggles against white supremacy, in different eras.

And finally, Holly M. Kent's chapter discusses an exercise in which students themselves become the creators of fashion media, collaborating on a course-run blog centered on different facets of historical and contemporary fashion. Blog post topics ask students to analyze how issues including race, class, gender, and age shape their (and others') experiences in fashion culture, in terms of daily dress practices, consumption, and popular images of fashionability. All of the chapters in this section offer a range of approaches for students to actively analyze the varied ways that fashion, identity, and diversity intersect in their daily lives, and shape the larger cultural environments of which they are a part.

18
INTERSECTIONALITY MAP ASSIGNMENT

Anya Kurennaya, Parsons School of Design

Contextualization

Because both fashion as an embodied practice and fashion as an academic field of inquiry engage with multiple subject positions such as age, gender, class, ethnicity, and so on, it is important for students and educators to consider these subject positions in detail. Furthermore, the intersection of these subject positions is crucial for an understanding of the complex ways diverse individuals engage with dress practices in everyday life. Using Kimberlé Crenshaw's notion of intersectionality, along with Susan Kaiser's examination of the concept with reference to fashion and cultural studies, this assignment asks students to create an intersectionality map that describes their own intersecting identities at the present moment.

As a precursor to the assignment, students should be exposed to both Crenshaw's notion of intersectionality and Kaiser's fashion-inflected discussion of the concept. Crenshaw conceived of the idea when attempting to reconcile her position as an outsider within two overlapping spheres: as a college student, she felt that the antiracism activist movements she was involved with did not consider gendered power relations as a key factor in struggles of women of color, and at the same time she felt that feminist groups did not sufficiently engage with race. Crenshaw argues that subject positions are always interrelated and can never be discussed in isolation. Furthering this work, Kaiser (2012b) applies the concept of intersectionality to dress practices, contending that "inevitably, people appear" and their appearances are structured through "multiple cultural discourses."[1] Drawing on the body of work within fashion studies that addresses everyday dress practice, Kaiser reminds us that individuals structure relationships to themselves and to each other through Entwistle's (2000) notion of "situated bodily practice."[2] In addition to this, as individuals balance the demands of social structures with their own sense of agency, their daily dress practices are affected by hegemonies (both overarching and scattered) that impact both their self-conceptualization and their social relationships. When originally implemented in my courses, I introduced these ideas to students via required readings and a lecture that reinforced key concepts and vocabulary with an interactive handout containing key terms.

This assignment asks students to choose seven different subject positions, some required and some self-supplied, and to reflect on their "position" within each category in a five- to seven-sentence paragraph, focusing on how each position impacts their dress practices. Students are also asked to include images that illustrate their relationship to these subject positions and to format their work in a visual map format that clearly indicates the relationship between their different subject positions. This encourages students to think of their subject positions as overlapping rather than isolated from one another, a goal that can be fostered by a follow-up in-class discussion or reflection assignment.

Additionally, combining visual components (images, photographs, and drawings) with written components (paragraphs explaining their subject positioning for each component of the map) allows students with various skillsets to excel. This assignment was originally delivered to students majoring in fashion design, fashion management, illustration, photography, and other design fields.

This exercise is particularly relevant in light of recent initiatives to foster inclusivity on college campuses and to consider the factors that structure diverse social interactions. Students are guaranteed to come into contact with others whose subjectivities differ from theirs, and this assignment asks them to unpack assumptions about appearances and visible differences as manifested through dress practices. This assignment oncourages students to break down the essentialist thinking that often pervades popular understandings of dress practices (e.g., mass media discourses that assume women are "naturally" preoccupied with fashion). Instead, students reflect on an often-overlooked part of their daily practice and articulate the complex and competing ways social structures imprint themselves on their embodied selves. Thinking through the impact of power structures on selfhood and social relationships prepares students for this assignment, which asks them to consider their own dress practices in an intersectional context, and guides them toward the goal of considering the ways in which their subjectivity intersects with the subjectivities of those around them. After completing the assignment, students are equipped to discuss the following questions:

- How can you describe yourself and your dress practice in terms of intersectional subject positions?
- How does your intersectional subjectivity compare to the subjectivity of those around you? What factors are similar, and what factors differ?
- How do individuals negotiate apparent contrasts in subjectivity through their embodied dress practices (e.g., how do individuals reconcile competing or contradictory discourses between the subject positions that make up their subjectivities)?

Appropriate courses and course levels for the assignment: Introductory courses in a variety of disciplines: American or regional studies, fashion studies, media studies, women, gender, and sexuality studies are a few examples. The exercise can also be adapted for upper-level courses in a number of ways, such as by asking students to interview someone and create an intersectionality map for that individual, or to incorporate outside research on intersectionality in their assignment.

Appropriate class size: This assignment will work for any class size. It was implemented in a survey course numbering 120 students, and findings were shared in recitation sections of 20 students.

Estimated time required: Time required is variable, but most students spent about three to four hours at home composing text, locating images, and formatting text and images into a visual layout.

Required materials: Students will need access to a computer to complete the assignment outside of class time. No materials are necessary within the classroom, although if instructors ask students to share some of their findings, then an in-classroom computer and projector will be necessary.

Learning goals

- Understand how fashion/style/dress operate in their personal lives and in diverse societies.
- Understand the concept of intersectionality and productively apply it to their personal experiences.
- Reflect on their dress practices in writing with reference to key concepts and readings.
- Engage in dialogue with others about commonalities and differences in dress practices and subject positions.

Assessment

When this assignment was originally implemented, students were assessed using a 100-point rubric assessing four key areas:

1. The ability to meet requirements as outlined in the assignment description
2. The depth and quality of writing
3. The connection to course ideas
4. The clarity of writing

The first area is meant to assess the overall comprehension of the assignment and the amount of work put into its completion. When assessing the second area, instructors should evaluate the clarity and depth of the student's explanation of each subject position, and they should expect the writing to clearly and fully answer the required questions. In the third area of assessment, instructors should look for explicit and thoughtful connection to Susan Kaiser's text and other ideas from class, as evidenced by a combination of quotes, paraphrased material, and the student's own reflections. Writing should make explicit rather than implicit reference to how dress practices are impacted by subject positions, using terminology drawn from the reading and lecture. Any outside material that is used should be integrated in a way that demonstrates student understanding of the concepts. Lastly, instructors should look for evidence of proofreading and attention paid to typographical errors, as well as evidence of editing and attention paid to technical aspects of writing. Instructors may specify their preferred format for quotation and citation and may require a bibliography accompanying the assignment.

Guidelines for instructors

- Readings to be covered prior to delivering the assignment prompt:
- Kaiser, Susan. "Fashion and Culture: Cultural Studies, Fashion Studies" in *Fashion and Cultural Studies,* 1–27. London; New York: Berg, 2012.
- Kaiser, Susan. "Intersectional, Transnational Fashion Subjects" in *Fashion and Cultural Studies,* 28–51. London; New York: Berg, 2012.
- In my courses, this assignment was introduced in the third week of the semester, as it works best as an introductory assignment that allows students to introduce themselves to the instructor and to each other. However, instructors should take care that the requisite readings and material have been covered prior to students undertaking this assignment, and that students are comfortable with the terminology needed to successfully complete the assignment.

Discussion questions

- How would you describe your relationship to each subject position on your map—where are you?
- When are you most aware of this subject position? How does it impact your daily life?
- What influence does this subject position have on your daily dress practices?
- Is this subject position fixed or has it changed? Will it change over time? How has this impacted/how will this impact your daily dress practices?
- How did this assignment affect your awareness of the subject positions you inhabit? Did you become aware of any competing discourses within your subjectivity?

Cautionary advice for instructors

- Instructors should consider the specific vocabulary necessary for completing this assignment and productively engaging in discussion. When piloted, these terms were introduced in lecture and supplemented with a handout that asked students to fill in definitions for specific vocabulary items as they listened to the lecture. Instructors may consider a prereading introduction to key terms, guided reading questions, or an in-class activity that reinforces the following key concepts:
    - Intersectionality
    - Subject position(s)
    - Subjectivity
    - Intersubjectivity
    - Agency/structure
    - Everyday dress practice
    - Situated bodily practice
    - Hegemony
- Additionally, instructors should be aware that this exercise, as with any introspective exercise, has the potential to highlight areas of personal concern for students, and they should keep this in mind when delivering content and debriefing about the exercise. When this exercise was originally implemented, students were not asked to present their findings in the form of a formal presentation so as not to put them on the spot or ask them to speak as a representative of any particular subject position. Instead, a full class discussion was implemented, during which students had the opportunity to volunteer information as they saw fit and refrain if they felt uncomfortable speaking to a particular experience. Instructors may consider beginning the discussion by asking about experiences the students are likely to have in common, such as those related to their age, before proceeding to a discussion of differences, such as those related to their gender or ethnicity.

Copy of the assignment

Introduction to fashion studies—intersectionality map

Earlier in our semester, we read about and discussed the concept of intersectionality and the different subject positions that make up our selves. This assignment asks you to create an intersectionality map that describes you at this present moment.

Some requirements:

- You must include at least seven subject positions on your map. There is no maximum.

- Of your seven subject positions, at least four should be from this list:
  - gender, sexuality, ethnicity, place, age, class, nationality
- The other three (or more) subject positions can come from the aforementioned list, or you can supplement with your own categories:
  - e.g.: religion, neighborhood, major, hometown, sports, music, and profession/internship
- For each subject position on your map, you must include a paragraph (about five to seven sentences) that answers the following questions:
  - How would you describe your relationship to this subject position—where are you?
  - When are you most aware of this subject position—how does it impact your daily life?
  - What influence does this subject position have for your daily dress practices?
  - Is this subject position fixed or has it changed/will it change over time? How has this impacted/how will this impact your daily dress practices?
- For each subject position on your map, you must include an image to illustrate your position. This can be an image of you, but it doesn't have to be.
- Your map can take a number of visual formats, as long as the relationship between the subject positions is clear. Follow Susan Kaiser's model or create your own (Figure 18.1). Be creative!

You will be graded on how well you meet the requirements listed earlier, as well as the following criteria:

- A clear and thoughtful explanation of each subject position that answers the required questions
- Explicit and thoughtful connection to Susan Kaiser's text and other ideas when we discussed these issues in class
- At least one direct quote from Susan Kaiser, cited according to the Chicago style
- Clear writing and evidence of editing and proofreading

Typical results and reflections on the assignment

When this assignment was originally implemented, students reported:

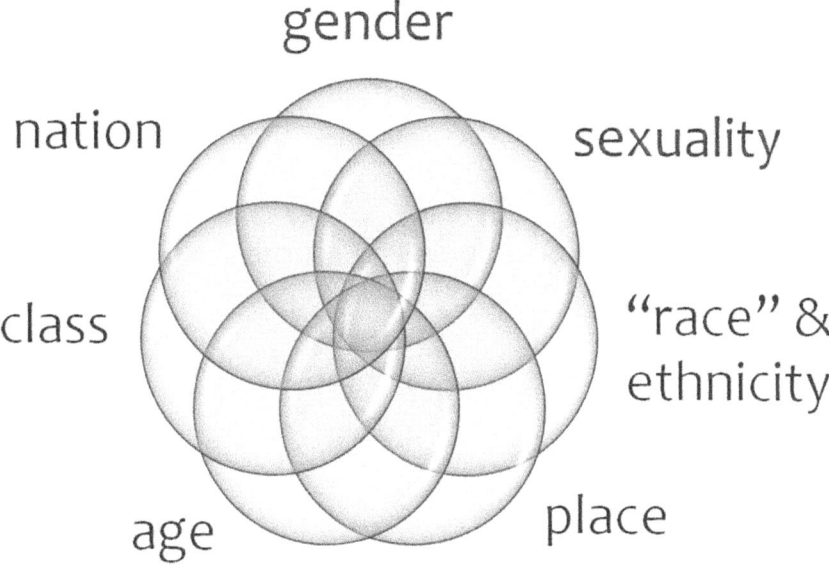

Figure 18.1 Susan Kaiser's model of intersectionality among subject positions.

- Although they had previously considered some of these subject positions, they had not considered their interconnected nature.
- They had not previously considered how their everyday dress practices were structured by their subject positions, and they had not considered the dynamic nature of their subject positions (how their relationship to subject positions and dress practice had changed or was likely to change over time).
- They found it easier to connect with the experiences and dress practices of others, because they understood that both commonalities and differences were to be found.
- They particularly enjoyed the visual format of the assignment, especially if they were visual learners. Some students went above and beyond to create inventive and original intersectionality maps, including collages, illustrations, and different conceptualizations of the map (e.g., some students formatted their maps in different shapes like the infinity symbol or a mindmap, whereas others expanded on Susan Kaiser's original illustration of the concept).

Notes

1. Susan Kaiser, *Fashion and Cultural Studies* (New York: Bloomsbury, 2012), 30, 28.
2. Joanne Entwistle, *The Fashioned Body: Fashion, Dress, and Social Theory* (Cambridge: Polity Press, 2000), 11.

Bibliography

Crenshaw, Kimberlé. "Mapping the Margins: Intersectionality, Identity Politics, and Violence Against Women of Color." *Stanford Law Review* 43, no. 6 (1991): 1241–1299. doi:10.2307/1229039.

Entwistle, Joanne. *The Fashioned Body: Fashion, Dress, and Social Theory*. Cambridge, UK: Polity Press, 2000.

Kaiser, Susan. "Fashion and Culture: Cultural Studies, Fashion Studies." In *Fashion and Cultural Studies*, 1–27. London; New York: Berg, 2012a.

Kaiser, Susan. "Intersectional, Transnational Fashion Subjects." In *Fashion and Cultural Studies*, 28–51. London; New York: Berg, 2012b.

19
ANALYZING REPRESENTATIONS OF FEMINIST AESTHETICS IN PRINT MEDIA

Elizabeth Stigler, University of Kansas

Contextualization

In both fashion studies and women, gender, and sexuality studies (WGSS), we are confronted by situationally specific understandings of what feminism has looked like and what it continues to look like. As philosopher Marjorie Jolles has pointed out, "Again and again, in popular debates concerning what feminism is and is not, fashion is invoked as a practice for both commenting on and enacting one's feminism."[1] This assignment asks students to select a contemporary (i.e., within the past five years) print advertisement and unpack whether it is representative of an empowering, feminist aesthetic or a disempowering, nonfeminist one. While it may seem reductionist to ask students to make such a binary distinction, they often gain a deeper understanding of clothing as approximating a code rather than clearly articulating a language, by drawing on this binary. Additionally, this assignment encourages students to explore how sexism, ableism, sizeism, racism, and classism are deployed in subtle ways via print media.

Students must address all aspects of their chosen advertisement, including composition, body position, background, color choice, text (if any appears), clothing or other products/props, and lighting. In order to determine whether this ad presents an empowering feminist aesthetic, students must use as many contextual clues as they can identify. For this assignment, students determine their own critical definition of feminism and defend it accordingly. Challenging students to formulate this definition builds on in-class discussions about intersectional feminism and the ways in which certain aesthetics are empowering for some and not empowering for others. This assignment is not intended to prove some definitions correct and others incorrect, but rather to demonstrate the multiple, possible ways that feminism can be read in/onto bodies through aesthetic and sartorial sensibilities. Once a student has selected a print advertisement, they are required to produce a 2,000-word response that includes an analysis of their chosen advertisement and three direct references to course texts. Their supporting texts must lend credibility to their reading of the ad as either feminist or nonfeminist.

One of the goals of this assignment is to effectively integrate Fashion studies into a WGSS classroom. This assignment assumes that students have had the opportunity to develop their independent research skills at the collegiate level, which is not something that all students have access to. At my university, there are no required prerequisites for taking my course, and WGSS courses are electives, not requirements, which means that, on average, more than half of my students have never taken a WGSS class before. Additionally, many of my students have had no previous exposure to the foundational concepts of WGSS such as the difference between sex and gender, the understanding that gender, race, and ability are all socially constructed, and theories of intersectionality. Therefore, I have had to design assignments with learning outcomes that could simultaneously be achieved by students with no WGSS experience alongside students who are WGSS majors.

This assignment was created to function as an accessible entry point for students new to WGSS concepts but also to afford enough complexity that advanced students could challenge themselves. In the past, more advanced students have used theories from Judith Butler, Michel Foucault, and Edward Said to support their analysis of their chosen advertisements. Because these students were already familiar with basic WGSS concepts, they felt comfortable utilizing complex theories to support their claims.

One of the key texts for this assignment and the larger course is Lars Svendsen's *Fashion: A Philosophy*, particularly his chapter on fashion and language. In this chapter, Svendsen cites the work of cultural theorists Roland Barthes and Alison Lurie. Lurie's work takes pains to convince readers that fashion is in fact a language, with clothing functioning as both vocabulary and a range of dialects. Svendsen systematically disassembles Lurie's argument and instead offers the idea that fashion is more like a code that is historically and contextually specific.[2] Svendsen also cites Fred Davis's chapter "Do Clothes Speak? What Makes Them Fashion?" which further dismisses the idea that fashion can be understood as a language. Davis's piece pokes fun at the idea that clothing can say one very specific thing about its wearer and thus act as a language, because there are no stable rules that govern fashion in the way that languages are governed. Davis, like Svendsen, suggests that fashion does not speak linearly but rather that it communicates meanings in a style that more closely approximates a code, albeit a weak code. Davis reminds us that the wearer is very rarely in charge of the messages that they are communicating, particularly if their self-styling is ambiguous or attempting to be subversive.[3] The conflicting perspectives offered by these texts further forces students to consider the juxtaposition of making judgments based on aesthetics and the impossibility of those same aesthetics to adequately communicate any one message.

The concepts of subversion and contradiction are also taken up in Marjorie Jolles's "Stylish Contradiction: Mix-and-Match as the Fashion of Feminist Ambivalence." Jolles uses the familiar "This is What a Feminist Looks Like" t-shirt to warn of the risks associated with stripping contradiction of its political power and reducing it to a sexy, one-size-fits-all aesthetic. Contradictory subject position, Jolles states, can be painful and difficult when one's identity cannot be reconciled due to cognitive dissonance. However, third-wave feminism's emphasis on personal choice and reluctance to articulate one stable identity have effectively diminished the power of contradictory subject position, reducing it to an assortment of sexy, aesthetic choices that reflect a casual aloofness. Jolles states, "Thus, precisely because a putative second-wave feminism is thought to insist upon what a feminist looks like, third-wave feminism insists only that 'This' is what a feminist looks like, whatever 'This' turns out to be."[4] Jolles's text demonstrates how a piece of clothing, or the mix-and-match aesthetic sensibility more broadly, can dilute the subversive power of contradiction and weaken its political effectiveness.

As a cultural studies scholar, analyzing visual media is a key part of my personal research as well as my pedagogical approach. This assignment asks students to engage in a number of critical skills, including independent research, critical thinking and writing, and application of course texts and theories to "real world" examples. Asking students to build and defend their interpretation of an image, without a clear indication of a "right" or "wrong" answer, forces them to reevaluate their personal criteria regarding critical constructs like sexism, racism, homophobia, sizeism, and ableism. I often find that students have a solid grasp on overt, nefarious forms of discrimination but have a more difficult time identifying and deconstructing covert, insidious discrimination. Additionally, using print advertisements forces students to consider the ways in which feminism and feminist values are employed and sold to consumers through carefully choreographed bodies and aesthetics. In my experience, this assignment spurs passionate conversations about ad campaigns and companies that students initially thought were empowering beacons of feminism but, after closer examination, have proven to be problematic.

Appropriate courses and course levels: I developed this assignment for a junior-level WGSS course with the understanding that the majority of my students come to my class from disciplines other than WGSS. This assignment would be appropriate for mid-level courses in departments like American or regional studies, media studies, human sexuality studies, or any courses that are cross-listed with WGSS and have an express interest in combining the critical perspectives of both fashion and feminist studies.

There are several ways that this assignment could easily be altered to better suit the needs of a lower-level course. In its current iteration, the assignment has a 2,000-word minimum and requires the incorporation of three scholarly texts from the course. The word requirement and the number of scholarly texts could both be reduced to better suit a 100- or 200-level course. Additionally, if there are concerns about the process, rather than charging students with finding their own print advertisement, instructors could assign the whole class the same advertisement, or offer a curated selection of advertisements to the students. Finally, this assignment could be altered to be an in-class activity rather than a homework assignment by showing one advertisement in class and asking students to verbally unpack the advertisement.

Estimated time required: This is an out-of-class assignment that builds on assigned readings and in-class discussions. It has been the most effective when assigned early in the term with a due date of approximately the middle of the term (my university is on a sixteen-week semester system, so this assignment is due on week eight). I distribute instructions for this assignment on the first day of my class, with the explicit understanding that the final assignment is not due for two months. However, by providing them with the instructions early in the semester, I can connect key concepts from readings that I think will be helpful to this assignment. Theoretically, this assignment could be completed in two weeks, but for my students at my university, a longer process has resulted in markedly better-quality work.

Learning goals

- Illustrate how feminist identity can be constructed through self-styling. Oftentimes students are initially resistant to the idea that their clothes are anything more than "just" clothes. This assignment asks students to make explicit connections between clothing and political, feminist subjectivity.

- Understand how clothing communicates multiple meanings that are not always clear. Because the print advertisement is a static one, students are forced to make decisions about the messages being disseminated without being able to confirm their interpretation with anyone else's input. This pushes them to be comfortable with a certain level of ambiguity as well as the potential that they have misread the advertisement and the bodies within it. The use of a print advertisement also helps to develop their critical thinking skills as they must make well-supported, insightful assumptions about a piece of popular media.

- Develop the ability to synthesize multiple theories and apply them to one example. In preparation for this assignment, students are exposed to a variety of complex theories like that of the gaze, Foucauldian discipline (Foucault, 1977), and the construction of rhetorical boundaries (Vats and Nishime, 2013). This assignment requires students to extract the important arguments from texts like those mentioned earlier and apply them to their analysis of an advertisement. This assignment compels them to yoke the work of other scholars with their own analysis.

Assessment

While definitions of success will vary somewhat from student to student, there are some evaluation criteria that are helpful to consider when assessing the completed assignment. As stipulated in the learning goals, students must demonstrate a nuanced understanding of their chosen ad. If a student cannot move beyond a simple "good" or "bad" value judgment or, similarly, if they are using broad, declarative statements (i.e., "This ad is clearly racist.") without offering any additional support, their work would not meet the learning goals. A successful assignment will thoughtfully and effectively incorporate the three required course texts. This means that students clearly demonstrate command over the key ideas of their chosen texts and rely on those ideas for substantial, textual support, rather than including one or two tangential quotes. In addition to using course texts effectively, a student must offer a strong explanation for their reading of their chosen ad. They must make a compelling case for why they believe their ad is or is not feminist. Finally, a successful assignment will adequately address issues of race, class, gender, ability, and size as they apply to the chosen ad.

Guidelines for instructors

- In order for this assignment to achieve its intended goals, you will need to ensure that your syllabus includes a sufficient amount of foundational texts in the fields of fashion studies and WGSS in order for students to have a strong base from which to perform their analyses.
- Caution students against conducting Google searches for "sexist ads." It took me a moment to realize when first using this assignment that my students were performing such online searches and grabbing the most overtly offensive ads for their papers. Since then, I have verbally instructed my students not to perform such searches, because it is important that they understand that not every affront to feminism or instance of sexism will be as obvious or nefarious as the ones that turn up when using those search terms.

Cautionary advice for instructors

- I would caution against allowing students to use video advertisements or commercials, because they frequently get caught up in analyzing what the characters are saying or how they are moving their bodies. The print advertisement forces students to draw a wide variety of conclusions from a static source.
- I would also emphasize that students need to understand that this assignment is not intended to be a competition about judging whether an advertisement is good or bad but, rather, they need to assess what about the clothing, self-styling, and subtext makes the advertisement appear to be feminist or not.
- It may be helpful to include a content warning in the assignment instructions, as students may encounter advertisements that can trigger past traumas.

Copy of the assignment

Is this what a feminist looks like?

This assignment is intended to help you apply the theories we've been reading about in class to an actual piece of print media. This assignment has two parts, and you must complete both of them to receive credit.

1. Locate one print advertisement featuring one person or multiple people. The ad can be for any product or company in the United States or internationally. The ad must be contemporary (meaning published within the past five years).
2. Write a critical analysis (minimum 2,000 words) of the ad using at least three of the course texts we have read to date to do so.

Your analysis should indicate whether your chosen ad communicates an empowering, feminist message or a disempowering, nonfeminist one. It is up to you to determine how you will judge whether this ad is empowering or not. In your analysis, you must communicate the criteria on which you judged the ad and how you crafted this criteria and reached your conclusion. Be sure to discuss how identity markers like race, class, gender, ability, size, and age are portrayed in the ad you have selected.

To receive full credit, you must go beyond saying what is "good" or "bad" about the ad and articulate what is being implied or communicated through the body (or bodies) in the ad. Through the use of direct quotes and references, you must explicitly connect your analysis to at least *three of the texts* we have read in class.

Your analysis must include a header with your name, the course, and the date as well as proper in-text citations and a Modern Language Association (MLA) -style work-cited page. You must also include a copy of the ad you have chosen to analyze. Failing to meet the word count requirement, include a copy of your ad, a header, or proper citations will result in a loss of points.

In the following text, you will find a list of questions that are intended to help you develop your analysis. You are not required to specifically address all of these questions in your paper; they are just meant to help generate ideas.

- What assumptions or stereotypes are presented in the ad?
- How is the body (or are the bodies) in the ad being used to sell the product?
- Are bodies used to represent "good" and/or "bad" behavior or habits?
- Are size, race, or ability used in an "inspirational" or "aspirational" way?
- To whom is the product marketed?
- Is the ad harmful? To whom?
- Who has the power in the ad?

Remember that you are not placing a value judgment on the ad or telling me what is "good" or "bad" about it. Rather, you are being asked to evaluate how feminist aesthetics are being used or negated to sell a product. Be sure you fully develop your argument. It is not enough to say "this ad is clearly sexist," you must explain what, exactly, makes it sexist.

Please make an appointment with me to discuss further questions.

Typical results and reflections on the assignment

- Students have expressed a deeper understanding of the complexities associated with judging feminism on purely aesthetic terms.
- Students are able to successfully apply course texts about feminism and fashion and embodied practice to a "real world" example.
- Students often initially express frustration at the difficulty of determining exactly what message was being communicated by their chosen advertisement. However, this frustration helps students to reflect on the multiple, often conflicting messages that can be interpreted and read onto aesthetic sensibilities.
- Students feel more comfortable in their use of scholarly sources, which helps better prepare them for subsequent papers and research assignments.

Notes

1 Marjorie Jolles, "Stylish Contradiction: Mix-and-Match as the Fashion of Feminist Ambivalence." In *Fashion Talks: Undressing the Power of Style*, ed. Marjorie Jolles and Shira Tarrant (New York: State University of New York, 2012), 227–243.
2 Lars Svendsen, "Fashion and Language." In *Fashion: A Philosophy*, trans. John Irons (London: Reaktion Books, 2006), 63–74.
3 Fred Davis "Do Clothes Speak, What Makes Them Fashion?" In *Fashion, Culture, and Identity*. (Chicago, IL: University of Chicago Press, 1992)
4 Marjorie Jolles, *Fashion Talks: Undressing the Power of Style* (New York: State University of New York, 2012), 235.

Bibliography

Barnard, Malcom, ed. *Fashion Theory: A Reader*. New York: Routledge, 2007.
Byrd, Ayana D., and Lori L. Tharpes. *Hair Story: Untangling the Roots of Black Hair in America*. New York: St. Martin's Press, 2001.
Davis, Fred. *Fashion, Culture, and Identity*. Chicago, IL: University of Chicago Press, 1992.
Foucault, Michel. *Discipline and Punish: The Birth of the Prison*. New York, NY: Random House, 1977. Translation copy, New York, NY: Random House, 1995.
Gurrieri, Lauren, and Helene Cherrier. "Queering Beauty: Fatshionistas in the Fatosphere." *Qualitative Market Research: An International Journal* 16, no. 3 (2013): 276–295.
Svendsen, Lars. *Fashion: A Philosophy*. Translated by John Irons. London: Reaktion Books, 2006.
Tarrant, Shira, and Marjorie Jolles, eds. *Fashion Talks: Undressing the Power of Style*. New York: State University of New York Press, 2012.
Vats, Anjali, and LeiLani Nishime. "Containment as Neocolonial Visual Rhetoric: Fashion, Yellowface, and Karl Lagerfeld's, 'Idea of China'." *Quarterly Journal of Speech* 99 (2013): 423–447.

20
THE "VINTAGE BLACK GLAMOUR" SHOWCASE: DEVELOPING MEDIA LITERACY AND CULTURAL COMPETENCY

Mel Michelle Lewis, Saint Mary's College of California

Contextualization

This chapter explores the central "showcase" assignment for the first-year seminar course, "Vintage Black Glamour." The course explores twentieth-century black fashion, culture, and entertainment in the United States. This assignment engages performing and visual arts of the period, and analyzes the impact of race, class, gender, sexuality, and other social formations on the lives and artistry of entertainers and cultural icons whose talents and images were revered in US culture.

The aim of this assignment is to develop media literacy and cultural competency by considering historical issues of activism, diversity, and inclusion and then connecting these issues to contemporary conversations. The assignment connects the foundations of vintage black glamour with prominent contemporary figures in popular culture and questions how their lives and works inspire us today. In the exercise, students also examine subversive or cutting-edge responses to cultural representations.

Vintage icons considered as a part of this assignment include Josephine Baker, Dorothy Dandridge, Harry Belafonte, and Diana Ross, among others. Prominent contemporary figures in popular culture include Beyoncé, Laverne Cox, and Lupita Nyong'o. The class also examined subversive historical representations, such as Black Panther posters and paired them with contemporary cutting-edge subversive acts, including Oakland's Queer Fashion Week and Kehinde Wiley's stained glass windows. The objective of this "timeline" approach is to illustrate the ways in which contemporary icons are inspired by and reference the past. Students learn how to trace influences and creative citation across time.

Examining vintage black glamour is an important intervention into the historical narrative of twentieth-century blackness. This lesson also provides a foundation for understanding the politics of contemporary black iconicity. Most students in the United States have limited exposure to twentieth-century figures in black history. The curriculum and programming for Black History Month or Martin Luther King, Jr.'s birthday may look back at Harriet Tubman and *Frederick Douglass*, or engage an incomplete and uncritical account of the civil rights movement of the 1960s, but rarely do students have the opportunity to engage influential figures in popular culture. In this course, students fill in some of the gaps by examining affirming images in black fashion and entertainment. This lesson offers a more complex and multidimensional understanding of black culture through fashion and political aesthetics.

Appropriate courses and course levels for the assignment: This course was designed as a part of the Frontiers: First Year Seminar series for incoming students in their first semester in college. A women, gender, and sexuality studies and Africana studies faculty member taught the course. In addition to these fields, the course was intended to introduce first-year students to topics and methods of inquiry in multiple interdisciplinary programs and areas of study, including communication, film and media studies, history, sociology, and visual and performing arts, among others.

Appropriate class size: The most desirable class size for this exercise is fifteen to twenty-five students.

Estimated time required: This is a longitudinal assignment; deliverables were due throughout the semester. The first deliverable, the proposal and outline, was due after foundational material had been covered, in the sixth week of the course. The second deliverable, the creative showcase presentation, was shared in the final weeks of the course, that is, weeks thirteen and fourteen. The final paper was due during the final exam period, allowing students to incorporate any feedback, new questions, or unexplored ideas following their showcase presentations to be addressed and integrated into the final paper.

Required materials: The proposal and final paper required library research. The creative showcase presentations required audio/visual computer access in the classroom, as well as a performance area at the front of the room.

Learning goals

- Students will develop media literacy and cultural competency by considering issues of activism, diversity, and inclusion. Prompts will highlight how early and mid-twentieth-century vintage representations of black culture and identity reshaped prevailing White supremacist misogynistic narratives, tropes, and images. Students will make connections between vintage representations and contemporary cultural icons, activism, and cultural issues.

- Students will acquire research, presentation, and writing skills, including the ability to develop structured arguments as part of their papers and presentations. Prompts will emphasize the ways in which early and mid-twentieth-century vintage fashion, entertainers, films, music, and other artistic expressions are foundational to contemporary cultural production.

- Students will identify, examine, and explain key interdisciplinary feminist and Africana studies concepts related to social constructions of gender, racial formations, frameworks of power and privilege, cultural production, social justice, activism, and the ways in which "the personal is political." Students will demonstrate their understanding of terms, theories, and concepts orally during in-class discussions, in presentations, and in written assignments.

Assessment

The assessment tool for this creative assignment is adaptable. My goal was to provide assessment that accommodated the various presentation formats students used to share their knowledge and talents during the showcase. The final paper assignment section of the rubric is also able to respond to varied modes of inquiry and research formats. Points were allotted in the following way:

Showcase presentation

- The presentation is well researched and illustrates a command of the material. 10 points
- The presentation is creative and dynamic in its approach to conveying the material. Exceeds or meets the requirements of the assignment (length and subject matter). Care and effort put into the process. 10 points

Final paper

- Themes and concepts are strongly supported by weekly course materials and cited materials with citations. 30 points
- Background context and idea development support the discussion. Insight, analysis, and illustration of the connections between concepts presented. 30 points
- Strong writing style presented. Clear ability to express thoughts and point of view, including grammar, syntax, and spelling. 10 points
- Exceeds or meets the requirements of the assignment. Care and effort put into the process. 10 points

Guidelines for instructors

In teaching the assignment, I found that it was a challenge to negotiate the generational divide between students and the material being discussed. It was important for me to recognize that many students have little to no knowledge of the cultural references from the early and mid-twentieth century. Although some black students reported that their parents or grandparents had introduced them to particular films, artists, or songs, almost all students felt the material was very unfamiliar.

Additionally, in a majority White classroom, it was important to allow for maturation and establish ground rules for discussion. Respect, inclusion, communication, and responsibility were consistently asserted as supporting guidelines for discussion. Introducing these at the beginning of the semester and referring to them when initiating discussion was helpful. Using reframing statements was also helpful: "what I hear you saying is" and "let's use more specific language rather than generalizations" were helpful clarifying statements.

Finally, during the showcase, many students used Internet access to play clips or audio, while others needed an audio plug for their cell phones or tablet media players to share music or videos. Having adapters for different devices on hand was helpful. Instructing students to email their work to themselves, have it on a flash, or having at least one backup method of retrieving their material was critical.

Discussion questions

Before the presentations, students were asked to consider the following prompts to shape their feedback and discussion for their classmates:

- Using examples from the presentations, discuss the significance of the images (visual) and sonic (audio) materials examined by the class. Consider both the historical significance and contemporary debates that apply to the photos, videos, lyrics, musical style, etc.
- Using examples from the presentations, compare and contrast the arguments about masculinity, femininity, and sexuality explored in the presentations.
- Using examples from the presentations, discuss the significance of presenting new narratives representing African American culture and identity in the early and mid-twentieth century. How do the musical, visual, stories, and/or performers themselves relay these new representations? How are the contemporary works an extension of the foundational films?

Cautionary advice for instructors

- Clarify historical contexts, language, and images: that is, early-twentieth-century materials and texts use the term "Negro"; mid-century materials, such as

Blaxploitation films, may use charged radicalized language. Be sure to discuss historical and culturally specific uses of language and set ground rules for class discussion, such as substituting the "N word" or referring to an author's use of a term indicating they are not pedestrian, contemporary uses of the terms.

- Deconstruct on-screen representations. This class emphasizes the debates around representations of black female sexuality as always already objectified, or as purposeful and empowering. For example, are the Ikettes simply "eye candy," or do they represent an empowering break from the conservative sexual politics of respectability? At the beginning of the showcase, remind students that they are engaging images and ideas rather than passively consuming them as viewers. This disrupts the practice of simply consuming the "other," in this context black performers, as a spectacle. Rather than seeing "difference" or "exotic," students are asked to develop a critical eye for acts of agency, transgression, and celebration.

Copy of the assignment

Vintage Black Glamour showcase assignment

1. Deliverable one: Research proposal and outline (approximately 400–500 words + outline)

In your proposal you will:

1. Name and discuss your topic and any subtopics of interest.
2. Offer a thesis statement regarding the significance of your topic.
3. Tell me how and why you have selected this topic.
4. Submit an initial outline of your paper.
5. Submit a description of your presentation/performance/creative work.

2. Deliverable two: Showcase presentation/performance/creative work

You will develop, research, and present a rigorous and dynamic project of your own design related to your vintage black glamour theme. This project should be creative. Examples may include a live dance, musical, or theatrical performance, a fashion show, an artistic portfolio, a resource guide, a mix tape, a website design, an art instillation, a short film, and an educational video game: the form is up to you. Enjoy your artistic freedom! You will present and discuss your creative work as a participant in the "vintage Black glamour showcase" with your classmates. When you present, you will discuss the relationship between your creative showcase presentation and your research paper (five to ten minutes max).

3. Deliverable three: Final research paper (five to seven pages)

You will compose a research paper related to your vintage black glamour theme. You will introduce your topic and propose your thesis statement regarding the significance of your topic. You will then explore the topic, using specific examples. The best papers will directly draw from the research materials and properly cite your references.

Typical results and reflections on the assignment

Examples of showcase and related paper topics included the following:

- A photo spread created by a student who curated a "collection" of vintage wear that transgressed gender norms and expressed genderfluid identity
- A pair of students composing a spoken word duet responding to contemporary hip-hop lyrics with vintage songs and praise for the women who sang them
- A comparison of artists who have used or referenced Josephine Baker's iconic banana skirt, including *Beyoncé and Nicki Minaj*
- A slideshow revealing the fashion statement and impact of the Black Panther Party

These presentations, among many others, illustrated the following goals:

- The development of media literacy and cultural competency by considering issues of activism, diversity, and inclusion. Students demonstrated the ability to analyze media representations (the vintage wear "collection" that transgressed gender norms) and consider the cultural significance of representations (the beret or afro hairstyle worn by the Black Panther Party).
- Final papers clearly articulated the ways in which early and mid-twentieth-century vintage fashion, entertainers, films, music, and other artistic expressions are foundational to contemporary cultural production (e.g., black female dancers and singers wearing or referencing Josephine Baker's iconic banana skirt).
- All papers and presentations illustrated student skill and ability to identify, examine, and explain key interdisciplinary feminist and Africana studies concepts related to social constructions of gender, racial formations, frameworks of power and privilege, cultural production, social justice, activism, and the ways in which "the personal is political." At its foundation, the spoken word duet incorporated terms, critiques, and key concepts from the course.

Bibliography

Baadasssss Cinema—A Bold Look at 70's Blaxploitation Films. [Film] Dir. Isaac Julien, USA: Docurama, 2003.
Carmen Jones. [Film] Dir. Otto Preminger, USA: 20th Century Fox, 1954.

Collins, P.H. *Black Sexual Politics: African Americans, Gender, and the New Racism*. New York: Routledge, 2004.

Davis, A.Y. *Blues Legacies and Black Feminism: Gertrude "Ma" Rainey, Bessie Smith, and Billie Holiday*. 1st edn. New York: Vintage, 1999.

Gainer, N. *Vintage Black Glamour*. London: Rocket 88, 2014.

Hammonds, E. "Black (W)holes and the Geometry of Black Female Sexuality." In *Feminism Meets Queer Theory*, edited by Elizabeth Weed and Naomi Schor. Bloomington, IN: Indiana University Press, 1997.

Stormy Weather. [Film] Dir. Andrew L. Stone, USA: 20th Century Fox, 1943.

Thaggert, M. "Marriage, Moynihan, Mahogany: Success and the Post-Civil Rights Black Female Professional in Film." *American Quarterly* 64, no. 4 (2012): 715–740.

Thompson, M.S. and V.M. Keith. "The Blacker the Berry: Gender, Skin Tone, Self-Esteem, and Self-Efficacy." *Gender and Society* 15, no. 3 (2001): 336–357.

Vogel, S. "Performing 'Stormy Weather': Ethel Waters, Lena Horne, and Katherine Dunham." *South Central Review* 25, no. 1 (2008): 93–113.

21
DISCUSSING DIFFERENCE IN STUDENTS' FASHION BLOGS

Holly M. Kent, University of Illinois-Springfield

Contextualization

In the twenty-first century, significant parts of the fashion media have migrated online, with major fashion periodicals and commentators developing substantial online presences and engaging extensively through social media. The proliferation of online spaces has opened up new opportunities for fashion writers to share their ideas through mediums such as blogging with a larger public than (in the pre-Internet age) would have been possible. While fashion blogs are no longer quite the same force in fashion as they were at the turn of the twenty-first century, online spaces nonetheless remain important for fashion commentators.

Diversity is a significant issue in the virtual fashion world, just as it is in the material one. Even though access to online culture has expanded, fashion blogs remain relatively homogeneous, with cisgender, white, affluent, able-bodied, thin, conventionally feminine-presenting, heterosexual women tending to predominate. This homogeneity has certainly not gone unchallenged, with blogs created by and focused on fashion and women of color, self-defined fat women, differently abled, genderqueer, non-binary, and trans people becomingly increasingly common. Such fashion bloggers, however, are still all too often marginalized in mainstream fashion spaces, and do not always garner the media attention granted to fashion writers from dominant social groups.

This assignment enables students to become creators of fashion media, to reflect on how fashion blogs have transformed the media landscape, and to consider how fashion blogs both succeed and fail in grappling with issues of diversity. The assignment consists of writing for a collective course blog. By themselves becoming creators of online fashion media, students have the opportunity to reflect on the diverse meanings fashion has for different individuals and groups and to reflect on the ongoing inequalities that pervade online fashion spaces.

Appropriate courses and course levels for the assignment: While I use this assignment in my upper-division history course on fashion in the United States, it could also readily be applied to lower- and upper-division courses in communication, English, media, sociology, and women, gender, and sexuality studies, and could focus on any country or region.

Appropriate class size: While my classes have typically had about fifteen students, smaller or larger classes could certainly tackle this assignment (instructors may, however, want to adjust the level of required commenting for the blog, depending on class size, to ensure that all students are engaging in conversations about one another's work).

Estimated time required: I typically encourage students to take at least one week to craft their blog posts (leaving themselves more time if it is a post for which they will need to conduct interviews or fieldwork).

Required materials: The instructor will need to set up a collective course blog (through a free site such as WordPress or through a blogging platform at their institution), and ensure that students have the necessary passwords and comfort levels to post and comment on these sites. Instructors may find it valuable to schedule a day in a computer lab on campus to have students experiment with posting to and commenting on the course blog.

Learning goals

- To think about the place of blogging in the fashion media landscape
- To reflect on how students' lived experiences with fashion culture tie into broader cultural and scholarly debates about fashion
- To interrogate how factors such as race, class, gender, sexual orientation, ability, age, and religion shape both fashion culture and individuals' and groups' experiences of it

Assessment

In my course, this assignment counts for 10 percent of students' final overall grades (that grade being comprised of an average of students' grades on each of their individual blog posts, and of points students receive for commenting on their classmates' blog posts). I grade each post out of 100 points, and each post comment out of 10 points. I assess posts and comments on several different criteria: professionalism of presentation, evidence of effort having been put into posts and comments, and success in tying the themes of posts and comments into the larger ideas and readings of our course. Successful posts and comments should be clearly organized and free from any typographical errors, should demonstrate that students dedicated time, care, and thought to considering the question or undertaking the exercise in their specific prompt, and should reflect on how the issues they are considering in their posts and comments connect to ideas that have been raised in course readings, lectures, and discussions.

I have found this system of assessment effective, as the blogging assignment counts for enough credit for students to take it seriously as an important course assignment, but not so much credit as to be intimidating, and to impede students from expressing themselves more freely and creatively through their blogging and commenting.

Guidelines for instructors

Depending on the course in which this assignment is being used, instructors may wish to preface these assignments with specific readings about fashion, blogging, and social media (suggested readings can be found in the bibliography).

Instructors will need to ensure that students have access to, and familiarity with, necessary technologies for this assignment (and that instructors make accommodations for students who do not have access to smartphones, personal computers, or regular Internet access).

Discussion questions: While it is optional, instructors can take time in class to discuss blog posts and comments. Possible questions include the following:

- What issues came up for you, as you were writing your blog post for this week?
- Did you find anything surprising, working on this particular assignment?
- For those of you who had read and commented on blog posts for this week, what kinds of patterns and themes did you notice in your colleagues' posts?
- How do you see our blog posts tying into our course readings, and the issues we have been discussing in class?

Cautionary advice for instructors

- Instructors will want to emphasize the necessity for courtesy in blog posts and comments. Several of the assignments call for students to interview those different from themselves about their experiences of fashion culture and to observe how fashion goods are sold in a range of different venues. These blog posts can therefore bring up sensitive issues of race, gender, class, and other forms of difference. Instructors should discuss the necessity of writing and engaging with their peers and other members of the public respectfully.
- Instructors should also be aware that since several of these assignments ask students to think about their lived experiences with dress, difficult experiences surrounding body image can arise. Instructors should be sure to emphasize that students can elect not to write on any prompt that raises difficult issues for them, and the necessity of engaging in respectful considerations of themselves and

each other (i.e., no self-denigration or commentary about classmates' physical appearance will be permitted). Instructors should be sure to stress that, even when discussing their own wardrobes, students are under no obligation to post images of themselves.
- As several of possible blog assignments involve students interviewing others, instructors should ascertain what their institutions' policies about oral histories are. Students should ensure they have their interviewees sign a consent form, and, depending on their institutions' policies, may need to submit this project to an Institutional Review Board (IRB).
- Instructors may also consider making their blogs private (some institutions use systems like Blackboard that enable instructors to create blogs that can only be accessed by members of the class), rather than use a public blogging platform.

Copy of the assignment

Blogging assignment sheet

Assignment overview

For this assignment, you will be selecting *four* of the six blogging prompts listed in this assignment sheet, and writing brief (approximately 500–700 words) about your chosen topic for our course blog. Your blog posts can be written in a colloquial style (while maintaining professional standards in terms of proofreading). You will upload your blog post to me directly, and I will post it on our course blog thereafter.

You will also be commenting a minimum of *eight* times on your colleagues' posts over the course of the semester. You are welcome to select whichever blog posts you wish to comment on. Your responses should be between about 100 and 200 words. Your comments must be posted *one week after the blog post you are commenting on was due*.

You will not be making formal presentations about your blog posts, but we will be discussing the blog posts in class, the week after your blog posts were due.

Your overall grade for this assignment will be calculated from the collective points you receive for each blog post and comment (you will be graded out of 100 points for each post and out of 10 points for every comment).

Blog posts: Specific guidelines

Option #1: Reflecting on my closet

For this assignment, you will be selecting a garment or object from your own closet, and reflecting on its significance in fashion history.

- Why is this specific object/garment important to you? Why did you initially purchase it (if you did), and why do you still keep it?

- If a fashion historian only had this object/garment to work with, what kinds of conclusions do you think they might draw, about you, and about culture in our era more broadly?

Option #2: Fashion interviewing

For this assignment, you will be finding a person to interview about their experiences with fashion culture. You will ask:

- Whether or not fashion seems relevant to their life (if so, how, and if not, why not?)
- How they make decisions about what clothing to wear and buy (is it about how much clothes cost? What is the most convenient? About personal style? About self-expression?)
- If they feel pressured (by family members, peers, or the broader culture) to dress a certain way (because of their age, gender identity, expectations in their workplace or school, etc.?) If so, what are those pressures and how do they respond to them? And if not, why do they think there aren't any pressures to dress a certain way?

For this assignment, in addition to writing your post, please be sure to have your interviewee sign the required consent form.

Option #3: Fashion on campus

For this assignment, you will be selecting a fellow campus community member to interview about fashion culture. You will ask:

- How they make their decisions about what to wear to campus. When they are getting dressed to come to school and/or work, how do they make choices about what to wear?
- What they think characterizes our campus' style. What do they notice about how students, faculty, and staff dress on campus? Do they notice any particular commonalities? Do people on campus dress similarly and/or differently? How and why?

For this assignment, in addition to writing your post, please be sure to have your interviewee sign the required consent form.

Option #4: Fashion fieldwork

For this assignment, you will be selecting any venue that sells clothing (so you can go to a thrift store, or a big box store like Target or Walmart, or a mall, or a smaller, specialty store, etc.). After choosing and visiting your venue, you will consider the following:

- The physical layout. How is the store designed, and why? How is it seeking to appeal to consumers, and how is it a success and a failure, in your opinion?
- The staff. How many staff members are there? Are they visible to you as a consumer? Do they engage with you? If so, how?
- The other clients. Who else is shopping in the store? How are your fellow customers behaving: Does shopping seem to be a pleasant leisure activity? An obligation to be gotten through quickly? Are they alone, or are they shopping with others?
- The goods. What do you notice about the garments/accessories in the store? Do you notice particular themes and commonalities? Which kinds of consumers are they seeking to reach with their garments? How do you think that their marketing is more (and less) successful?

Option #5: Fashion culture on the Internet

For this assignment, you will be identifying a fashion website and reflecting on what we can learn from it about fashion in the digital age. This site can take any form you wish: it can be the website of a major fashion periodical like *Vogue*, an independent fashion blog, the site of an Etsy retailer, someone documenting on street style on Instagram, the Twitter feed of a fashion journalist ... anything you like, as long as it is online! Please be sure to provide the URL for your site in your post. Once you have identified your site, you will:

- Analyze its content. What are the content available on the site, in terms of images, text, etc.? Who do you think this site is seeking to appeal to?
- Reflect on your site and consider if there are things the "new media" of the Internet can do which are different from the "old media" of magazines, etc. If so, what are these things, and if not, how do "new" and "old" media seem similar?

Option #6: Reflecting on contemporary fashion

For this assignment, you will be reflecting on what you think characterizes our era in fashion history. For this assignment, you will discuss the following:

- What do you think defines contemporary fashion (in terms of aesthetic, attitude, trend, etc.)?
- When fashion historians look back on our decade 25, 50, 100 years from now, how do you think they will describe it?
- If you had to project forward, what do you think the coming decades have in store, fashion-wise (in terms of trends, shifts, and developments)?

Blog comments: Specific guidelines

When you are commenting on your colleagues' posts, please observe the following guidelines:

- Be as specific as possible.
- Be sure to be respectful in terms of how you engage with your classmates. Raising questions or disagreeing with a point one of your colleagues has raised is totally fine; just make sure to do so in a courteous way.

Typical results and reflections on the assignment

- Students have typically found this assignment empowering, as it has enabled them to not just read about and study online fashion culture, but themselves become part of it.
- This assignment has proven useful in giving students the opportunity to apply abstract concepts about fashion from class concretely, through reflecting on their experiences.
- This assignment has been valuable, as it has enabled students to learn about fashion experiences of individuals different from themselves. (Students are often struck, for example, about how significantly factors such as age and region can shape experiences of fashion culture.)
- This assignment can sometimes be challenging for students because, since it asks them to consider fashion as an embodied practice, it can bring up issues of body image. Instructors will need to be sensitive to these issues, having more generalized discussions in class about fashion and the body, and encouraging students not to write on prompts that might be triggering for them.
- This assignment can also sometimes be challenging since it asks students to grapple with issues of fashion and difference, particularly along the lines of race and class. Instructors should be aware that discussions of these issues can sometimes become fraught (with students sometimes "othering" the dress practices of those unlike themselves). Instructors may wish to preemptively have conversations with students about being respectful in terms of how they grapple with issues of dress and difference.

Bibliography

Chittenden, Tara. "Digital Dressing Up: Modeling Female Teen Identity in the Discursive Spaces of the Fashion Blogosphere." *Journal of Youth Studies* 13, no. 4 (August 2010): 505–520.

Connell, Catherine. "Fashionable Resistance: Queer 'Fa(t)shion' Blogging as Counterdiscourse." *WSQ: Women's Studies Quarterly* 41, no. 1 and 2 (Spring/Summer 2013): 209–224.

Entwistle, Joanne. "Fashion and the Fleshy Body: Dress as Embodied Practice." *Fashion Theory: The Journal of Dress, Body, and Culture* 4 (2000): 323–347.

Harp, Dustin, and Mark Tremayne. "The Gendered Blogosphere: Examining Inequality Using Network and Feminist Theory." *Journalism and Mass Communication Quarterly* 83 (2006): 247–264.

Pham, Minh-Ha. "Blog Ambition: Fashion, Feelings, and the Political Economy of the Digital Raced Body." *Camera Obscura* 26, no. 1 (2011): 1–36.

White, Michele. *Producing Women: The Internet, Traditional Femininity, Queerness, and Creativity*. New York: Routledge, 2015.

PART SEVEN

ETHICS AND SUSTAINABILITY

Introduction

This section grapples with the complex topics of fashion, ethics, and sustainability, offering exercises designed to help students identify and think through vital moral questions central to fashion production and consumption, and consider how to effectively address these problems. These chapters tackle difficult issues surrounding the fashion industry's impact on the environment, workers' rights in an ever-accelerating fast fashion economy, and the persistent, pernicious nature of cultural appropriation in fashion culture. In her chapter, Alice Payne invites students to reflect on the complicated issues surrounding ethical and ecofashion, having them take on the roles of fashion buyers deciding between a range of potential brands to collaborate with (each of them uses different materials and processes to create their garments). This exercise allows students to engage in valuable discussions about the complex factors that shape how a garment or collection is (or is not) judged to be eco-friendly and ethically produced.

    Amanda Sikarskie's chapter brings students into important conversations about cultural appropriation in the fashion world. Sikarskie's assignment enables them to reflect on the ways in which cultural appropriation manifests itself in decisions made by designers, marketers, models, and other fashion professionals. Having students identify and analyze a specific example of the appropriation of indigenous fashion by a Western designer, Sikarskie's chapter allows students to think about the ways in which cultural appropriation in the fashion world ties into the long-standing history (and ongoing realities) of colonialism and racial inequality.

    And finally, June-Ann Greeley's chapter allows students to consider the significance of their decisions as consumers within the global fashion marketplace. Enabling students to engage in independent research into the environmental impact and labor practices of the brands they buy and the businesses where they shop allows them to reflect on the national and global implications of their own fashion choices, and to consider how individual consumers can help to build a more ethical, eco-friendly international fashion system.

22
WEIGHING UP SUSTAINABLE FASHION

Alice Payne, Queensland University of Technology

Contextualization

Sustainability in fashion is a highly complex issue in which students must grapple with ethical considerations such as workers' rights, as well as environmental issues such as waste and pollution of air, water, and soil. As Bennie, Gazibara, and Murray note, although fashion and the fashion industry can "create wellbeing, embrace creativity and connect global communities," fashion has also many negatives, "characterized at its worst by factories exploiting workers, generating throwaway fashion, wasting resources and encouraging unsustainable consumption."[1] In the past decade, although many fashion companies have worked to alleviate their environmental and social impact, there are still intractable problems to overcome.

In this exercise, students are asked to engage in a role-playing task around the topic of fashion and sustainability. As buyers for an online retailer, they must select three garments to feature on the website's sustainable fashion feature page (inspired by ASOS's Green Room). In groups, they are provided with images of ten garments from fictitious brands that are each engaged in activities aligned with sustainable fashion. Students must determine which three garments would be best to feature, and why. The aim of the exercise is not to merely classify garments as more or less "sustainable," but rather for students to rigorously examine and debate the many dimensions of fashion and sustainability that can be applied to the discussion.

The task is underpinned by a life cycle approach to sustainable fashion. Life cycle thinking, highlighted by both Alison Gwilt and Kate Fletcher, allows one to trace fashion and sustainability issues through fiber choices (cradle), design, manufacturing, use phase, and finally end of life including disposal (grave) or reuse and recycling.[2] The notion stems from formal Life Cycle Assessments (LCAs), a quantitative analysis in which environmental impacts of a product may be measured within set parameters.[3] The LCA methodology underpins tools such as the Material Sustainability Index in which textiles are indexed according to environmental impact.[4]

The qualitative approach to life cycle thinking is also important. Beyond metrics, producers and consumers can ask: Where was the garment manufactured and under what conditions? Is the garment able to be recycled? Is the garment reusable? How long will it last? Can I trust the claims of a brand? The sustainable characteristics explored in the task are intentionally diverse, and include local production, traceability and supply chain transparency, second-hand items, recyclability, social justice and fair trade, organic fibers, classic garments designed for longevity, and more. These examples are drawn from the work of Black, Gwilt, and Rissanen and Brown, in which best practice case studies of companies and designers demonstrate the breadth of possible approaches in the area of sustainable fashion.[5] *A Practical Guide to Sustainable Fashion*, by Gwilt, provides an excellent and accessible overview of the key issues.[6]

Engaging with this task will encourage students to think critically about the "what" and "how" of ethical fashion production and enable them to distinguish measurable actions from marketing speak. To become future industry leaders, fashion students require a nuanced understanding of contemporary sustainability practices, including the need for companies to have rigorous and measurable standards. Through role-playing buyer decision-making processes, students can gain an appreciation of the sheer diversity of possible approaches: there is not one road toward sustainable fashion, but a myriad.

Appropriate courses and course levels for the assignment: This exercise is designed for an undergraduate cohort in a fashion design, fashion business, or fashion communication course. However, with the focus on how firms communicate corporate social responsibility (CSR), the exercise would also be valuable for business students studying advertising and marketing, supply chain management, or international business.

Appropriate class size: A tutorial class of approximately twenty to twenty-five students is appropriate. Students can be divided into groups of four students.

Estimated time required: This exercise is designed to run over a fifty-minute class, including briefing, group work, and then final presentation and discussion.

Required materials

- Each group will need a hard copy set of the ten clothing brand cards and a copy of the starting point form (see "Copy of the Exercise" section).
- Pen and paper for note-taking.
- The students will ideally have access to a smartphone, tablet, or computer in each group, but this is not essential.
- The facilitator may wish to sign up to an online collaboration tool such as Padlet.com, which allows all student groups to post to it like a giant online whiteboard. This works well if there is more than one class being run on the topic as all students enrolled in the course can see how other classes tackled the task.

Learning goals

- Understanding approaches to quantifying a company's engagement with sustainable practices.
- Understanding the inherent complexity of the social and environmental issues involved in fashion production.
- Understanding that there are multiple ways of viewing and assessing a company's self-described ethical values from the measurable (e.g., certifications and audits) to the less measurable (e.g., marketing and "brand story"[7]).

Assessment

This task is well suited for an in-class discussion exercise. It could however be extended for assessment through inclusion of a reflective written component in which the students examine their decision-making process and what insights they formed regarding their perspectives on sustainable fashion.

The task could also form the premise for an individually assessed report, in which the student develops a written analysis of their chosen brands including a rationale for their choice, supported by research in the form of industry tools, reports, and scholarly literature. Criteria for assessment may include the student's ability to

- Draw upon high-quality, highly relevant research to support findings and analysis;
- Synthesize environmental and ethical issues into sophisticated, insightful, and substantiated recommendations for sustainable industry approaches.

Guidelines for instructors

This task should ideally be placed midway through a module on fashion and sustainability in which students have been introduced to environmental and social impacts of fashion production and consumption. Key issues covered in the unit of study prior to running this exercise could include the following:

- Basic introduction to clothing fibers and materials including ways of measuring environmental impact
- Conditions for workers in the fashion industry including factory conditions, company CSR, and fair trade practices
- Waste in fashion production and consumption and various strategies to eliminate, reduce, reuse, or recycle waste including downcycling, upcycling, and cradle-to-cradle approaches[8]

For this exercise, each group will be given ten fictitious brand cards and the "starting point" form. We invented the ten fashion brands, providing each with a garment featuring a variety of sustainable fashion characteristics (see Table 22.1). To bring them to life, we gave the labels evocative names (chosen from Lou Reed songs), and each card was illustrated with an image sourced online from a fashion forward, youthful brand (see Figure 22.1 for suggested card format).

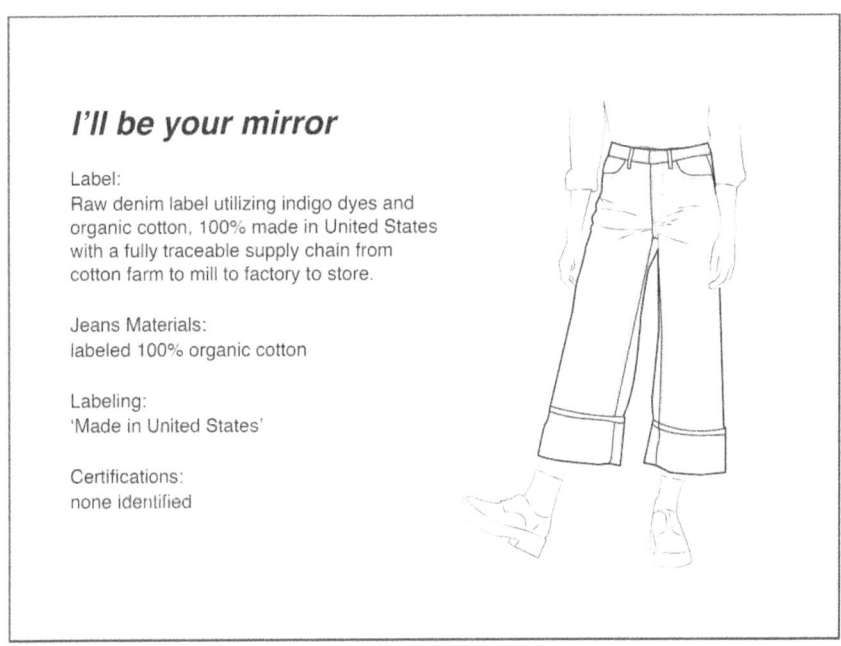

Figure 22.1 Example of brand garment cards to hand out (image: Alice Payne).

Table 22.1 *Description of brands and garments*

Brand name	Description of brand and garment
Venus in Furs	Brand: Curated collection of vintage garments Jacket material: 100 percent cotton Country of origin: unknown Certifications: None
Sunday Morning	Brand: Will collect the garment at end of life; offers repair and alteration service in store. Coat material: 100 percent lightweight, high-performance polymide (nylon) Labeling: Made in China Certification: Oeko-Tex Standard 1000 "Confidence in Textiles"
I'll be your mirror	Raw denim label utilizing indigo dyes and organic cotton Made in the United States Traceable supply chain from cotton farm to mill to factory to store. Jeans material: Labeled 100 percent organic cotton Labeling: "Made in United States" Certifications: None identified

Brand name	Description of brand and garment
White Light	Brand: Youthful and fun—partners with Bionic yarns to collect ocean plastic used in collections; target for 100 percent recycled materials by 2018; investing in waterless dyeing Jacket material: 100 percent recycled polyester Labeling: "Made in China" Certifications: Independent factory audits through Fair Wear Foundation
All Tomorrow's Parties	Brand: Fair Trade brand committed to providing living wage with a portion of profits donated to supporting schooling for their factory workers' children Material: Suede skirt of vegetable tanned goat leather; lining 100 percent polyester Labeling: "Made in Bangladesh" Certifications: Fair Trade certified
Loop	Brand: Social enterprise label providing the opportunity to work and learn in the fashion industry for young people who have experienced being a refugee. Nonprofit organization. Material: Skirt—50 percent wool, 50 percent acrylic Top—100 percent cotton using natural dyes Labeling: "Made in Australia" Certification: Ethical Clothing Australia
Satellite of Love	Brand: Uses eco-friendly fabrics with nontoxic dyes Dress Material: 100 percent Lyocell Labeling: "Made in India" Certification: Oeko-Tex Standard 1000 "Confidence in Textiles" Independent factory audits through Fair Wear Foundation
Run Run Run	Brand: Uses only factory offcuts and ends of rolls to make limited edition collections Material: Preconsumer waste in cotton, viscose, and polyester Labeling: "Handmade in UK" Certification: Global Recycle Standard
Sweet Jane	Brand: Uses only organic fabrics and dyes that are cradle-to-cradle certified to be safely biodegradable; seeds embedded into garment labels for composting at end of life Shirtdress Material: 100 percent organic cotton Labeling: "Made in Turkey" Certification: Cradle-to-Cradle Certified™

Discussion questions

As students present their three garment choices, ask:

- Why did you choose the brands you did? On what criteria did you and your group base your decision?
- Where did you place the most weight: in aspects that can be measured and quantified, for example, classifications of one fiber over another? Or in less tangible aspects such as brand philosophy?
- What role did certifications and labeling play in your decision-making?
- Did you choose to focus on reduced environmental impact or social impact or both?

Cautionary advice for instructors

- This exercise may cross into political debates surrounding globalization and economic development, and as such students should be sensitive to others from different cultural backgrounds.
- Additionally, students should be encouraged to move beyond simplistic box-ticking and instead engage in a fulsome discussion within their group about their own values and how these may determine the criteria they select for choosing their garments. A simple method to encourage this kind of discussion is to move around the room and ask casual prompt questions of student discussion groups to encourage them to voice their perspectives.

Copy of the assignment

Student brief

You are assistant buyers for a fashion-forward online retailer.

Your job is to select three garments to feature in a curated page of eco/ethical fashion. In front of you are your choices.

What criteria do you use to choose which brands' garments to select over others? (Materials? Processes? Where the garments are made? How they are made? Consideration of impact across the garment life cycle?)

Choose your three garments, and tell us why you have selected them.

Typical results and reflections on the assignment

- This is a highly engaging task for students, prompting lively discussion in their groups around which garments to select and why—why is one garment "better" than another? Students need a good amount of time to sort through the cards and begin determining their groups' criteria.
- Some students used the "starting point" table (Table 22.2) to simply give a score to all brands and then pick the top scoring ones. In contrast, others determined particular issues to privilege over others, for example some chose waste reduction and recyclability and other groups chose based on social justice principles such as treatment of workers.
- Students realized the complexity inherent in making decisions on one garment's "sustainability" relative to another. Given this complexity, many students noted that they made their decisions based on certifications that they knew and trusted,

Table 22.2 *Choosing your ethical/sustainable brands—starting point!*

	Material?	Processes?	Labour?	Certifications?	Recycled?
Venus in Furs					
Sunday Morning					
I'll be your mirror					
White Light					
All Tomorrow's Parties					
Satellite of Love					
Run Run Run					
Loop					
Sweet Jane					

- or based on the quantitative measures from fiber and textile rankings such as MADE-By's environmental benchmark for fibers or the Materials Sustainability Index.[9]
- Interestingly, some groups selected the same labels but for different reasons, which sparked thoughtful discussions around the narrative of choice: Are choices driven by environmental concerns, social justice concerns, trust in a brand's claims, or measurements that can be quantified? The Padlet approach allows multiple classes to view how other groups selected their three garments.
- It can be interesting to discuss why some labels were not chosen. For example, in one class, no group selected the Venus in Furs label (all vintage garments), although from a quantitative LCA perspective, reusing existing garments has a lower environmental impact than buying new items.[10] Also, no group selected "Loop," the social enterprise label based on Australian organization The Social Studio that provides training to young people who have experienced being a refugee.[11] This led to a discussion around the diverse narratives, values, and metrics that can be applied to sustainable fashion choices.

Notes

1. Fiona Bennie, Ivana Gazibara, and Vicky Murray, *Fashion Futures 2025: Global Scenarios for a Sustainable Fashion Industry* (Forum for the Future and Levi Strauss, 2010), 5.
2. Alison Gwilt, "Producing Sustainable Fashion: The Points of Positive Intervention by the Fashion Designer," in *Shaping Sustainable Fashion: Changing the Way We Make and Use Clothes*, ed. Alison Gwilt and Timo Rissanen (London: Earthscan, 2011); Kate Fletcher, *Sustainable Fashion and Textiles: Design Journeys* (London: Routledge, 2014).
3. Mary Ann Curran, *Life Cycle Assessment Handbook: A Guide for Environmentally Sustainable Products* (Hoboken: Wiley, 2012).
4. Sustainable Apparel Coalition, "Materials Sustainability Index: Base Materials Score." Available online, http://msi.apparelcoalition.org/ (accessed November 12, 2015).

5   Sandy Black, *The Sustainable Fashion Handbook* (London: Thames & Hudson, 2012); Alison Gwilt and Timo Rissanen, eds., *Shaping Sustainable Fashion: Changing the Way We Make and Use Fashion* (London: Earthscan, 2011); Sass Brown, *Eco Fashion* (London: Laurence King, 2010).
6   Alison Gwilt, *A Practical Guide to Sustainable Fashion* (London and New York: Bloomsbury, 2014).
7   Joseph Hancock, *Brand/story: Ralph, Vera, Johnny, Billy and Other Adventures in Fashion Branding* (New York: Fairchild, 2009).
8   William McDonough and Michael Braungart, *Cradle to Cradle: Remaking the Way We Make Things* (New York: North Point Press, 2002).
9   MADE-By, "Environmental Benchmark for Fibres." Available online, http://www.made-by.org/consultancy/tools/environmental/ (accessed November 12, 2015); Sustainable Apparel Coalition, "Materials Sustainability Index: Base Materials Score." Available online, http://msi.apparelcoalition.org/-/ (accessed November 12, 2015).
10 Anne Woolridge, Garth D. Ward, Paul S. Phillips, Michael Collins, and Simon Gandy, "Life Cycle Assessment for Reuse/Recycling of Donated Waste Textiles Compared to Use of Virgin Material: An UK Energy Saving Perspective," *Resources, Conservation and Recycling* 46 (2006): 94–103.
11 The Social Studio, "The Social Studio." Available online, http://www.thesocialstudio.org/ (accessed November 12, 2015).

Bibliography

Bennie, Fiona, Ivana Gazibara, and Vicky Murray. *Fashion Futures 2025: Global Scenarios for a Sustainable Fashion Industry*. Forum for the Future and Levi Strauss, 2010. Available online, http://www.forumforthefuture.org/files/FashionFutures_2025_FINAL_SML.pdf (accessed March 6, 2010).
Black, Sandy. *The Sustainable Fashion Handbook*. London: Thames & Hudson, 2012.
Brown, Sass. *Eco Fashion*. London: Laurence King, 2010.
Curran, Mary Ann. *Life Cycle Assessment Handbook: A Guide for Environmentally Sustainable Products*. Hoboken: Wiley, 2012.
Fletcher, Kate. *Sustainable Fashion and Textiles: Design Journeys*. London: Routledge, 2014.
Gwilt, Alison. *A Practical Guide to Sustainable Fashion*. London and New York: Bloomsbury, 2014.
Gwilt, Alison. "Producing Sustainable Fashion: The Points of Positive Intervention by the Fashion Designer." In *Shaping Sustainable Fashion: Changing the Way We Make and Use Clothes*, edited by Alison Gwilt and T. Rissanen. London: Earthscan, 2011.
Gwilt, Alison and Timo Rissanen, eds. *Shaping Sustainable Fashion: Changing the Way We Make and Use Fashion*. London: Earthscan, 2011.
Hancock, Joseph. *Brand/Story: Ralph, Vera, Johnny, Billy and Other Adventures in Fashion Branding*. New York: Fairchild, 2009.
MADE-By. "Environmental Benchmark for Fibres." 2015. Available online, http://www.made-by.org/consultancy/tools/environmental/ (accessed November 12, 2015).
McDonough, William, and Michael Braungart. *Cradle to Cradle: Remaking the Way We Make Things*. New York: North Point Press, 2002.
Sustainable Apparel Coalition. "Materials Sustainability Index: Base Materials Score." 2015. Available online, http://msi.apparelcoalition.org/ (accessed November 12, 2015).
The Social Studio. "The Social Studio." 2015. Available online, http://www.thesocialstudio.org/ (accessed November 12, 2015).
Woolridge, Anne C., Garth D. Ward, Paul S. Phillips, Michael Collins, and Simon Gandy, "Life Cycle Assessment for Reuse/Recycling of Donated Waste Textiles Compared to Use of Virgin Material: An UK Energy Saving Perspective." *Resources, Conservation and Recycling* 46 (2006): 94–103.

23
THINKING ABOUT CULTURAL APPROPRIATION AND INDIGENOUS FASHION

Amanda Sikarskie, University of Michigan-Dearborn

Contextualization

In the spring semester of 2015, I piloted a course that I designed on Native North American Art at the Gwen Frostic School of Art at Western Michigan University. In the course, my students and I explored both traditional and contemporary Native North American art, including contemporary fashion designers such as Jamie Okuma (Luiseño and Shoshone-Bannock) and Bethany Yellowtail (Northern Cheyenne and Apsaalooke "Crow").

To be aware of any news items related to the course that I might want to bring into class discussion, I followed many of these artists and designers on social media. It was in this way that I discovered the *Apsaalooke Nights* controversy. In February 2015, during New York Fashion Week, London-based label Kokon to Zai (KTZ) debuted a beaded dress on the runway that incorporated traditional Crow designs and showed a strong influence of Bethany Yellowtail's *Apsaalooke Nights* dress from 2014. Yellowtail told *Indian Country Media* that she was "gutted" by the appropriation of not only her work, but also her tribe's designs.[1]

My students and I had some great conversations about the use of non-Western designs by Western artists and designers.

The appropriation of Crow designs, as evident in the *Apsaalooke Nights* controversy, was only the beginning. Several days later on a runway in Milan, Dsquared2 introduced its Fall/Winter 2015 line, which adapted many aspects of traditional Native North American fashion, including materials such as beadwork and feathers and interpretations of tribal motifs. Such adaptations of indigenous and Western design are second nature to shoe designer James Okuma, whose own high-fashion shoes combine Parisian couture with traditional beadwork techniques. But upon seeing the show, Okuma alleged that Dsquared2 copied a bag design created by her mother,

Sandra Okuma.[2] According to Minh Ha T. Pham, prolific author on cultural appropriation and issues of race in the fashion world, this is usually how debates about cultural appropriation begin.[3] Writing for *The Atlantic*, Pham noted, "Typically, it begins with a fashion event that raises issues of race, gender, or class: a new designer collection in the genre of 'exploitation chic,' a blackface/yellowface/redface magazine spread, the use of people of color as props on the runway, etc."[4] Even more upsetting to Okuma and other native designers, however, was the hashtag that Dsquared2 used in their social media surrounding the show: "#dsquaw." Etymologically, the word "squaw" comes from the Algonquin suffix for "woman," but was used in a derogatory manner by nonnative men in the nineteenth century to refer to American Indian women. For many indigenous women in North America, "squaw" has become the equivalent of the "c-word."

These controversies inspired me to create an exercise that uses the lens of the #dsquaw controversy to explore the history of the appropriation of indigenous fashion by Western haute couture. Cultural appropriation is often done with little or no regard for indigenous designers, indigenous cultural property and cultural heritage, or indigenous women's dignity and self-worth. Similarly, discussions of cultural appropriation are often done with little or no thought about what appropriation really means. Pham argues:

> The popular chorus of *cultural appropriation! cultural appreciation!* quickly becomes a performance, in which neither side misses a cue nor forgets a well-learned line. This continues for several days and maybe weeks until it peters out or until the next racist fashion event crops up—whichever comes first. The debate around the event often gets more press and social-media attention than the event did itself, and nobody seems to change opinions for the next go-round.[5]

This assignment gets students thinking critically about cultural appropriation, beyond the binaries of cultural appropriation versus cultural appreciation that are so often played out in the media.

Appropriate courses and course levels for the assignment: This lesson is designed for an undergraduate course in Native North American Art, but can be readily adapted for a variety of courses, including courses on dress and culture, apparel or surface design studio, history of dress and textiles, art history, Canadian and/or US history, and histories of fashion in Canada and the United States.

Estimated time required: One class period is required, ideally between forty-five minutes and one hour and fifteen minutes. Alternately, if there is room in the syllabus, instructors may wish to do the lesson twice, once at the beginning of the semester and once toward the end, allowing students to chart how far their thinking has come on issues relating to cultural appropriation over the duration of the course.

Required materials: There are no particular required materials, apart from the materials which students will find online in advance and bring to class.

Learning goals

- Think about cultural appropriation in the context of the "3 Ps": perspectives, practices, and products.
- Understand cultural appropriation and how it functions within contemporary high fashion.
- Understand how cultural appropriation can be hurtful to indigenous people, including native designers.
- Form an educated opinion about cultural appropriation that will guide students' future practices—as consumers and/or as designers or artists.

Assessment

Traditionally, classroom assessment techniques focus on assessing course-related knowledge and skills. This includes assessment of prior knowledge, recall, understanding, analysis and critical thinking, synthesis and creative thinking, and problem solving.[6] The goal of this assignment, however, which focuses on developing awareness of cultural appropriation, is a different sort of result than these traditional kinds of learning outcomes. Angelo and Cross (1993) suggest assessment techniques specifically for assessing "learner attitudes, values, and self-awareness," both "students' awareness of their attitudes and values" and "students' self-awareness as learners."[7] Angelo and Cross propose a variety of methods for assessing attitudes, values, and self-awareness, including classroom opinion polls, double-entry journals, profiles of admirable individuals, posing the students with ethical dilemmas, focused autobiographical sketches, and goal ranking, among others.[8] While instructors are encouraged to get creative and try any or all of these techniques, in practice, asking students to write double journal entries, either one before and one after the lesson or one at the beginning and one at the end of the semester (if other course content deals with the theme of cultural appropriation), works well.

Guidelines for instructors

Students should be assigned the task of finding an example of the cultural appropriation of indigenous dress before class as homework and bring it to class to facilitate discussion. (Note that there are enough examples of appropriation for students to find easily.) It is also helpful to have students do a reading in advance of class that foregrounds the issue of cultural appropriation and indigenous fashion. Minh Ha T. Pham's article "Fashion's Cultural-Appropriation Debate: Pointless," referenced earlier in this chapter, is a great place to start. The two news stories cited earlier in this chapter, "Bethany Yellowtail 'Gutted' by Crow Design on Dress at New York Fashion Week" and "Oh No They Didn't:

Designers Show 'Squaw' Fashion in Milan," are helpful in contextualizing the lesson for students.

Alternately, if the instructor is using a textbook that includes material on contemporary design, it might be good to assign those pages prior to this lesson. Instructors will likely also wish to show slides or websites of designs and designers that clearly appropriate indigenous motifs or forms. The website of Inukt, a Canadian luxury fashion brand that celebrates (and heavily appropriates) Canadian First Nations design and material culture, is one such example.[9] If this lesson will be done in a course that is not devoted to Native American art or material culture, showing a map of the traditional lands of various tribes would be particularly helpful for locating where various patterns, motifs, and forms come from, as would a discussion of the basic groups of indigenous peoples of North America—Eastern Woodlands, Plains, Southwest, Pacific Northwest, and Inuit—Inupiaq. Be prepared for students to have varying degrees of background knowledge on Native North American History. Many students, for example, might be unfamiliar with even the concept of Indian Removal and most all will be unaware of Native American Graves Protection and Repatriation Act (NAGPRA) and other forms of legal protection. Be prepared also for a wide variety of degrees of sensitivity (or lack thereof) to other cultures.

Art history, and especially the history of dress, can be quite colonial in both its practice and pedagogy. For example, little Native American, African-American, and Chicana/o art is typically taught in most US and Canadian high schools and colleges, compared with European and Euro-American art. Art historians (along with artists, designers, and even art viewers) can unwittingly perpetuate violence against other cultures. I have found it helpful in teaching about the artistic productions of non-Western cultures to take a cue from the discipline of foreign language studies. Given that their field is based on cross-cultural awareness, scholars of foreign languages often lead the way in this area. The "standards for cultures" from the *ACTFL Standards for Foreign Language Learning* (a set of guidelines adopted by the American Council on the Teaching of Foreign Languages) are very relevant for this lesson.[10] These standards deal with what are known in foreign language pedagogical circles as the "3 Ps" of perspectives, practices, and products, and are as follows:

- Standard 2.1: Students demonstrate an understanding of the relationship between the practices and perspectives of the culture studied.
- Standard 2.2: Students demonstrate an understanding of the relationship between the products and perspectives of the culture studied.[11]

The goal here is to guide a class discussion on the cultural appropriation of indigenous fashion by Western designers in a way that focuses not just on *products* of culture (e.g., the fashions themselves) as scholars tend to do in art history and related disciplines, but also on the perspectives of the indigenous designers and their unique practices: everything from beadwork traditions to different ideals of female beauty when it comes to models. (The casting calls for models for Santa Fe Fashion Week, for example, typically look for women sized US 6 or 8, well above standard "model weight.")

Discussion questions

- What is cultural appropriation?
- How does appropriation differ from plagiarism?
- When (if ever) is it acceptable for Western designers to use non-Western motifs or forms in their designs?
- Why might the appropriation of the so-called "tribal" motifs be popular among high fashion designers (and consumers) at present?
- Why do you think that the "#dsquaw" hashtag was used in conjunction with Dsquared2's Milan Fashion Week show? Do you suppose that the designers had any idea how upsetting such a term might be for some people?
- Is it possible for Western appropriation of indigenous design to be positive and celebratory, instead of negative and colonial? Why or why not?
- Where do we draw the line between cultural insider and outsider? What about, for example, indigenous designers appropriating motifs or forms from another tribe and region (such as an Ojibwe woman wearing a Navajo squash blossom necklace)?
- Does viewing all cultural appropriation as misappropriation help to perpetuate the belief that some marginalized cultures need special protections that others do not? Or would a more conscientious approach be more respectful to all involved?

Cautionary advice for instructors

- The region in which a college or university is located and the ethnic makeup of its student body could potentially change the nature of this assignment dramatically. Students studying in New York City, a major fashion capital and cultural melting pot, might reflect very differently on these issues than students studying on or near an Indian Reservation, for example.
- Instructors should remain mindful that it is not the students' fault if they bring in strong (and often quite colonial) preconceptions to class. This exercise should help students to explore, unpack, and question such preconceptions.
- Instructors should be prepared for very strong viewpoints on both sides of the issue. Instructors can work with such strong viewpoints productively by encouraging reasoned and respectful dialogue before beginning the discussion.
- Any indigenous students in class will obviously feel particularly close to the issue of cultural appropriation of indigenous design. Instructors can help to ensure that their viewpoints and perspectives are respected, in what often become difficult conversations. Remind students that these are living cultures being discussed.
- No matter the makeup of the class, instructors should try to facilitate a discussion in which all students feel comfortable expressing multiple viewpoints on cultural

appropriation in fashion, and not let students who plan to continue to wear or design "tribal" forms or patterns come away from class feeling persecuted. That said, while students with these views should not leave feeling persecuted, instructors should also refrain from validating or condoning blatant cultural appropriation as "okay," but rather ensure that all students leave the class with an understanding of why cultural appropriation is so hurtful for many indigenous people, and to raise productive questions about nonnative people's wearing and design work using native motifs, and the ethics thereof. Instructors can do this in terms of their own statements and how they direct the conversations.

While I have only taught this course in spring semesters, faculty teaching this lesson in the fall semester may want to do the lesson in October, in the days leading up to Halloween, as the cultural appropriation of indigenous dress for Halloween costumes is fairly common on some college campuses.

Copy of the assignment

Thinking about cultural appropriation and indigenous fashion

Cultural appropriation of indigenous design is very much in fashion these days, with "tribal" styles prevailing on the runways in the twenty-first century. Cultural appropriation, in its most basic definition, is simply one culture borrowing from another. It need not necessarily be violent or colonial or derogatory, though it can certainly be all of those things (and can and does differ in terms of its impact and how it is perceived based on those receiving it).

Cultural appropriation is all around us, and has been vitally important in the world of fashion for centuries (and I am not just talking about non-Germans wearing lederhosen). Examples include Kimono sleeves from East Asia, caftans from Africa, and paisley from India, most prints that are not simple stripes or polka dots, among many others. Though cultural appropriation is all around us, it takes on a negative connotation when it seems unethical, makes us uncomfortable, or conjures images of colonial or racially motivated violence.

For this assignment, go online and find an example of the cultural appropriation of indigenous fashion by a Western designer. Print it out, bring it to class, and note the designer (if known) and the culture/tribe whose motifs or forms have been appropriated. Be prepared to discuss both the aesthetic impact and sociocultural implications of the ensemble/piece.

Typical results and reflections on the assignment

- Students begin to think of cultural productions not just as a set of end products, but also as intricately related to a set of cultural perspectives and practices.

- Many students have never thought before about what it means to wear a "tribal" print or piece of jewelry. Mindfulness tends to be the major result of this lesson.
- Some nonnative students have a false perception that native cultures are no longer living cultures, and many will never have considered the idea of contemporary indigenous fashion designers. Again, mindfulness is a major outcome here.
- Students also tend to dispel some long-held myths about indigenous dress. Invariably, students have come to class with an image of native dress in mind that correlates with that of *Pocahontas* in the animated Disney film. Many students are surprised to learn how much clothing women in the Eastern Woodlands actually wore.
- Students studying art or design have indicated that this knowledge will influence the choices that they make in their future work.

Notes

1. ICTMN Staff, "Bethany Yellowtail 'Gutted' by Crow Design on Dress at New York Fashion Week," *Indian Country Media* (February 2015), http://indiancountrytodaymedianetwork.com/2015/02/20/bethany-yellowtail-gutted-crow-design-dress-new-york-fashion-week-159319.
2. Vincent Schilling, "Oh No They Didn't," *Indian Country Media* (March 2015), http://indiancountrytodaymedianetwork.com/2015/03/03/oh-no-they-didnt-designers-show-squaw-fashion-milan-159446.
3. See also Minh Ha T. Pham's 2015 book *Asians Wear Clothes on the Internet: Race, Gender, and the Work of Personal Style Blogging*.
4. Minh Ha T. Pham, "Fashion's Cultural-Appropriation Debate: Pointless," *The Atlantic* (May 15, 2014), https://www.theatlantic.com/entertainment/archive/2014/05/cultural-appropriation-in-fashion-stop-talking-about-it/370826/.
5. Ibid.
6. Thomas A. Angelo and K. Patricia Cross, *Classroom Assessment Techniques*, 2nd ed. (San Francisco: Jossey Bass, 1993), x–xi.
7. Ibid., xi.
8. Ibid.
9. *Inukt*. Accessed March 5, 2017. http://www.inukt.com.
10. I'd like to thank my husband, Matthew Sikarskie, a scholar of German, for the idea to use the ACTFL Standards in my own classroom.
11. American Council on the Teaching of Foreign Languages, *ACTFL Standards for Foreign Language Learning*, last modified 2012, http://www.actfl.org/sites/default/files/pdfs/public/StandardsforFLLexecsumm_rev.pdf.

Bibliography

American Council on the Teaching of Foreign Languages. *ACTFL Standards for Foreign Language Learning: Preparing for the 21st Century*. 2012. Available online: http://www.actfl.org/sites/default/files/pdfs/public/StandardsforFLLexecsumm_rev.pdf. Accessed January 14, 2018.

Angelo, Thomas A., and K. Patricia Cross. *Classroom Assessment Techniques: A Handbook for College Teachers*. 2nd ed. San Francisco: Jossey Bass, 1993.

Berlo, Janet C. and Ruth B. Phillips. *Native North American Art*. Oxford: Oxford University Press, 1998.

Bernstein, Bruce. "The Booth Sitters of Santa Fe's Indian Market: Making and Maintaining Authenticity." *American Indian Culture and Research Journal* 31, no. 3 (2007): 49–79.

Croteau, Susan Ann. *"But it Doesn't Look Indian": Objects, Archetypes and Objectified Others in Native American Art, Culture and Identity*. Doctoral Dissertation, University of California Los Angeles. ProQuest, 2008.

Daves, Jessica, ed. "Fashion: Beach Plums: Native American Fashions." *Vogue* 127, no. 2 (February 1, 1956): 190–191.

ICTMN Staff. "Bethany Yellowtail 'Gutted' by Crow Design on Dress at New York Fashion Week." *Indian Country Media*, February 2015. Available online: http://indiancountrytodaymedianetwork.com/2015/02/20/bethany-yellowtail-gutted-crow-design-dress-new-york-fashion-week-159319.

Indyke, Dottie. "Jamie Okuma." *Southwest Art* 30, no. 12 (May 2001): 60–62.

Indyke, Dottie. "Jamie Okuma." *Southwest Art* 32, no. 3 (August 2002): 188–191.

Inukt: Men and Women's Canadian Style Clothing, Footwear, Accessories and Home Decor. Accessed March 5, 2017. http://www.inukt.com.

Kramer, Karen. *Nativo Fashion Now: North American Indian Style*. London: Delmonico Books, 2015.

Penney, David W. *North American Indian Art*. London: Thames & Hudson, 2004.

Penney, David W., and George C. Longfish. *Native American Art*. New York: Hugh Lauter Levin, 1994.

Pham, Minh Ha T. *Asians Wear Clothes on the Internet: Race, Gender, and the Work of Personal Style Blogging*. Durham, NC: Duke University Press, 2015.

Pham, Minh Ha T. "Fashion's Cultural-Appropriation Debate: Pointless." *The Atlantic*, May 15, 2014. https://www.theatlantic.com/entertainment/archive/2014/05/cultural-appropriation-in-fashion-stop-talking-about-it/370826/

Schilling, Vincent. "Oh No They Didn't: Designers Show 'Squaw' Fashion in Milan." *Indian Country Media*, March 2015. Available online: http://indiancountrytodaymedianetwork.com/2015/03/03/oh-no-they-didnt-designers-show-squaw-fashion-milan-159446 (accessed January 14, 2018).

Wood, Margaret. *Native American Fashion: Modern Adaptations of Traditional Designs*. New York, NY: Van Nostrand Reinhold Company, 1981.

24
A SYSTEMIC ANALYSIS OF THE ETHICS OF FAST FASHION CONSUMERISM AND A CALL TO SUSTAINABILITY

June-Ann Greeley, Sacred Heart University

Contextualization

Since the mid-1990s, the fashion industry has observed a marked increase in the amount of clothing people have been purchasing, as well as an acceleration in the rate of clothing purchases. The result has been that competing brands have evolved a segment of the fashion industry known as "fast fashion," or clothing that is manufactured at an accelerated rate in multiple collections, with an eye to lower and lower costs—by whatever means—for the consumer. Consumers now demand wider variety of fashion styles in larger quantities throughout the year and that situation has pressured buyers of national and international clothing chains to make available a larger range of clothing products more often but also at reduced prices. Such an accelerated process has resulted in the boom of "fast fashion," a situation that has proved beneficial for consumers of clothing and lucrative to certain clothing chain stores that feature "fast fashion" products, as well as to major corporations. However, this accelerated production schedule has also proven disastrous for the environment, the social and economic standards and conditions of workers, and efforts toward normalizing human rights on a global scale.

The consequences of fast fashion on the environment have been swift and apparent. Landfills throughout developing nations have witnessed annually increased tonnage of discarded and otherwise unwanted clothing with the result that mounds of clothing made of synthetic materials fill acres of land without decomposing, and other mounds of clothing that, on decomposition, increase the emission of toxic gases that lead to global warming. It is also true that in the creation of certain textiles (like cotton, for example), regulations imposed on farmers by companies like Monsanto (which hold the patent on the cotton seeds) eventually destroy the fertility of the soil by overseeding the land and ruining the livelihood of the farmers who, by contract with Monsanto, cannot use any other seeds.

Also, in many developing countries, the production of certain fashion items, like leather bags, leads to massive pollution of local water supplies. This pollution has resulted in alarming increases in birth defects and human illnesses such as cancer, among the populations relying on those sources of water. There is, of course, little access to health care in those regions, since most companies that manufacture the textiles and the articles of clothing for "fast fashion" brands commonly outsource their factories to the most impoverished, least politically influential areas of developing nations.

The fast fashion industry is no stranger to the goal of high profitability that drives the policies and procedures of most corporations. That key incentive, combined with the pattern of quick collection turnover that is the hallmark of fast fashion, has resulted in labor practices that violate the universal statement of workers' rights promulgated by the United Nations.[1] Not only is the illegal use of child labor rampant, but adults also are compelled to work in unsanitary, unsafe conditions as the pressure to produce more clothing at a quicker pace intensifies and some workers spend up to fourteen hours a day in sweatshops and other sites of clothing production.[2]

There are several explicit reasons for including this assignment unit in a curriculum of fashion studies. Primarily, the project is an opportunity for students to explore ethical questions that are both related to fashion, especially fast fashion, and that extend beyond the world of fashion to include other dimensions of social interaction, cultural and global values, and the moral intricacies of an increasingly interconnected and intersected global environment. Thus, at the evident center of the study is a protected space for students to become informed and to ask comprehensive questions about private, civic, and human principles, personal and social accountability, and the feasibility of the common good, all within the context of deconstructing a rather quotidian activity (i.e., the purchase of clothing).

The assignment will also afford students a focus to realize the intersection of most ethical problems: for example, in this study, the intersecting dilemmas of private, national, and international economic needs, options in consumer behavior, corporate accountability, and labor practices that the fast fashion industry of the "first world" has engendered. Students will discover that the seemingly minor decision to purchase an article of clothing is, in fact, part of a larger confluence of processes that have global effects (with relation to labor practices, gender and family traditions, environmental and medical concerns, and political interests) and very human consequences beyond their own lives. Of course, the reason for the assignment is not simply to assign blame to any single person or group entity, or pose a daunting set of incorrigible circumstances; rather, the intention is to provide students with a platform from which they can expand self-awareness of themselves as consumers and consider ways of reforming personal behavior when a difficult array of factual information adjudicates such behavior negatively, as well as develop possible solutions to the ethical problems that fast fashion has presented.

Finally, the assignment should alert students to the dense connectivity of the many different aspects of daily life, for while the assignment addresses daily (fast) fashion specifically, it can lead to an interrogation of other dimensions of human existence: similarly examining the interrelated dimensions of the production, economy, advertising, and consumption of food or shelter or transportation, for example, may clarify to students that what people wear or what they eat or how they live or what transportation they use has wider ramifications for their own lives and the lives of others. Thus, the assignment also encourages a range of conversations about intergenerational/intra-generational and intercultural/intracultural justice and care.

Appropriate courses and course levels for the assignment: This assignment is geared primarily for undergraduate students in courses such as economics, sociology, ethics, global studies, and environmental studies.

Required materials: This section can vary according to the specific interests of the instructor and the academic level of the students. Instructors should review news sites as well as special interest organizations online. In this chapter's bibliography, please see a list of foundational readings and references, arranged by topic.

Learning goals

- Acquaint students with the ethical issues surrounding the production of "fast fashion" and for those in developed nations specifically.
- Encourage students to develop sets of ethical inquiries for consumer- and product-related studies and disciplines.
- Engender in students' critical self-awareness, as well as critical consciousness about consumerism and "first-world" privilege.
- Inspire students to formulate positive solutions for unjust or unethical conditions from which first-world privilege benefits.

Assessment

Assessment for an assignment of this sort should be at the discretion of the instructor and what dimensions of the exercise the instructor wishes to emphasize. Since the assignment calls for group presentations and a group report, the assessment protocol may take the form of grading, ranking, rating, or scoring students in two capacities: as presenters and as audience. The learning goals offer some indication of the elements of content that the students undertaking the assignment should come to understand (of course, individual instructors may wish to supplement to delete from those goals), and instructors may want to ascertain whether and to what degree students as audience members of the group presentations have incorporated that content by essay quizzes/exams, reflection posts, peer review, or some other means suitable to the specific classroom and/or course.

For the group presentations and the group report, the following rubric offers some guidance for assessing both the content and the delivery of the content by each designated group. Again, the rubric is only a general standard and may be revised as each instructor deems most relevant for the class and for personal instruction.

Grading

	"A" range	"B" range	"C" range	Failure
Discussion of content	Fully explains the text(s), thinker(s), or theorist(s), choosing very effective passages and/or examples.	Makes many accurate statements the text(s), thinker(s), or theorist(s), based on appropriate passages and/or examples.	Makes some accurate statements, but more detail is needed. Choice of passages and/or examples is ineffective at times.	Makes several inaccurate statements and/or chooses poor examples and/or gives little support from the relevant texts.
Deliberation on concepts	Supports a particular viewpoint on the question, problem, or issue insightfully and persuasively, showing a facility with the conceptual tools of the course.	Supports a particular viewpoint soundly, making proper use of the conceptual tools of the course.	Offers a viewpoint and says why, but use of the conceptual tools of the course is brief or thin. More "opinion" than analysis.	Struggles with identifying and/or articulating a central idea.
Expression	The essay/presentation is clear, well organized, and virtually error free. Accurate use of proper text citations throughout composition.	The essay/presentation is generally clear and organized. It has some errors, but they do not detract from the reader's understanding. Use of proper citations frequent and usually accurate.	The essay/presentation needs improvement in clarity and/or organization. Flaws detract from the reader's understanding at times. Little use of citations and/or citations are not accurate.	Grammatical or stylistic flaws in writing often hinder the reader's understanding. No text citations or reference to sources.

Guidelines for instructors

The nature of this unit of study is very interdisciplinary, so the primary instructor is encouraged to engage in the delivery of the unit with colleagues in such disciplines as economics, international business, environmental science, sociology, agronomics and agricultural business, international relations/politics, consumer relations and consumer studies, and psychology.

Given that it could be argued that there is a kind of political "skew" to this assignment, the instructor will want to be very careful with his/her/their research: it will be important to gather the most recent data and information about the fast fashion industry from reliable but nonpartisan sources, and to supply students with any information about corporate redress of some of the worst offenses (like cleaning water supplies, assuring basic workers' rights in factories, etc.). The point of the assignment is not to create a political argument, but to awaken students to the hard choices and problematic decisions of the fashion industry, and to carry that awareness into other realms of ethical inquiry, whether relative to food supply, medical, and pharmaceutical industry or natural resources and energy industries.

Finally, it is critical that the instructor, with students, develops a unit on strategies for improvement and possible solutions to the "fast fashion" dilemma. One site that provides some practical suggestions and possible policies for countering the ill effects of fast fashion can be found at the "Ethical Fashion Forum," although instructors should also have students generate their own ideas about clothing sustainability and appropriate resolutions to the ethical quandaries that fast fashion and "first world" hyper-consumption pose.[3]

For this assignment, students should be divided into groups of four to five (depending on class size) at the instructor's discretion.

Discussion questions

- What do you consider the most pressing ethical problem associated with fast fashion? Why? What do you believe to be the most effective and reasonable solution to that ethical problem?
- Does being a consumer (of any product) make an individual complicit in any sustained and integrated ethical and legal malfeasance committed by the producers of that product, or is the consumer an innocent bystander in such situations?
- How do you understand the concept of "first world" privilege? Do you believe it exists? If so, what do you consider other examples of first world privilege apart from rampant consumerism? If not, what examples of privilege can you offer by way of contrast?
- Reflect on your own purchasing by keeping a log/video blog for a month: what you buy, when, where, why, the cost, and how often the article(s) has/have been worn/used. What have you learned about your own trajectory of product consumption?

Cautionary advice for instructors

- Probably the most important caveat in this assignment is the care which should be taken with the students who are likely to be consumers of fast fashion themselves: the instructor needs to step gingerly between addressing the ethical problems of fast fashion and creating a safe environment in which students who might very well be consumers of fast fashion feel able to address the broader ethical concerns and implications without censuring themselves—or feel that they are being censured—in the process. There are a few different strategies an instructor might use in such circumstances, the most obvious being a consistent insistence on the project as an exercise in understanding those systemic conditions within the fashion industry that should elicit conversations about ethical issues and complexities on a global scale and in terms of class and gender. The project is meant to afford an opportunity for the students to engage in critical analyses that might otherwise not arise, and not to dwell on judgment. The fact is, the fast fashion industry has provided easy access to cheap and available clothing and most college students are not in any financial circumstance to purchase boutique or even "slow fashion"–curated clothing, and instructors should ask students to share their understanding of that complex nexus of personal identity/clothing/social acceptance and how fast fashion purchases become the most apparent option. In this regard, the instructor should admit of her/his own purchases of fast fashion and, if such is not the case, then offer some suggestions about the value and implications of purchasing in alternate venues such as thrift stores or selective outlets, or use that instance as an opportunity to reflect on the meaning of clothing, personal identity, conventional standards, and individual expression. There are online resources such as *Mamahuhu* that offer young people sites to visit and (young) bloggers to read: such resources address global ethics and environmentally sound alternatives to fast fashion, as well as new ways to think about clothing and general attire.[4]

Copy of the assignment
"From seed to shopping bag"

- Your group will select an article of clothing or accessory that you have seen (or perhaps purchased) at a "fast fashion" store such as Forever 21, H&M, Target, Zara, etc.
  - In your group, you will assign a "coordinator," who will maintain the progress of the group and report to the instructor any difficulties the group encounters during the duration of the project.
  - Based on group consensus, each group member will select a segment in the creation of the item to research in actual terms. Examples include the acquisition and planting of the cotton seeds; the harvesting of the cotton and the experiences of the agricultural community; the creation of cotton cloth; the cutting and design of the article of clothing; the manufacture of the article of clothing; the distribution of the article to franchise stores; the marketing and advertising of the product; and finally its purchase.

- Each member of your group should include in her/his/their research at least two sustainability solutions to the ethical lapses apparent in the specific segment of fast fashion production.

- Your group will then create a report based on the aggregate findings of your group members. Your group will present its report in two formats: as a group paper submitted to the instructor and as a PowerPoint presentation presented to the class. Each group will also be responsible for generating class discussion based on its presentation.

Typical results and reflections on the assignment

- Students report that the assignment itself is very accessible, and an important aspect of fashion studies in general.

- Students were generally appalled by what they learned about the failings of the fast fashion industry and the broader consumerist culture in which they live (and perhaps even participate), yet it is not clear that such awareness has completely altered their shopping habits. Prior to undertaking this exercise, students are usually unaware of the real "cost" of the clothing they purchase and the practices of the industry that relies on them for its revenue, and when they realize the true price of fast fashion and its global, environmental, labor, psychological, political, and cultural impact they are naturally shocked and dismayed.

- Students in class are even able to formulate several "slow fashion" alternatives and sustainability models to counteract the effects of fast fashion. However, outside the classroom, many students do not report significant changes in their purchasing: it seems that the condition of being able to buy several items of clothing at (seemingly) reduced costs is too attractive to refuse or is their given reality: limited funds can be applied in only so many ways and so many young people lack the freedom or option to shop elsewhere for clothing, including clothing necessities.

Notes

1   http://www.un.org/en/ecosoc/docs/2008/resolution%202008-18.pdf
2   https://labs.theguardian.com/unicef-child-labour/
3   http://www.ethicalfashionforum.com/
4   https://www.mamahuhu.online/blogs/news/top-10-influencers-of-ethical-and-sustainable-fashion

Bibliography

1. On modernity, the culture of consumerism and fashion, and the fallout of rampant consumerism that is "fast fashion" (and its implications thereof)

Biehl-Missal, Brigitte. "Art, Fashion, and Anti-consumption." *Journal of Macromarketing* 33, no. 3 (2013): 245–257.

Brooks, Andrew. *Clothing Poverty: The Hidden World of Fast Fashion and Second-Hand Clothes*. London: Zed Books, 2015.

Bruce, Margaret, and Lucy Daly. "Buyer Behavior for Fast Fashion." *Journal of Fashion Marketing and Management: An International Journal* 10, no. 3 (2006): 329–344.

Cline, Elizabeth L. *Overdressed: The Shockingly High Cost of Cheap Fashion*. Rpt. New York, NY: Portfolio Books, 2013.

Eckhardt, Giana M., Russell Belk, and Timothy M. Devinney. "Why Don't Consumers Consume Ethically." *Journal of Consumer Behavior* 9 (2010): 426–436.

Elliott, Richard, and Clare Leonard "Peer Pressure and Poverty: Exploring Fashion Brands and Consumption Symbolism Among Children of the 'British Poor.'" *Journal of Consumer Behavior* 3, no. 4 (2004): 347–359.

Joergens, Catrin. "Ethical Fashion: Myth or Future Trend?" *Journal of Fashion Marketing and Management: An International Journal* 10, no. 3 (2006): 360–371.

McNeill, Lisa, and Rebecca Moore. "Sustainable Fashion Consumption and the Fast Fashion Conundrum: Fashionable Consumers and Attitudes to Sustainability in Clothing Choice." *International Journal of Consumer Studies* 39, no. 3 (2015): 212–222.

Minney, Safia. *Slow Fashion: Aesthetics Meet Ethics*. Ottawa, Ontario: New Internationalist, 2016.

Siegle, Lucy. *To Die for: Is Fashion Wearing Out the World?* London: Fourth Estate, 2011.

Von Drehle, David. *Triangle: The Fire That Changed America*. New York, NY: Grove Press, 2004.

Wilson, Elizabeth. *Adorned in Dreams: Fashion and Modernity*. London and New York: I.B. Tauris, 2013.

2. Environmental themes

Luz, Claudio. "Waste Couture: Environmental Impact of the Clothing Industry." *Environmental Health Perspectives* 115, no. 9 (2007): A449–A454.

Minney, Safia. *Naked Fashion: The New Sustainable Fashion Revolution*. Oxford, England: New Internationalist, 2012.

Morgan, Louise, and Grete Birtwistle. "An investigation of young fashion consumers' disposal habits." *International Journal of Consumer Studies* 33, no. 2 (2009): 190–198.

Myers, Norman, and Jennifer Kent. "New Consumers: The Influence of Affluence on the Environment." *PNAS* 100, no. 8 (2003): 4963–4968.

Weber, Sabine, Jennifer Lynes, and Stephen B. Young. "Fashion Interest as a Driver for Consumer Textile Waste Management: Reuse, Recycle or Disposal." *International Journal of Consumer Studies* 41, no. 2 (2017): 207–215.

Zhi-Hua Hu, Qing Li, Xian-Juan Chen, and Yan-Feng Wang. "Sustainable Rent-Based Closed-Loop Supply Chain for Fashion Products." *Sustainability* 6, no. 10 (2014): 7063–7088.

3. Corporate practices, globalization, and responses to fast fashion

Hira, Anil, and Maureen, Benson-Rea. *Governing Corporate Social Responsibility in the Apparel Industry After Rana Plaza*. New York, NY: Palgrave MacMillan, 2017.

Lavergne, Michael. *Fixing Fashion: Rethinking the Way We Make, Market and Buy Our Clothes*. Gabriola Island, BC Canada: New Society Publishers, 2015.

McArdle, Louise, and Pete Thomas. "Fair Enough? Women and Fair Trade." *Critical Perspectives on International Business* 8, no. 4 (2012): 277–294.

Srikantia, Jessica. "The Structural Violence of Globalization." *Critical Perspectives on International Business* 12, no. 3 (2016): 222–258.

4. Marketing and advertising policies and practices

Hyllegard, Karen, Jennifer Ogle, and Ruoh-Nan Yan. "The Impact of Advertising Message Strategy – Fair Labour v. Sexual Appeal—upon Gen Y Consumers' Intent to Patronize an Apparel Retailer." *Journal of Fashion Marketing and Management: An International Journal* 13, no. 1 (2009): 109–127.

Taplin, Ian M. "Who is to blame? A re-examination of fast fashion after the 2013 factory disaster in Bangladesh." *Critical Perspectives on International Business* 10, no. 1/2 (2014): 72–83.

PART EIGHT

EMBODIMENT AND DAILY FASHION PRACTICES

Introduction

The chapters in this section help students to reflect on the interconnections between the larger fashion world and their daily experiences surrounding dress, self-presentation, and style. In these exercises and assignments, students consider how their decisions about dress shape their sense of self and their identities and how they navigate the communities in which they live and work. In her chapter, Anya Kurennaya details her assignment in which students keep a daily log about their dress and style practices, actively reflecting on the factors that shape their decisions about self-presentation. Having students analyze their experiences of dress as embodied practice, as Kurennaya demonstrates, helps them to consider their agency in terms of their self-presentation choices, as well as the broader social and cultural factors that influence individual fashion practices.

Laura Snelgrove's chapter sends students out into different environments, to consider the intersections between diverse public spaces, self-presentation, and embodied fashion practices. Having students select particular public spaces, Snelgrove asks students to analyze how they adopt their fashion choices according to these specific locations, and what their experiences are navigating potentially unfamiliar environments (and how and why they dressed, either to seek to avoid or to draw attention, and to consciously reflect on their bodily experiences of confidence, discomfort, or vulnerability as they navigate specific public spaces).

And finally, Eileen Boris's chapter provides a framework for students to craft individual, creative final projects centered on how individuals and groups experience fashion and dress in their daily lives. Boris reflects on the wide range of different types of projects students can undertake in order to productively reflect on fashion and daily embodied practice through independent research, including personal experiments (of wearing others' clothes, choosing to wear or not wear makeup or bras for a designated period of time), and crafting participatory events for other students to engage in (such as a queer fashion show, providing space for LGBTQIA+ campus community members to display and reflect on their diverse fashion practices). Each of the chapters in this section enables instructors to consider new, innovative ways to bridge the gap between theory and practice, enabling students to better understand how larger cultural factors and social structures shape their daily experiences of and decisions about dress.

25
AN EXERCISE IN REFLECTING ON DAILY DRESS PRACTICES

Anya Kurennaya, Parsons School of Design

Contextualization

Dress, as social theorist Joanne Entwistle (2002) writes, "forms part of our epidermis—it lies on the boundary between self and other."[1] Therefore, the comprehensive study of dress must necessarily engage with and consider its embodied nature. At the same time, such a study must also "acknowledge the social nature of [dress]—how it is shaped by techniques, attitudes, aesthetics and so on, which are socially and historically located."[2] This assignment asks students to engage with their own embodied experience of dress and interpret their findings in the context of their social and cultural surroundings.

The assignment is comprised of two written components that work together to demonstrate both the embodied and the social dimension of dress practice. The first component is a dress practice log, a seven-day journal in which students record their daily dress practices, noting both what items they use to fashion themselves and why they make the dress and appearance decisions they do. Students should be familiarized with Pierre Bourdieu's discussion of the *habitus,* consequently including within their dress practice logs a variety of techniques of the body that relate to their daily subject formation, from the selection of garments and accessories to the styling of hair and application of makeup and from bodily techniques such as exercise to the techniques of management, such as laundry or closet (re)organization. The second component of the assignment is a final overall reflection in which students consider their dress practices as a whole and reflect on the social and cultural contexts of their embodied dress practices.

In addition to engaging with embodiment and the social and cultural aspects of dress practice, the assignment asks students to consider the importance of two other areas of fashion studies scholarship, namely material culture and the study of dress in everyday life. By asking students to consider the physical experience of wearing and moving through time and space in their garments, this assignment reinforces the study of fashion as an object whose materiality is of evidential value. Working with Cheryl Buckley and Hazel Clark's (2012) imperative for the study of fashion as "a manifestation of routine daily lives that remains with people over time," this assignment reinserts the everyday life into academic discourse and asks students to encounter it directly.[3] This assignment locates social and cultural ideas directly on the body and provides tangible evidence of the discourses at work in structuring lived reality. Combining these often-overlooked dimensions of the study of dress, this assignment has the potential to alter students' perceptions of fashion's materiality and its prevalence in everyday life. After completing the assignment, students will be equipped to discuss the following questions:

- What patterns and themes can you locate in your daily dress practices?
- How are your daily dress practices impacted by social and cultural factors?
- What role does your body and movement play in your dress decisions, and why is it important to consider dress and the body in conjunction?
- What is the importance of studying dress practices in everyday life?

Appropriate courses and course levels for the assignment: This is appropriate for any course on the lower- or upper-division level that engages with the themes of fashion studies and dress practices in everyday life. It is particularly applicable for courses in the following fields: cultural studies, fashion studies, sociology, and women, gender, and sexuality studies.

Appropriate class size: This assignment will work for any class size. It was originally implemented in two separate contexts: one iteration was implemented in a senior writing seminar numbering 17 students and the other was implemented in a survey course numbering 120 students, with findings shared in recitation sections of 20 students. The assignment can be adapted for upper-division courses by asking students to write longer responses or to incorporate supporting evidence for their ideas with outside research.

Estimated time required: Time required is variable, but most students spent about thirty minutes per log entry and two to three hours composing the final overall reflection, in addition to any time they spent composing and taking photographs. They were given two weeks to work on the assignment: one week to log dress practices for seven consecutive days and one week to reflect on their dress practice and compose their final overall reflection.

Required materials: Students will need access to a computer to complete the assignment outside of class time. No materials are necessary within the classroom, although if instructors ask students to share some of their findings, then an in-classroom computer and projector will be necessary.

Learning goals

- Consider the embodied, habitual, and routine nature of dress practice in everyday life.
- Reflect on their everyday dress practices in writing with reference to key concepts and readings.
- Engage in dialogue with others about commonalities and differences in everyday dress practices and subject positions.

Assessment

When this assignment was originally implemented, students were assessed using a 100-point rubric assessing four key areas:

1. The ability to meet requirements as outlined in the assignment description
2. The depth and quality of writing
3. The connection to course ideas
4. The clarity of writing

The first area is meant to assess the overall comprehension of the assignment and the amount of work put into its completion. When assessing the second area, instructors should evaluate the clarity and depth of the student's log entries, and they should expect the final overall reflection to clearly and fully answer the required questions. In the third area of assessment, instructors should look for explicit and thoughtful connection to relevant course texts and other ideas from class, as evidenced by a combination of quotes, paraphrased material, and the student's own reflection on the material. Writing should make explicit rather than implicit reference to how their dress practices were embodied and structured by their subjectivities, using terminology drawn from the reading and lecture. Any outside material that is used should be integrated in a way that demonstrates student understanding of the concepts. Lastly, instructors should look for evidence of proofreading and attention paid to typographical errors, as well as evidence of editing and attention paid to technical aspects of writing. Instructors may specify their preferred format for quotation and citation and may require a bibliography accompanying the assignment.

Guidelines for instructors

Readings to be covered prior to delivering the assignment prompt:

> Entwistle, Joanne. "The Dressed Body." In *Real Bodies: A Sociological Introduction,* ed. Mary Evans and Ellie Lee, 133–150. Hampshire, UK: Palgrave, 2002.
>
> Woodward, Sophie. "Hanging Out in the Home and the Bedroom." In *Why Women Wear What They Wear,* 31–49. London; Oxford: Berg, 2007.
>
> Selected passages and excerpts of the instructor's choosing: Heti, Sheila, Heidi Julavits, and Leanne Shapton. *Women in Clothes.* New York: Blue Rider Press, 2014, and/or from Spivack, Emily. *Worn Stories.* New York: Princeton Architectural Press, 2014.

Thematically, students should be aware of the wide variety of activities that constitute embodied dress practices and should be familiarized with Pierre Bourdieu's discussion of the *habitus* (introduced in Entwistle (2002); see also Bourdieu (1977)). This can be done through class lecture and supplemented with discussion or a class activity that asks students to supply examples of activities that fit within the defined framework of the *habitus*.

This assignment can be undertaken at any point in the semester, although it is useful as an introductory assignment so that students can consider their own dress practices before reflecting on those of others. It also serves to introduce the students to the instructor and to one another. Additionally, instructors should be aware that this exercise, as with any introspective exercise, has the potential to highlight areas of personal concern for students, and they should keep this in mind when delivering content and debriefing about the exercise. See the "Cautionary advice for instructors" section for suggestions.

Discussion questions

As students compose their daily log entries, they should consider the following questions:

- Why are you making the dress choices you're making?
- What social and cultural factors influence those decisions?
- What level of agency or what level of restriction are you encountering?
- Why did you choose to wear what you wore and not some alternative?
- How did you feel about what you wore, and how did you feel in those clothes?

As students compose their final overall reflection, they should consider the following questions:

- What themes emerged in your dress practice log?
- What did you notice about daily dress practice that you hadn't noticed before?
- How did the dress practice log impact your understanding of the relationship between dress and the body?

When debriefing about the dress practice log in class discussion, instructors should consider posing the above-mentioned questions to students, in addition to the following:

- What did you learn about yourself in the process of completing this assignment?
- Was there anything you felt particularly proud of or embarrassed by in the process of completing this assignment? Why? Do you think other students have similar experiences?
- Why is it useful for designers and professionals in the fashion industry to consider everyday dress practices? What do these practices tell us about fashion and the body?

Cautionary advice for instructors

- Instructors should be aware that this exercise, as with any introspective exercise, has the potential to highlight areas of personal concern for students, and they should keep this in mind when delivering content and debriefing about the exercise. Particularly because this assignment asks students to reflect on their embodied dress practices and report on these practices in writing, it has potential to be triggering for students struggling with body image issues, anxiety, and/or depression. Students should feel empowered to discuss any potential concerns with their instructor, and the instructor should exercise caution when asking students to share their findings in class so as not to unintentionally put students on the spot. Instructors can also easily devise an alternative version of the assignment, which asks students to chronicle a friend's dress practices and conduct an interview about the choices made in dressing on a daily basis. Because these assignments require additional planning time for the student and entail more writing, I suggest a reduction in the total number of entries.

Copy of the assignment

Introduction to fashion studies—Dress practice log

In our class, you have read about everyday dress practices and we discussed the importance of studying everyday routines and habits associated with dress. This assignment asks you to document your dress practices for a one-week period and to reflect on the subject positions and larger cultural and social influences that impact those dress practices.

Some requirements:

- You must log at least seven days in your dress practice log. I recommend spending one consecutive week logging entries so you have one week to format your log and further reflect on it.
- Each entry in the log should include some level of description and some level of reflection. Aim for roughly 200–300 words per entry.
- Description:
  - Who: who you're seeing/noticing, who you're dressing "for"/"as"
  - What: what you're wearing, what you're doing
  - When: when you're dressing/changing clothes/making decisions about dress
  - Where: where you're getting dressed, where you're headed to and from

- Reflection:
  - Why: Why are you making the dress choices you're making? What social and cultural factors influence those decisions? What level of agency or what level of restriction are you encountering? Why did you choose to wear what you wore and not some alternative? How did you feel about what you wore, and how did you feel in those clothes?
  - You should incorporate at least two images in your dress practice log—feel free to include more. These could be images of your closet, selected garments/objects from the closet, or images of you in the garments, but they don't have to be.
    - Think about other images that relate to your dress practice log in some way, and think creatively about how you can use images to document your dress practices.
  - At the end of your dress practice log, you should include a final overall reflection (200–300 words) using these questions as a guide:
    - What themes emerged in your dress practice log?
    - What did you notice about daily dress practice that you hadn't noticed before?
    - How did the dress practice log impact your understanding of the relationship between dress and the body?

Suggestions:

- Pay attention to aspects of your routine you don't normally think about—all the "taken-for-granted" aspects of daily life. Why do these things, and what would change if you did them differently?
- Think about times when you feel "uncomfortable" in your clothing, or when you become particularly aware of your body in your clothing—what is really going on in these moments?
- Pay attention to the difference between what you feel you "should" do/wear and what actually happens.

You will be graded on how well you meet the requirements listed earlier, as well as the following criteria:

- Clear and thoughtful explanation of your dress practices and their larger social/cultural context
- Explicit and thoughtful connection to relevant readings (i.e., Entwistle, Woodward, or Heti et al.)
- At least one direct quote from a relevant course reading in your final overall reflection, with Chicago-style citation
- Clear writing and evidence of editing and proofreading

Typical results and reflections on the assignment

- Students reported that their perception of their everyday dress practices was different than the reality. Many students reported that they did not realize how much they relied on a "uniform" set of clothes and practices from day to day.
- They thought about the physical nature of their clothing more. Although many of the students completing this assignment in my course were majoring in fashion design, they felt the assignment caused them to consider anew the way they felt, physically and emotionally, in their garments. This was even more revelatory for students who engage less directly with the materiality of fashion, such as fashion marketing or fashion management students.
- They expanded and refined their language for talking about daily dress practices. For example, rather than considering "comfort" a value with universal meaning and intelligibility, they could recognize how their understanding of "comfort" differs from someone else's, and they could distinguish between varying conceptions of comfort in physical, psychological, or social terms.
- They perceived a close link between their dress practices and their social context. Many students reported very different dress practices for days when there was ample or diverse social interaction than for days when social interaction was limited. Students particularly found it interesting to discuss their "home clothes" (i.e., the clothes they wore privately around the house but would never let others see).
- They measured their individual experiences against what they perceived as common for others in similar positions. However, in class discussion, many students realized that they had much more in common than not. Many also observed that they did not conform—and did not wish to conform—to imagined ideals (e.g., women who spent five minutes getting ready in the morning and men who spent an hour getting ready compared themselves against gendered social norms concerning the "appropriate" amount of time one should spend getting ready).
- They particularly enjoyed the visual components of the assignment. Some students went above and beyond to include inventive and original photographs to document their dress practice.

Notes

1. Joanne Entwistle, "The Dressed Body," in *Real Bodies: A Sociological Introduction*, ed. Mary Evans and Ellie Lee (Hampshire, UK: Palgrave, 2002), 133.
2. Ibid., 134.
3. Cheryl Buckley and Hazel Clark, "Conceptualizing Fashion in Everyday Lives," *Design Issues* 28, no. 4 (2012): 18–28. doi:10.1162/DESI_a_00172.

Bibliography

Bourdieu, Pierre. *Outline of a Theory of Practice*. Cambridge, UK: Cambridge University Press, 1977.

Buckley, Cheryl, and Hazel Clark. "Conceptualizing Fashion in Everyday Lives." *Design Issues* 28, no. 4 (2012): 18–28. doi:10.1162/DESI_a_00172.

Entwistle, Joanne. "The Dressed Body." In *Real Bodies: A Sociological Introduction*, edited by Mary Evans and Ellie Lee, 133–150. Hampshire, UK: Palgrave, 2002.

Entwistle, Joanne. *The Fashioned Body: Fashion, Dress, and Social Theory*. Cambridge, UK: Polity Press, 2000.

Heti, Sheila, Heidi Julavits, and Leanne Shapton. *Women in Clothes*. New York: Blue Rider Press, 2014.

Spivack, Emily. *Worn Stories*. New York: Princeton Architectural Press, 2014.

Woodward, Sophie. "Hanging Out in the Home and the Bedroom." In *Why Women Wear What They Wear*, 31–49. London; Oxford: Berg, 2007.

26
EXPERIENCING THE CLOTHED BODY IN PUBLIC SPACE

Laura Snelgrove, Parsons School of Design

Contextualization

As an undergraduate student, I enrolled in a course called "The Body in Cultural Studies," in which we were introduced to the figure of the *flâneur*. The source text was Michel de Certeau's chapter "Walking in the City" from *The Practice of Everyday Life,* though the concept had been passed down from Charles Baudelaire's *The Painter of Modern Life*, and filtered through Walter Benjamin. De Certeau's *flâneur* (loosely translated to "stroller") was presented as someone who embodies and defines the everyday experience of walking in urban spaces, bringing the rhetoric of city planning down to the human scale. We were given an assignment to stroll around any part of our city and reflect upon the interaction between our bodies and that space.

I developed a version of this assignment for my "Fashion and Violence" seminar course that I taught at Parsons School of Design in New York. This course was concerned with how fashion, dress, violence, and fear are all embodied experiences, subject to changes across space and time. The students undertook a *flâneur* assignment that shifted the focus to the *dressed* body, using Joanne Entwistle's introductory chapters of *The Fashioned Body* as context to consider the themes of the urban, the everyday, and fear. Students traveled to spaces in which they felt uncomfortable, exploring urban space to think through the ways in which danger's *frisson* acts upon the dressed self. Prior to undertaking this fieldwork, students read Hille Koskela's foundational work in feminist geography, "Bold Walks and Breakings: Women's Spatial Confidence Versus Fear of Violence." This article details how gendered power structures can shape the experience of walking in urban spaces, and how women can and do resist the construction of public space as fearful. It also explains how women sometimes use dress to convey—or even prompt—a lack of fear and how repeated use of certain spaces can create a sense of ownership that further dispels fear.

However, the assignment is more broadly applicable than just to the experience of urban fear. I have used it to introduce other seminal fashion studies texts, including Elizabeth Wilson's *Adorned in Dreams*, which emphasizes the way that dress creates and maintains boundaries between personal and public space. Wilson writes that fashion "was always urban (urbane), became metropolitan, and is now cosmopolitan," having taken root in the "early capitalist city," and now finds itself an agent of the globalization of a singular modern ideal.[1] This perception narrows the range of what can be considered spaces of *fashion* to those within the borders of urban centers (as opposed to *dress*, which inhabits every human space). Applying these concepts in my classes, I asked students to consider this assertion critically: that is, could they see fashion existing in spaces outside of the city? How do they conceive of dress and fashion differently in either type of space? Particularly as most of them come to New York from smaller cities, students tended to frame the assignment as being about themselves as people inhabiting differing spaces across time, responding to changes in their environment.

In the lecture I have used to introduce this assignment, I expand upon the connection between fashion and urban space with the help of Benjamin and Baudelaire's descriptions of Paris in the nineteenth century. The *flâneur* emerges in these writings as a figure observing the modern fashion parade from a cool distance, absorbed in the rhythm of city streets, without inserting himself into its action. The department store and the strolling version of shopping it produced are seen as the natural outcome of this mode of city living. Reading these works, students are thereby asked to view their own *flâneurie* as implicated in the late-capitalist city and their "street clothes" as part of its guiding economic system and cultural norms.

Georg Simmel's 1903 essay "The Metropolis and Mental Life" is also key to understanding the relationship between embodiment, identity, and space. This essay outlines his view of the essential problem facing the modern subject: the tension between individual identity and group dependence. The modern city, with its increased pace and scope of human relations, forced citizens to distinguish themselves by new means, including by the manipulation of image through fashion. Urban spaces, including sidewalks, public transportation, shops, and restaurants are viewed as akin to stages where identity is performed in public.

I asked students to consider Simmel's ideas when choosing the location for their stroll. How public is it? How much of themselves are they required to manipulate in advance, in order to achieve a goal of either fitting in or standing out? Which of these strategies do they prefer in this space, and why? What do they expect to witness from the other people/bodies they'll encounter in that space? Ideally, their chosen space would be representative of (in the case of my students) a particular aspect of New York City's unique sociology.

To encourage thinking *through* the body, I introduced Merleau-Ponty's idea of the body as the first location of perception: a thing not only *in* space, but *of* space. Students were asked to question how their sensorial experience of being in public space shaped their sense of their cultural identity, that is, their *habitus*. Could this experience help them untangle the threads of their socialization and its shaping of their body and their dress?

I asked students to situate their reflections about their experiences in relation to Entwistle's clear explication of dress and embodiment from *The Fashioned Body*. In the chapters I assigned, she introduces the definition of dress as a "situated bodily practice," the daily environment of the self, and the way in which we learn to live in our bodies (and therefore the spaces our bodies inhabit).[2] When asked to detail how they dressed for their outing, students were required to situate all dress decisions in meaningful reflection.

Appropriate courses and course level: Since the length of this paper can be adjusted significantly, it is easy to scale up or down for different levels of undergraduates. When I provided this assignment to an upper-year seminar, students were required to reference more course readings, while sophomores needed only a minimum of three. In both cases, the courses were in fashion studies departments, but this could also work in urban geography or women, gender, and sexuality studies classes, with slightly adjusted emphases on urban space or the gendered aspects thereof. Seeing as the assignment is also an ethnography of the self and of a neighborhood, it could also fit within certain anthropology courses, particularly if there is any focus on the body. And of course, developed as it was from an original cultural studies course, I believe this assignment could find a place in any course that explores semiotics, with a focus directed more toward the signs and signifiers of dress and away from the phenomenological aspect of being a dressed body.

Appropriate course size: This assignment can be used in a class of any size.

Estimated time required: Given that a self-directed outing is required, I recommend giving a minimum of three weeks for this assignment to accommodate students' individual schedules. The writing itself is best done very shortly (if not immediately) after the outing, a time management strategy I always encourage when explaining the assignment to students.

Learning goals

- Recognition of the phenomenological aspects of everyday dress.
- Ability to describe bodily sensations in a coherent way with respect to clothing
- Comprehension of the concept of the *flâneur* and its place in fashion history
- Reconciliation of the continuity between this history and the present through dress
- Awareness of how gendered power structures operate on the body in public

Assessment

In order to privilege the above-mentioned learning goals, grading should favor papers that are organized well with respect to balance between description and reflection; description should take up no more than one and a half pages, or about one-third of the total length. The reader should be able to picture the space and the ensemble in whole and in detail. The portion dedicated to reflection should be written clearly, with thoughtful, deep, and explicit connections to the theories outlined. In particular, it should engage with the concept of the *flâneur* and provide evidence of understanding both why this is a unique figure in urban space (rather than just a pedestrian) and whether or not they feel they achieved the goal of inhabiting such a role.

The body must play a central role in the narrative as well, to show comprehension of basic phenomenology and the view of dress as a situated bodily practice rather than just a tool for outward communication. Students should be able to describe the feeling of being themselves in space rather than just a series of assumptions about how they appeared.

Proper sourcing and citations according to the requirements assigned by the instructor should take up a portion of the evaluation.

Guidelines for instructors

Though I have given this assignment in a large urban center, it does not have to be. It would be just as interesting to ask students to compare their own place of residence to that of the traditional *flâneur*. Can one be a *flâneur* when everyone else is in a car, for instance? How does walking in a rural area compare to walking in an urban one? Or, does a suburban shopping mall recreate any of the conditions of city shopping and strolling? The interaction between body, dress, and space is what matters: the city is merely the established, not the only possible, home of the *flâneur*.

I would recommend covering, in class, the material on space and embodiment that is referenced in the "Contextualization" section of this chapter before assigning this outing, as it would be difficult for undergraduate students to work from the readings alone, as many of these readings are dense and/or historical. In my courses, this assignment has been given mid-semester, after some basic grounding in the difference between fashion and dress, the materiality of garments, the role of the consumer, and the function of semiotics in our "reading" of others' dress.

A small number of students always request to write about excursions outside the city (i.e., to their hometowns, on holidays, or on visits to friends at other colleges). I ask that they approach me with this request in advance, along with an angle they expect to explore, to be sure that they are still thinking through the same issues as the rest of the class, and making productive comparisons between the other space they propose examining and New York.

Cautionary advice for instructors

- Considering the age group of traditional-aged undergraduates, reflections on the self in public can often focus on the perceived judgment of others. Students undertaking this exercise should be reminded that not every look they receive from a stranger is negative, and to maintain their focus on their own experience of dress in space, rather than what they imagine others are thinking about them.
- Given that students are asked to explore spaces with which they are less familiar, there is an issue of potential liability. They should be encouraged to go

beyond their comfort zone, though never to court danger. Making sure a nearby friend is aware of their whereabouts and ready to answer a phone call in case of emergency would be useful for students undertaking this assignment. The instructor should thoughtfully discuss with them how they might interpret the directive to stretch beyond the familiar in safe ways, proposing examples of nonthreatening discomfort like that found in new social settings. Being safe and sensible must be stressed.

- Encouraging students to be aware of the different forms of privilege they possess is an important aspect of preparing them to undertake this assignment. I've found it best to emphasize how the intersection of multiple identities shapes our experience of our bodies in space: for instance, if a student is a young white woman writing about the catcalls she experiences in a neighborhood with a majority population which is of color, remember that the student's class and racial privilege may mark her as an oppressive outsider as much as her femaleness may mark her as an object to sexualize, and for her to consider this even as she reflects upon the visceral discomfort of feeling targeted on the sidewalk.

Copy of assignment

Spatial dress reflection

This assignment is intended to deepen your understanding of the connection between dress, the body, and space and to ground the concepts from class readings and discussions in your real, lived experience of the city. If you would like to propose undertaking the assignment in another location (for instance, if you are traveling before the deadline), please speak to instructor as soon as possible to discuss the approach you plan to take.

Assignment

Choose a place in the city to go and walk around. This could be a neighborhood you haven't been to, a park, a building, or part of a building. It can be a social space such as a store (maybe one selling clothes you can't afford, or would never choose to wear), or a party full of new people. Consider your choice of place carefully: it will be most rewarding to try to push yourselves *beyond your comfort zone*. (Though please note: going beyond your comfort zone does not mean entering into any space in which your bodily autonomy or physical safety are compromised. Be sure to make your personal safety a priority as you seek out spaces that are new to, and potentially uncomfortable for, you.)

Keep in mind the figure of the *flâneur*, a person who thrives on the energy of the city's public spaces and maintains a cool emotional distance from the scene around them. This should help you stay in the headspace required for observing the sensations of your own dressed experience.

Details

Begin by briefly describing (*one paragraph*) the space you will be heading to, and the conditions under which you are going (alone or with others, day vs. night, distance and method of transportation, etc.). Tell us why you've chosen this particular space, and what makes it uniquely urban.

Consider carefully your clothing choices before heading out. Describe (*one paragraph*) your outfit and the thought process behind it. Some questions to guide you: Do you feel conspicuous, or do you hope to blend in? Are you choosing clothes for practical reasons (such as weather), or style reasons? Dark colors or tough materials? Obviously expensive clothing or accessories? Clothing with sentimental value or many associated memories? Gender-conforming or gender-defying dress?

The remainder of the paper should be divided between an account of what happened once you reached your destination, and a reflection on how this experience did or did not reflect the theories and themes we have read about and discussed in class.

Ask yourselves: Did you feel conspicuous in the space? Did your body feel comfortable or vulnerable? Why and how? Did your clothing make you feel more or less protected or confident? Can you describe how the space around your body feels affected by you being in it? If there were others there, did any react to you in an overt way? Did you feel warm, cold, itchy, or another physical sensation that affected how you interacted with the space or other people?

You should write the account in first person, and feel free to be creative with the prose. We are looking for evidence of some deep thinking about yourself as a dressed body in public space, so use an active rather than a passive voice.

Parameters

1. The paper should be four to five pages in length, double-spaced, using twelve-point font. Please use one-inch margins.
2. Use the Chicago style for citations (footnotes and bibliography).
3. You must quote from the Entwistle chapters and at least two other course readings.

Typical results and reflections on the assignment

- Choices of spaces range from economically depressed neighborhoods (where class difference often reared its head as students felt conspicuous or embarrassed in clothing that had felt normal to them in their bedroom mirrors), to house parties full of strangers, to upscale boutiques (where class consciousness appeared in reverse to the that mentioned previously, with students writing of

- the shame they felt at their scuffed shoes or cheap handbags), to students' own apartments with no one else home overnight.
- Students rethought spaces around them according to the ways that power structures public space and often reflect on how invisible boundaries around themselves became perceptible to them through the exercise. In particular, young women and queer-identified men often wrote about how clothing made them feel more or less vulnerable to harm in male-dominated spaces.
- Students carefully considered their own everyday dress in ways that reframed common experiences of their bodies, by being conscious of that which is often done unconsciously.
- The best work managed to integrate bodily sensations like touch and temperature with the strictly visual, to capture the many ways that dress operates at once.
- Students rethought style definitions like "tough," "badass," or "goth" based on their semiotics and the complex identities they sometimes represent.
- Students often wrote about discovering the function of clothing as protective armor, which fundamentally reimagines the possibilities of dress in their lives.

Notes

1 Elizabeth Wilson, *Adorned in Dreams: Fashion and Modernity* (Berkeley and Los Angeles: University of California Press, 1985), 9.
2 Joanne Entwistle, *The Fashioned Body: Fashion, Dress and Modern Social Theory* (Cambridge: Blackwell, 2000), 34.

Bibliography

Baudelaire, Charles. "The Painter of Modern Life." In *Modern Art and Modernism: A Critical Anthology*, edited by Francis Frascina and Charles Harrison, 23–28. New York: Harper & Row, 1982.
Benjamin, Walter. *The Arcades Project*. Translated by H. Eiland and K. McLaughlin. Cambridge: Harvard University Press, 1999.
De Certeau, Michel. "Walking in the City." In *The Practice of Everyday Life*, translated by Steven Rendall, 91–110. Berkeley and Los Angeles: University of California Press, 1984.
Entwistle, Joanne. *The Fashioned Body: Fashion, Dress and Modern Social Theory*. Cambridge: Blackwell, 2000.
Goffman, Erving. *The Presentation of Self in Everyday Life*. Garden City, NY: Anchor, 1959.
Koskela, Hille. "Bold Walk and Breakings': Women's Spatial Confidence Versus Fear of Violence." *Gender, Place and Culture* 4, no. 3 (1997): 301–319.
Merleau-Ponty, Maurice. *Phenomenology of Perception*. Translated by Colin Smith. London and New York: Routledge, 2002.
Simmel, Georg. "The Metropolis and Mental Life." In *The City Cultures Reader*, edited by Malcolm Miles and Tim Hall, with Iain Borden, 12–19. London: Routledge, 2000.
Wilson, Elizabeth. *Adorned in Dreams: Fashion and Modernity*. Berkeley and Los Angeles: University of California Press, 1985.

27
FASHIONING DRESS FROM THE RAG TRADE TO THE RUNWAY

Eileen Boris, University of California, Santa Barbara

Contextualization

Teaching about fashion is to confront large issues of political economy and urgent questions of social responsibility and personal ethics. As the 1911 Triangle Shirtwaist Fire in New York City[1] and the 2013 Rana Plaza collapse in Bangladesh[2] made all too clear, women sometimes pay with their lives for the clothes they have sewed for others to wear.[3] As disapproving media comments on the outfits of women politicians, wives of political leaders, black youth, and genderqueer individuals underscore, dress stands as a terrain for struggles over respectability, expression, and proper deportment.[4] Fashion is about style but it is also about production, consumption, and the social reproduction of identity and culture. The challenge is to connect the personal to the political. How can students understand individual choice in relation to local and global economies of production and consumption and see that the gender systems shaping their lives operate in the making of clothes as well?

Design exists as part of a larger fashion system that includes the envisioning, manufacturing, displaying, selling, and wearing of clothing and accessories.[5] This system developed over time and across space. It has encompassed ateliers and schools; textile mills, workshops, sweatshops, and computerized factories; fashion weeks, runways, and photo shoots; boutiques, discount chains, and department stores; and glossy magazines, personal blogs, and e-commerce.[6] There are numerous players: designers, sewers, machine operators, pressers, distributors, publicists, agents, models, storeowners, bloggers, buyers, and wearers. The making of clothes has crossed borders: from city to countryside and back to urban spaces; from the United States to Central America and Mexico and then to China, Bangladesh, and elsewhere in Asia. Used clothes travel to thrift stores and charities and to Africa, where they are repurposed. Middlemen of all sorts take their cut while those who do the cutting (and sewing) too often earn less than a living wage and labor without proper ventilation and with poor lighting under the harsh eyes of supervisors. However, the contractors and subcontractors who manufacture fashion for the many, in a kind of trickle-down style, themselves are trying to make ends meet as they scramble to fulfill just-in-time production contracts and various demands of retailers, who, in their own race to the bottom, squeeze producers.[7]

Allowing for choice among material objects, some unavailable from price and others deemed culturally inappropriate, fashion has reinforced but also challenged normative gender, class, race, age, and other social positions. It forces us to ask: Can there be personal agency in a mass-produced world? Is appearance power? What does law and social policy have to do with fashioning dress? Are we what we wear? Do clothes make the woman, the man, or the genderqueer person? What do we have in common with those who design, sew, assemble, display, and sell dress?

Studies of gender, sexual, and race/ethnic meanings attached to dress often neglect the rich historical and sociological literature on the garment industry,[8] but some cultural analysis brings production and identity together.[9] The evolution of the making of clothing and the emergence of the fashion maker and seller as specific occupations opens a window also into dominant conceptions of male and female, first embodied in aristocracies and then national and international bourgeoisies.[10] The emergence of alternative practices that subvert or recreate style to suit the fancies, laboring conditions, and resources of subaltern or subcultures has inspired designers. Appropriation of "native" patterns (as in Aztec and African prints), ethnically associated looks (such as corn rows and baggy pants), or working-class apparel (like denim and blue jeans) can commodify self-expression or announce a political agenda.[11]

But borrowing of motifs, fabrics, and clothing items (like suits or kimonos) has never moved in only one direction. For example, the rise of Asian-American designers during the last decades of the twentieth century signaled the transfer of skill from an immigrant generation employed in the garment industry to their children and fictive kin with advanced educational attainments (university as well as art school) and the opportunities afforded by lower rents in some New York City neighborhoods. Also central were the establishment of training schools in China and the prominence of Japanese artists and designers in the fashion capitals of Paris, Milan, and New York.[12] It is possible to trace "modest dressing" among Muslim, Orthodox Jewish, and Mormon women in Britain and the United States by charting the influence of Middle Eastern populations in London and Turkish designers setting the standards for those in Northern Europe and North America.[13]

While much of the scholarship condemns labor practices throughout the rag trade and fashion system, notably garment assembly in the global South and modeling, popular biographies and autobiographies nonetheless celebrate fashion pioneers. It is important to recognize the accomplishments of individual artists and brands, even after making a political economy turn in analysis. Similarly, acknowledging a new world of personal blogging suggests a multiplicity of tastemakers. The power of individual combinations of articles assembled by self-announced fashionistas has impacted displays of retailers and promotions of online distributors. Niche markets—for the plus-sized, professional, religiously observant, or ethnic associations—testify to a multivocal market.

Style, identity, and economics take concrete shape by going to virtual museum exhibits that introduce a material culture counterpart to fashion and feminist theory. The Museum of American History's "Between a Rock and a Hard Place" offers a tour of garment-making conditions from 1820 to 1997, including "the Fashion Food Chain" or what scholars now name the global supply chain for the production and distribution of items.[14] The Fashion Institute of Technology's "A Queer History of Fashion: From the Closet to the Catwalk" exemplifies gender bending and genderqueer design.[15] By studying the timelines of these exhibits together, the mapping of gender presentation with garment manufacturing becomes possible, thus enhancing the study of the fashion system in its multiple dimensions.

Our own experiences as purchasers and wearers of clothing offer an entrée into studying the fashion system. Students are able to approach theoretical concepts by translating the abstract into familiar dilemmas, such as worry over messages of sexual availability conveyed by a favorite blouse or pair of shoes or whether an ethnic print must signal insensitive appropriation of another culture. Many would never sign up for a course on political economy, but they emerge from one on the fashion system with new insights precisely because they learn to connect the personal to the political. A final course assignment, preferably carried out as a group project, draws upon fascination with fashion by asking students to connect political and social structures to individual opportunities, tastes, and ethical conundrums.

Appropriate courses and course levels: Undergraduate courses in cultural studies, fashion studies, feminist studies, globalization, history, and labor studies and history.

Appropriate class size: Twenty-five to thirty students in order to allow sufficient time for each group to present their project during the last week of class.

Estimated time required: This is a term project and requires minimum of twenty hours of work over the course of ten weeks.

Required materials

- Note: Materials will depend on the direction of the project. They can include examples listed here or consist of traditional library or digital resources (such as books, academic articles, and web pages).
- Sewing machine, needles, cloth, thread, and other materials.
- Video or digital camera and computer programs to edit video.
- Computer and Internet connection.
- Art supplies.

Learning goals

- Understand garment production over time and space and the fashion industry.

- Identify key theoretical lenses by which scholars consider "the fashion system."
- Discuss the ways that clothing express and define gender and other social identities.
- Connect individual meanings and social/political contexts, learning the ways that the personal is political.
- Improve research, critical thinking, and presentation skills by engaging with concrete aspects of the designing, making, distribution, circulation, and wearing of fashion.

Assessment

Given that students have leeway to create a final project and may work in groups, what is assessed will vary, but the criteria should be constant: Has the project advanced critical thinking and research skills as seen in the final object? Does it display creativity and originality? Did the students learn to develop an idea and carry it out, even if there were mishaps and readjustments along the way? Did they draw upon concepts and readings from the class? Instructors should supplement evaluation of the process and product of the group with evaluation of individuals within it, including analysis of their self-evaluations (and their assessment of the group work process) which should be part of a write-up accompanying the project that discusses their contributions, the key findings of the project, and what they learned. Those who do individual project and more traditional research papers still should provide a self-assessment.

A checklist can help the instructor be consistent. The first section should measure adhering to timelines, including scheduled subassignments and meetings. The second section should evaluate the process of project development: research question or topic, methods used, and readjustments along the way. Were methods appropriate to goals? The third section should judge form as well as the content. The criteria for a paper differ from a well-shot video and a survey from a collage, but both can be graded on "production values." The final section focuses on the individual student. Did they do their share? Did they offer a compelling self-assessment?

Guidelines for instructors

Allowing maximum flexibility in choice of projects is a pedagogical strategy to encourage investment and excitement, but it does require monitoring to see if students are analyzing their interests in the context of the larger fashion system. The instructor should have a wide familiarity with the fashion system, its structures, and its meanings across time and space or be willing to investigate resources for suggested projects. Particularly important is an ability to convey gender theory in its various components as well as to explicate the political economy of the various branches of the system and pinpoint the operations of gender therein.

The instructor may compile a list of possible projects to suggest a range of possibilities. For ethnographies and videos that show the face or reveal private information about student informants, the instructor should guide project members through human subject protocols and devise informed consent forms even if their particular campus does not require approval by its human subjects research committee for classroom assignments. This precaution is important to maintain the rights of informants and protect the research group since videos and other materials could go viral on social media. The instructor may wish to provide an honor code for project groups to sign when the final product has such a potential to expose information about other students that otherwise might be considered personal (such as their sexual or gender identity, class background, or exposed body).

Discussion questions

Instructors may want to ask the students to formulate an explicit question that their project will address, elaborate the means they will use to answer the question, list the resources and skills required to accomplish the project, and consider the roles of each member within multiperson groups. During class presentations of final projects, the instructor might ask the students to reflect on how the outcome measured up to their proposal outline and work plan, what they had confirmed, what they were surprised by, what challenges they faced, and what they learned about the subject, objects interrogated, and themselves in the process.

Cautionary advice for instructors

- The assignment was designed for a course given on the quarter system and would have to be adapted for a semester term.
- The instructor will have to recognize that some students have scheduling and other reasons for wanting to be a one-person group.
- Group projects require safeguards against "free-riding" students who let others do the work and can hamper the overall quality of the project. Thus, it is essential to have an individual paper and self-reflection to hold all accountable as well as to alleviate any anxiety about group work and to facilitate fair grading.
- The tendency was for students to analyze themselves and the use of fashion in the nearby student-dominated area where many lived. There are advantages to letting students essentially write about themselves and those around them: research subjects for surveys and interviews are available and the motivation to learn more about one's self or one's cohort is strong. There was great enthusiasm for such projects.
- The challenge is to push students to think critically about their own world (whether a queer student group, sorority houses, or an ethnically based culture) and to consider social structures, cultural power, and economic clout in moving

from description to analysis while recognizing where they are approaching the subject from and respecting their identities.

- The limit of student-defined projects comes from their lack of articulation of goals, their lack of experience with the topic, and their inability to move from the micro to the macro level of analysis, and their newness at connecting gender expression and other identities to political economy.
- When appropriate to the project, be sure that students distribute participation consent forms that fully explain the project and how it will be displayed (on an unrestricted student web page, on a class page that is restricted to enrolled students, just an oral presentation, or other venues).
- When students become aware of exploitative labor practices in the garment and fashion industries, some become very guilty and upset if they feel they cannot purchase ethically because they buy at discount and lower-priced stores, even though high prices are not necessarily an indicator of socially responsible production. Instructors can respond by leading the class in a discussion about the ethical implications of consumption. By emphasizing the political, social, cultural, and economic constraints under which consumption occurs, the instructor can show that the problem is more than an individual one. The class then might brainstorm about concrete ways to respond to these dilemmas, while the instructor might present examples of past and current actions taken by organized consumers, unions, and concerned individuals.

Copy of the assignment

Term group project/individual commentary

Overall project guidelines: This project will be presented during the last week of class to all of your classmates, and collected by me at that time. In terms of the form your final project will take: use your imagination! You can undertake a fashion show, a gender-bending design collection, a clothing swap or collection drive, a solidarity campaign, a corporate responsibility investigation, a survey, or a traditional term paper (this medium is especially appropriate, for a single-person group). Those who do research papers will also devise an appropriate class presentation. Try to connect your personal concerns to the larger structures of the designing, producing, distribution, and selling of fashion.

Requirements: Prior to undertaking work on your project, your group will submit a topic project plan to me, which will be due during week 2 of the term. This two-page document with attached bibliography will present your topic and means of investigation, clearly discussing the specific roles that will be undertaken by each group member. The project plan should connect the topic to the course themes by suggesting how its pursuit illuminates a key question.

Schedule: Each group will be coming to meet with me during week 3 of our term, to discuss their topic project proposal. At this meeting, we will go over my response to your project plan and students should discuss their division of labor and conceptualization in greater detail. During the term, your group will also be submitting one-page progress checks with updates about the current state of your projects to me. These updates will list sources consulted, actions taken (i.e., surveys given, interviews made, and scripts written), and challenges faced. Progress Check 1 will be submitted during week 4, and Progress Check 2 will be submitted during week 6. We will also be having a work day and a class meeting before break in which groups can resolve research issues, review findings, and prepare for final write-ups.

Individual commentary guidelines: On the day your group presents, you will also be submitting a one-page self-evaluation discussing your contribution to the project and assessing your efforts (this self-evaluation will be required of both group project and individual projects/papers). You will also provide a commentary on your project of three to four pages, drawing on appropriate assigned class readings in discussing the goals, outcome, and meaning of your project.

Typical results and reflections on the assignment sheet

- Student projects mostly either addressed the political economy of fashion or explored personal identity expression through clothing. Some successfully connected the two.
- One student made an item of clothing, as an experiment on reusing materials.
- An outstanding project on the political economy of fashion sought to educate purchasers of cheap clothes by giving the consumer campaign against worker exploitation a concrete form through the use of paper dolls: it consisted of a bulletin board with male and female paper dolls that could be dressed with articles of cutout clothing. On the other side of these pieces was information on style, materials, method of production, cost of production, working conditions of makers, and price.
- Another project displayed as a poster a timeline that connected the introduction of fashion styles to a history of US imperialism.
- Combining political economy with identity expression, a project in the form of a traditional term paper discussed cultural appropriation by fashion brands of dress and design associated with indigenous peoples.
- Video projects recorded fashion shows to capture student identity. "The Queer Fashion Show" shot a catwalk and interviews with queer-identified students on their clothing choices. The "Greek Apparel Catwalk" presented sorority sisters in a candid camera format and also included interviews with members on why and on what occasions they wore sorority emblems.
- "The Bra and Nipple Freedom Project" surveyed women on their wearing of bras and displayed findings in a PowerPoint. The "Make-up Experiment"

photographed a student's own looks with and without makeup, chronicling the reactions of onlookers and self-reflections over a two-week period. "The Wearing Other Women's Outfits" videoed clothing switching and individual reactions to be in another person's chosen garments. Both of these projects involved ethnographic observation. The students were pushed to reflect on larger systems of gender and work informing these choices.

- Overall, students gained insight into a variety of research methods (survey, ethnography, cultural analysis, and web and archival research). The best incorporated objects and deployed media for presentation of results, whether through PowerPoint, video, or web pages. They also took off from readings.

Notes

1 "Remembering the 1911 Triangle Factory Fire," https://trianglefire.ilr.cornell.edu/, last accessed August 23, 2017.
2 "Rana Plaza," Clean Clothes Campaign, https://cleanclothes.org/safety/ranaplaza, last accessed August 23, 2017.
3 Elizabeth Cline, *Over-Dressed: The Shockingly High Cost of Cheap Fashion* (New York: Portfolio/Penguin, 2013).
4 Susan B. Kaiser and Sarah Rebolloso McCullough, "Entangling the Fashion Subject Through the African Diaspora: From Not to (K)not in Fashion Theory," *Fashion Theory: The Journal of Dress, Body & Culture* 14, no. 3 (2010): 366–368; Tanisha C. Ford, *Liberation Threads: Black Women, Style, and the Global Politics of Soul* (Chapel Hill: University of North Carolina Press, 2015).
5 Rebecca Arnold, *Fashion: A Very Short Introduction* (New York: Oxford University Press, 2009).
6 Elizabeth Wissinger, *This Year's Model: Fashion, Media, and the Making of Glamour* New York: New York University Press, 2015); Thuy Linh Nguyen Tu, *The Beautiful Generation: Asian Americans and the Cultural Economy of Fashion* (Durham: Duke University Press, 2011).
7 Cline, *Over-Dressed*. For a powerful resource, see "China Blue," http://www.pbs.org/independentlens/chinablue/, last accessed August 23, 2017.
8 Nancy Green, *Ready-to-Wear, Ready-to-Work: A Century of Industry and Immigrants in Paris and New York* (Durham: Duke University Press, 1997).
9 Angela McRobbie, *British Fashion Design: Rag Trade or Image* (New York: Routledge, 1998); Nan Enstad, *Ladies of Labor, Girls of Adventure: Working Women, Popular Culture, and Labor Politics at the Turn of the Twentieth Century* (New York: Columbia University Press, 1999).
10 Arnold, *Fashion*; Tu, *The Beautiful Generation*.
11 Ford, *Liberation Threads*.
12 Tu, *The Beautiful Generation*.
13 Reina Lewis, *Muslim Fashion: Contemporary Style Cultures* (Durham: Duke University Press, 2015).
14 Museum of American History, "Between a Rock and a Hard Place," http://americanhistory.si.edu/sweatshops/, last accessed August 23, 2017.
15 Museum at Fashion Institute of Technology, "A Queer History of Fashion: From the Closet to the Catwalk," http://exhibitions.fitnyc.edu/, last accessed August 23, 2017.

Bibliography

Arnold, R. *Fashion: A Very Short Introduction*. New York: Oxford University, 2009.

Cline, E. *Over-Dressed: The Shockingly High Cost of Cheap Fashion*. New York: Portfolio/Penguin, 2013.

Enstad, N. *Ladies of Labor, Girls of Adventure: Working Women, Popular Culture, and Labor Politics at the Turn of the Twentieth Century*. New York: Columbia University Press, 1999.

Ford, T.C. *Liberation Threads: Black Women, Style, and the Global Politics of Soul*. Chapel Hill: University of North Carolina Press, 2015.

Green, N. *Ready-to-Wear, Ready-to-Work: A Century of Industry and Immigrants in Paris and New York*. Durham: Duke University Press, 1997.

Kaiser, S.B., and S.R. McCullough. "Entangling the Fashion Subject Through the African Diaspora: From Not to (K)not in Fashion Theory." *Fashion Theory: The Journal of Dress, Body & Culture* 14, no. 3 (2010): 366–368.

Lewis, R. *Muslim Fashion: Contemporary Style Cultures*. Durham: Duke University Press, 2015.

McRobbie, A. *British Fashion Design: Rag Trade or Image*. New York: Routledge, 1998.

Tu, T.L.N. *The Beautiful Generation: Asian Americans and the Cultural Economy of Fashion*. Durham: Duke University Press, 2011.

Wissinger, E. *This Year's Model: Fashion, Media, and the Making of Glamour*. New York: New York University Press, 2015.

PART NINE

HISTORY AND LITERATURE

Introduction

The chapters in this section provide insight into the vital importance of fashion in understanding past eras, societies, and cultures. The exercises contained in these chapters enable students to consider what descriptions of dress in the fiction of different time periods reveals about expectations about class, gender, and religious identities, how leaders have used fashion as a means of crafting public personas, and what historical costume reveals about ideals of beauty, the body, and social and cultural change during different eras. Diana Saiki's exercise allows students to engage in a hands-on exercise, in which they create different versions of the draped Greek garment, the chiton. In addition to engaging students in this kinetic form of learning and helping them to develop their skills in collaborative work and garment construction, Saiki's assignment enables them to think consciously about what types of garments are worn within specific cultures during particular eras, how specific garments evolve and change over time, and what a garment such as the chiton reveals about the expectations of gender, class, and status in the culture from which it comes.

Catherine Howey Stearn's chapter uses an exercise centered on British monarch Queen Elizabeth I as a means of engaging with key questions about how public figures use fashion to shape their personas, how these representations are reinforced and contested in the larger culture of their era, and how conceptions of gender and power are shaped through decisions about dress and self-presentation (and how dress and self-presentation, in turn, serve as important sites through which notions of femininity, masculinity, and authority are formed). Stearn's exercise has students imagine themselves to be contemporaries of Queen Elizabeth I, tasked with creating their own images of her. The assignment thus enables students to critically reflect on, and participate through hands-on learning about, the complex ways in which public images of political and cultural figures are created and contested.

Amber Chatelain's chapter allows students to consider the connections between dress and larger historical context, by selecting a specific region and era in fashion history to analyze, and considering how political, economic, cultural, national events, and trends impacted dress in this place and time. Chatelain's chapter also helps students to reflect on how changing ideas about gender and sexuality impact modes of dress in the era students have selected. In her exercise, Catherine Bradley likewise considers how reflecting on broader cultural forces can enrich understanding of historic costume from different eras. Bradley's exercise helps students to analyze how factors such as scientific developments, popular culture, and politics shape the rise and fall of particular trends, and to present their insights to their peers in dynamic, kinesthetic ways (giving them the chance to try on styles and engage in dances which were popular during particular time periods).

Finally, Patricia Lennox's chapter discusses her exercise in which students read diverse literary texts and analyze how, where, and why these works include descriptions of fashion and dress. Lennox's chapter guides students through creating a chart noting each mention of dress in particular texts, enabling them to reflect on how place and era shape discussions of dress, and what clothing in these literary works reveal about characters' wealth and status, their political and religious affiliations, and their characters' conformity to (and/or their defiance of) gendered norms of their era and culture. As with all the chapters in this section, Lennox's exercise facilitates students drawing connections between the choices made about fashion by individual people in specific regions and eras, and how these choices are both shaped by and help to shape larger understandings of gender, race, class, sexuality, and identity during specific historical periods.

28
MAKING MODELS TO UNDERSTAND ANCIENT GREEK HISTORIC COSTUME

Diana Saiki, Ball State University

Contextualization

A traditional lecture approach is common in teaching fashion history, with students taking notes, examining images or artifacts, and taking objective tests.[1] Some attempts have been made to make the topic more stimulating to students with hands-on activities. For example, Marcketti, Fitzpatrick, Keist, and Kadolph had students in a fashion history course work with an apparel and textiles collection to engage in material cultural analysis and applied curatorial work.[2] These hands-on experiences helped students make personal, meaningful connections to the past. In another example, Saiki, Nam, and Beck had students make an online display to learn about historic clothing.[3] Other educators have used team-based learning to teach fashion history.[4] The results of these activities are increased engagement with the material, enjoyment in learning about fashion history, and a deep understanding of course material.

This exercise is most directly related to the hands-on teaching strategy of making models, which has been noted by several educational theorists to be an enjoyable approach to learning.[5] It is often employed in science courses and helps students reason and understand concepts by developing analogies.[6] It also helps with reteaching concepts that are difficult to understand.[7] It has been employed in fashion history courses in which students made paper models of bustle changes over the course of the nineteenth century. This model-making activity positively impacted student learning and resulted in improved test scores.[8]

This assignment is just such a hands-on activity to be used in a fashion history course. The activity incorporates students working in teams to make a Greek chiton or tunic out of provided materials. In groups of two to three, students use a sheet, safety pins, and a tie (belt) to make an assigned version of the Greek chiton (e.g., doric peplos and ionic chiton) on a designated student. Then each group presents to the class how they made the assigned garment. As the students in the audience listen to the presentation, they make comparisons between the particular garments they were assigned to create, the ones presented by the classmates.

If time permits, it is useful to have the students remove the sheet from their model student and also work on making outer garments, in addition to the chiton. The himation (a rectangular cloth thrown over the shoulder and worn across the body) is an easy garment to drape and is important for students to understand. Similar to the chiton, the himation influences garments in other ancient cultures. The chlamys (a cloak pinned at one shoulder) is another simple outer garment to make at the end of the class period, if time allows. All of these garments help students to learn not just about Ancient Greece, but also other regions and cultures, as they were subsequently adapted by Etruscan and Roman cultures. The garments also resemble later fashions, such as the light dresses worn during the early 1800s.

The activity produces a lively environment in the classroom and assists students with remembering and distinguishing between varying types of chitons. The activity enables students to learn from a three-dimensional model rather than a two-dimensional picture. They are able to take components of the two-dimensional picture and understand how garments such as the chiton were actually made. For example, when making the Doric chiton, a portion of the sheet is folded prior to draping the sheet on the body. After making the garment, students understand that, given a pictured statue wearing a chiton, a line above the belt is the edge of the folded sheet. Later, in a lecture about Greek costume, the instructor can identify the student who modeled a particular chiton. The instructor can also make reference to the activity when discussing other ancient cultures that wore the chiton (i.e., the Romans and Etruscans). It also becomes a memorable point of reference for later periods where Greek costume is referenced in a fashion history course, such as the French Revolution of the late eighteenth century.

Appropriate courses and course levels for the assignment: Courses in the history of Western fashion, fashion construction, international dress and markets, textiles for apparel, and fashion product analysis at the sophomore and junior levels

Appropriate class size: Twenty to forty-five students

Estimated time required: Fifty minutes

Required materials

- Several large sheets
- Safety pins
- Strips of fabric
- Textbook *Survey of Historic Costume* by Tortora and Marcketti[9]

Learning goals

Broad objectives of the assignment include the following:

- Assess features of draped garments.

- Understand how meaning in different cultures is achieved through dress (e.g., status).
- Recognize the variety in features that can be achieved through draped garments.
- Comprehend the impact technology has on garment construction.
- Evaluate the fabrics used in draped garments.

Specific objectives of the assignment include the following:

- Understand how an ancient garment, the chiton, was made.
- Compare and contrast the features of different types of Greek chitons.
- Identify costume worn during ancient Western cultures.
- Recognize historic terms related to Greek historic dress.

Assessment

The assignment is assessed during the student presentation and by grading the completed handout (see feedback form). During the presentations, the instructor ensures that the students have discussed the contextual influences on the Greek clothing presented. In addition, the instructor will ensure the garment is made accurately by either confirming the construction presented or correcting it. The handout is graded after the activity. The instructor examines whether or not the student has identified critical similarities and differences between the garment assigned and the garment presented (e.g., the Hellenistic chiton has a belt placed under the bosom). The graded handout is returned to the student for further referencing. Objective tests are also used to assure students understand the construction of and influences on the Ancient Greek chiton.

Guidelines for instructors

Students should read about Greek costume prior to arriving to class. This activity should take place prior to a course lecture on Greek costume and after defining the chiton. First, the instructor introduces Greek culture and defines the chiton or the Greek tunic for students. Students are then divided into groups of two to three students. Each group is given one full-sized bedsheet, safety pins, a strip of fabric (for a belt), and instructions and visuals on how to make a chiton (see the table in this chapter). The chitons the class makes include the following six varieties of the basic garment: (1) chitoniskos, (2) doric peplos, (3) Hellenistic chiton, (4) doric chiton, (5) ionic chiton, and (6) exomis.

The students are asked to dress one of their group members in the assigned garment, using the materials provided. They also prepare a presentation highlighting how they made the garment and how the textbook describes the garment (e.g., which genders it was worn by and what materials it was constructed from). Then they present their garments to the class overall. Groups assigned to the chitoniskos present first, demonstrating how they made the garment and discussing related historical facts. The instructor explains any variations among the garments made by the students and guides the presentations to assure accuracy. The presentation process is repeated until all garments have been explained.

While the groups of students present their garments, the students in the audience complete a worksheet. The worksheet asks the students, "How would you change your garment to" create the presented one? A student might note, for example, the belt of the doric peplos (assigned to their group) would need to be positioned under the bosom for the Hellenistic chiton (presented by another group). If there is time, the activity can also include each group also making outer garments (e.g., the himation and chlamys). In this case, the students would remove the sheet from the model student, and then make the outer garment as the instructor demonstrates how to make these garments from the front of the room. The instructor can also be scanning the room to ensure each student is draping the outerwear accurately. Students' completed worksheets are collected and reviewed by the instructor. Instructors can optionally follow this exercise with a lecture that discusses Greek clothing (e.g., himation and ionic chiton) and period film clips featuring Greek fashions (e.g., *Helen of Troy* and *Troy*).

This activity can be applied to other historic forms and eras. For example, the exercise could be broadened to include draped garments from Mesopotamian, Egyptian, Etruscan, and Roman cultures. Students could then witness changes in technology (e.g., skirt of the Sumerian culture in Mesopotamia vs. the Greek chiton) and variations in draping fabric on the body as given in each culture (e.g., an Egyptian wrapped garment vs. a Greek chiton).

Instructors can direct students to (and/or make copies for students) the resources listed in the following table, as students are creating their garments in class.

Garment	Website
Ionic, Doric Peplos, Doric Chiton, Chitoniskos	Lowell, L. (2015), "Greek clothing," *THD 331 Costume History: Antiquity to 19th Century*. Available online:http://www.cfa.ilstu.edu/lmlowel/THE331/Greeks.html
Doric Peplos, Doric Chiton	*Roman Life*. (2015), Greek Dress. Available online: http://www.dl.ket.org/latin1/things/romanlife/greekdress.htm
Doric Peplos, Doric Chiton Ionic Chiton	Thomas, P.W. (2001–2014), Ancient Greek Costume History Greek Dress—The Chiton. *Fashion-Era*. Available online: http://gaeabooks.com/gb/content/wearing-ionic-chiton
All chitons can be found on Pinterest	Pinterest. Available Online: https://www.pinterest.com/pin/144818944239954282/

Copy of the assignment

Assignment sheet: Greek wrapping activity

In your group of two to three students, you will make a presentation about the garment that you have been assigned. Complete the following steps to develop your presentation:

1. Dress one individual in the group in a chiton or Greek tunic.
2. List the following information for each garment (see textbook for this information):
    a. Who wore the garment (along the lines of gender, age, social status, etc.)?
    b. When was it worn (Archaic, classical, all periods)?
    c. What materials the garment was made from?
    d. Discuss hairstyle, shoes, and jewelry that would have been worn with it.
3. Prepare a short presentation about your garment, including how it was made and the information listed in #2.

Feedback form for students to fill out during student presentations

Name _____
  I have which garment? _____
  How would you change your garment to create a:

1. Doric Chiton?
2. Exomis?
3. Hellenistic Chiton?
4. Ionic Chiton?
5. Doric Peplos
6. Hellenistic Chiton?

Typical results and reflections on the assignment

The assignment has worked effectively in the course by providing

- an enjoyable exercise;
- an alternative from traditional methods to teach fashion history;
- a break from lectures;
- a memorable reference point to understand similar garments discussed later in the course.

The exercise has helped students meet learning goals by providing students with a/an

- hands-on experience with historic costume;
- three-dimensional example of different types of chitons worn in Ancient Greece
- understanding of a two-dimensional picture in a three-dimensional manner;
- memorable experience with concepts that will be referenced at later points in the course;
- understanding of the influence of technology on apparel (e.g., pins rather than zippers and woven cloth vs. knitted cloth);
- understanding of how culture influences dress (e.g., length of skirt indicated status and gender and women wore the Hellenistic chiton)

In conclusion, this activity assures that students will learn about the construction of the chiton, a critical garment worn in ancient Greek and later in ancient Etrucan and Roman culture. It is an important garment to understand in ancient history of costume because it influences several cultures. The activity also allows students to understand the limited construction technologies available at the time and how ancient cultures were able to differentiate themselves from others. In addition, the activity can be a memorable reference point for students in understanding later time periods where ancient dress influenced fashion, such as the period of the French Revolution (late 1700s to early 1800s). The time period was marked by a shift in focus from the aristocracy to the middle class as democracy prevailed. Women's fashion reflected the Ancient Greek chiton in support of the democratic political system of ancient Greek and Rome. Students will understand not only the construction elements of the eighteenth and nineteenth centuries, but how they reflect garments of Ancient Greece.

Notes

1. K. Johnson, J. Yurchisin, and D. Bean, "The Use of Writing in the Apparel Curriculum: A Preliminary Investigation," *Clothing and Textiles Research Journal* 21 (2003): 41–48.
2. S. Marcketti, J.E. Fitzpatrick, C.N. Keist, and S.J. Kadolph, "University Historic Clothing Museums and Collections: Practices and Strategies," *Clothing and Textiles Research Journal* 29 (2011): 248–262.
3. D. Saiki, J. Nam, and J. Beck, "Student Directed Learning: An Online Exhibition for a Historic Costume Collection," *Journal of Family and Consumer Sciences* 104 (2012): 34–39.
4. J. Banning and H.J. Gam, "Redesigning a Fashion History Course Through Team-based Learning," *Clothing and Textiles Research Journal* 31 (2011): 182–194.
5. P. Ross, D. Tronson, and R. Ritchie, "Modelling Photosynthesis to Increase Conceptual Understanding," *Journal of Biological Education* 40 (2005): 84–88.
6. S. Glynn, "Conceptual Bridges: Using Analogies to Explain Scientific Concepts," *The Science Teacher*, 62 (1995): 25–27.
7. Ross et al., "Modelling Photosynthesis to Increase Conceptual Understanding," 84–88.

8   D. Saiki, "Models Enhance Student Learning in FCS Lecture Courses," *Journal of Family and Consumer Sciences* 99 (2007): 54–58.
9   P.G. Tortora and S.B. Marcketti, *Survey of Historic Costume* (New York: Bloomsbury Publishing, 2015).

Bibliography

Banning, J., and H.J. Gam "Redesigning a Fashion History Course Through Team-based Learning." *Clothing and Textiles Research Journal* 31 (2011): 182–194.

Glynn, S. 'Conceptual Bridges: Using Analogies to Explain Scientific Concepts." *The Science Teacher*, 62 (1995):25–27.

Johnson, K., J. Yurchisin, and D. Bean. "The Use of Writing in the Apparel Curriculum: A Preliminary Investigation." *Clothing and Textiles Research Journal* 21 (2003): 41–48.

Marcketti, S., J.E. Fitzpatrick, C.N. Keist, and S.J. Kadolph. "University Historic Clothing Museums and Collections: Practices and Strategies." *Clothing and Textiles Research Journal* 29 (2011): 248–262.

Ross, P., D. Tronson, and R. Ritchie. "Modelling Photosynthesis to Increase Conceptual Understanding." *Journal of Biological Education* 40 (2005): 84–88.

Saiki, D. "Models Enhance Student Learning in FCS Lecture Courses." *Journal of Family and consumer Sciences* 99 (2007): 54–58.

Saiki, D., J. Nam, and J. Beck. "Student Directed Learning: An Online Exhibition for a Historic Costume Collection." *Journal of Family and Consumer Sciences* 104 (2012): 34–39.

Tortora, P.G., and S.B. Marcketti. *Survey of Historic Costume*. New York: Bloomsbury Publishing, 2015.

PUTTING THE "I" IN ICONOGRAPHY: PROJECTS ON QUEEN ELIZABETH I'S ROYAL IMAGE

*Catherine Howey Stearn,
Eastern Kentucky University*

Contextualization

It is very difficult to find innovative and meaningful ways for students to apply what they have learned in a history class, but it is a challenge worth meeting because students more successfully absorb new information through creative assignments. This assignment is part of a semester-long course on the reign of England's Queen Elizabeth I (r. 1558–1603). I developed this exercise to assess how well students learned an integral part of this course: through lecture, films, portraits, and a variety of secondary and primary historical reading assignments, the class examines the different symbols and messages Elizabeth used to convey a positive, political, and public image of herself, which changed over time to meet the specific needs of her reign.[1] I teach students that to decode the visual messages being expressed in these images they must identify the period's dress. Analyzing Elizabeth's appearance also starts discussions on how gender shaped the exercise of political power for both the queen and her courtiers, and students come to realize that women too participated in Elizabethan politics through the medium of dress.

To learn the fundamentals of Elizabethan dress and accessories, the scholarship of Janet Arnold and Jane Ashelford is essential. Their work identifies the garments being worn and the larger cultural context in which early modern English dress functioned. Many of Janet Arnold's publications analyze Elizabeth's portraits and include seminal primary sources.[2] Jane A. Lawson also focuses on dress in Elizabeth's portraiture and on courtly gift-giving.[3] Lisa M. Klein's article on women's homemade gifts to the queen, as well as my own work, highlights the roles women played helping Elizabeth fashion her image.[4] These readings get incorporated into my lectures and are sometimes assigned as supplementary readings for students.

Ultimately, this project's purpose is to provide students with an opportunity to become active learners. Instead of merely regurgitating the information they heard in class lecture or read for the course in a traditional expository essay, this three-part project requires students to understand on a deeper level the connections between material culture, politics, and the intricacies of the process of identity building at the court of Elizabeth I. In this assignment, they are not simply replicating what they studied, but creating an original piece of scholarship that when successfully completed shows their understanding of how clothing worked within the larger social, economic, and political worlds of sixteenth-century England.

Appropriate courses and course levels for the assignment: This exercise is for an upper-division course since students at that level have already developed some critical reading skills and could fit into a wide range of courses that might analyze how dress is used to create a politicized, public image such as anthropology, art history, history, literature, political science, or sociology.

Appropriate class size: It is best for a class no bigger than fifty students to accommodate the oral presentations without sacrificing too many class periods.

Estimated time required: At least two to three weeks of preparation outside of the classroom are required since students revisit previously assigned texts and read new supplementary material to flesh out their projects and papers. Time is also needed to create the object itself.

Required materials: Computer access is mandatory for the typed paper component, and Internet access is helpful as many of the supplementary readings must be downloaded through the JStor database. If JStor is unavailable, the instructor can place additional readings on library course reserve. No specific art materials are required; a pencil sketch will suffice.

Learning goals

- Identify and explain the various symbols that Elizabeth incorporated into her imagery.
- Understand and explain the different media the queen and her subjects used to create, maintain, and perpetuate Elizabeth's iconography.
- Trace the different stages Elizabeth's iconography underwent throughout her reign.
- Identify the groups of people who helped create Elizabeth's public image.
- Realize that not all images of the queen were positive.

- Understand and explain the role of dress in courtly politics, especially in terms of gift-giving.
- Understand and explain the roles gender, race, and social class played in defining the way monarchs and their subjects participated in fashioning the queen's public image.

Assessment

Each of the three parts receives a separate grade.

- Part I: Image. To receive an "A," several of the themes and symbols identified in class were incorporated. Time and thought clearly went into its making. Taking less-popular options such as creating a negative image or incorporating more arcane symbols/themes, or using a less-obvious format such as creating a literary image in the scene of a play, earn higher marks. "B" projects tend to show a basic mastery of a few of the themes/symbols, but do not exhibit as much creativity or thought. "C" projects tend to focus on only one or two themes/symbols and look hastily put together. "D" or "F" projects did not correctly use any of the themes/symbols or the image too closely resembled an already-existing object.
- Part II: Paper. "A" papers clearly and correctly explain the imagery used, have a backstory accurately reflecting Elizabethan court culture, and meet all the basic requirements laid out in the directions. "B" papers tended to have vaguer backstories and more awkward writing, and do not analyze the symbolism as deeply, but the basic requirements are still met. "C" papers are awkwardly written with little backstory and often missing one of the required sources. "D" and "F" papers are poorly written with few sources used or cited.
- Part III: Oral presentation. Students are evaluated on their eye contact with the audience, their ability to speak about their project and its backstory without heavy reliance on notes, and the length of their talk. Those who speak between five and seven minutes, and are clear, well organized, and engaged with the class, earn an "A"; those who speak between three and five minutes in length and are dependent on notes are in the "B" and "C" ranges; and those who speak for only a minute or two receive "D"s or "F"s.

Guidelines for instructors

Timing is important for this assignment since it is the culmination of all that the students have learned. Students first study the main people, political issues, events, and dates of the reign. Then the class focuses on Elizabeth's iconography by closely examining her portraits and how clothing was used in them. An entire class period is spent on the courtly system of sartorial gift-exchange that provided the queen with garments and jewels that fashioned her image and forged bonds of loyalty between her and her subjects. For that class, I assign primary source excerpts that list the types of gifts Elizabeth received from her subjects on New Year's Day such as J.L. Nevinson's 1975 article that includes the 1584 New Year's gift list, as well as some contextualizing remarks, and makes an excellent in-class assignment to guide the students through the process of translating sixteenth-century English.[5] I also get access for students to a (facsimile) sixteenth-century emblem book to ensure that they utilize symbols from the period instead of modern ones in their projects.[6]

Since it is not a research class, but students need material other than class lecture to aid them, I provide the class with a list of supplementary texts. Finally, I model the essay as an extended museum exhibition catalogue entry and supply students with access to exhibition catalogues that can also assist students in their research.[7]

Cautionary advice for instructors

- Many students worry that they will be judged based upon their artistic (in)abilities. Instructors should reassure students that artistic skills are not the basis for their grade, but it must be evident that effort was put into the project and that it accurately reflects what was taught in class. I also allow students to use anachronistic techniques to construct their image such as creating a collage or using a computer to cut and paste existing images of Elizabeth into a new, original one.

- I hand out this assignment on the first day of class so that students know this is expected of them from the very beginning and have time to get comfortable with the exercise.

- Some students might go overboard on their project. I emphasize that students must do the work themselves, and if they cannot physically create the object itself, they can always create plans for the item such as a sketch. Instructors should stress that they will use their imagination when assessing student work: that is, cardboard can represent gold.

- Some students find the creative writing elements disconcerting but providing general guidelines helps to give them direction. For example, they can fabricate a fictional artist or patron, but one who fits the profile of the type of person associated with the Elizabethan court. Students can also use actual historical figures, but pretend that they commissioned a fictional gift.

- A danger exists that all of the student's efforts goes into the production of the image at the expense of creating a solid backstory. Students usually do well in identifying and explaining Elizabeth's iconography but have very vague explanations as to who commissioned the piece and why.

Copy of the assignment

Name:
Due Date:

Part I: Image/object (50 points)

This assignment has three parts. The first part requires you to go back in time to the court of Elizabeth I (1558–1603) or James I (1603–1625), where you are an artist who has just been commissioned to paint a portrait or miniature, make an engraving, carve a statue, or in some way create an image of Queen Elizabeth I. Or you must create something (a gift) that Elizabeth I can use to create her image. I will allow for some artistic anachronism in the way you create your image (i.e., collage, graphic design, etc.), but double-check your method with me first. You will not be judged on your artistic ability, but rather on how you implement what you have learned about the symbolism used in Elizabeth's portraits, use of color, whether Elizabeth is portrayed alone or with other figures, etc. Although you can use past images as inspiration, you must create an original image. Keep in mind that images of Elizabeth were used to praise her, denounce her, or suggest how she should shape her public image and political policies.

Part II: Written essay (100 points)

After creating your image, you must fast-forward to the present day; you are no longer an artist, but a historian. Your local museum has just purchased "your" portrait or object and ask that you write a catalogue entry describing and analyzing this artifact. In this essay, you must tell the reader who commissioned the portrait or object, the title of the work, and the date of the work. The essay should describe the image and its context and discuss what symbolism was used in it and why. It is also important to address who commissioned the portrait and for what purpose. (Create a backstory.) Depending upon how you decide to construct the story behind the image, you may need *additional* secondary or primary sources than the ones assigned. There will be a folder on the Blackboard Readings Tab that will direct you to approved articles and PDF files of some primary sources that can help you with your project. *I will provide examples of what museum catalogue entries/ essays look like so that you have a format to follow on my Blackboard link.*

Paper requirements

- You *must* use a minimum of two secondary sources and two primary sources (one of which must be textual). All sources must meet my approval. Class lecture can also be used in addition to, *but not in place of*, the two secondary sources required for the paper!

- The paper *must* be a minimum of three full pages and no longer than a few lines on a sixth page.
- Font, New Times Roman; font size, twelve; double spaced; one-inch margin all around; and stapled.
- The paper must have a bibliography and use footnotes or endnotes following *The Chicago Manual of Style*.

Part III: Paper presentation (50 points)

The last part of the assignment requires that in a five- to seven-minute presentation you discuss your image with the class. You may use notecards, but do not read from your paper.

Typical results and reflections on the assignment

- Most students produce a positive image of Elizabeth I that incorporates dress and jewelry. Fewer students create an article of dress but often create something extraordinary. One student sewed a miniature outfit with sleeves, bodice, petticoat, and ruff. Other students created handkerchiefs that corresponded with the materials, such as metallic lace, listed in some of the New Year's gift rolls they had read. Another handkerchief included a hand-embroidered copy of Elizabeth's coronation portrait. Necklaces, pendants, gloves, tapestries, and jewelry boxes have been turned in as well as collages that incorporate preexisting images of the queen, but refashioned to create a unique image of their own.
- Overall, almost all my students enjoy this assignment. Even the ones who were initially trepidatious about creating an image of their own often find themselves getting into constructing their project and its backstory.
- The papers benefit students by having them master a broad range of critical skills as they blend creative writing with scholarly analysis. However, my students were the ones who initiated expanding the original project parameters when they asked if they could produce garments or jewelry that the queen would have used to create her persona instead of just making an image. As is so often the case with teaching, it was the students who taught me the true value of this exercise and made my assignment such a success.

Notes

1. Two key studies include Roy Strong's work on Elizabeth's image, *The Cult of Elizabeth: Elizabethan Portraiture and Pageantry* (London: Pimlico, 1999) and *Gloriana: The Portraits of Queen Elizabeth I* (London: Thames and Hudson, 1987; reprinted Pimlico, 2003).

2. Janet Arnold's most useful publications are, "The 'Coronation' Portrait of Elizabeth I," *The Burlington Magazine* 120 (1978): 727–741, *Queen Elizabeth's Wardrobe Unlock'd* (Leeds, UK: Maney & Son, Ltd., 1988), which includes a complete transcription of the inventory made of Elizabeth's clothes and jewels upon her death, and *"Lost from Her Majesties Back" Items of clothing and jewels lost or given away by Queen Elizabeth I between 1561 and 1585 entered in one of her day books kept for the records of the Wardrobe of the Robes*, Costume Society Extra Series No. 7 (Wisbech, Cambridgeshire: Daedalus Press, 1980). Jane Ashelford's two most important contributions are *A Visual History of Costume: The Sixteenth Century* (London: B.T. Batsford, Ltd., 1983; reprinted 1993) and *Dress in the Age of Elizabeth* (London: B.T. Batsford, Ltd., 1988). Maria Hayward also works on Tudor dress and Henrician court culture in "Fashion, Finance, Foreign Politics and the Wardrobe of Henry VIII," in *Clothing Culture, 1350–1650*, ed. Catherine Richardson (Burlington, VT: Ashgate, 2004), 165–178, "Gift-Giving at the Court of Henry VIII: The 1539 New Year's Gift Roll in Context," *The Antiquaries Journal* 85 (2005): 125–175, and *Rich Apparel: Clothing and the Law in Henry VIII's England* (Burlington, VT: Ashgate, 2009). Additional helpful secondary scholarship includes Susan Vincent, *Dressing the Elite: Clothes in Early Modern Europe* (New York: Berg, 2003) and Ann Rosalind Jones and Peter Stallybrass, *Renaissance Clothing and the Material of Memory* (New York: Cambridge University Press, 2000).

3. Jane A. Lawson, "Rainbow for a Reign: The Colors of a Queen's Wardrobe," *Costume* 41 (2007): 26–44, and her book *The Elizabethan New Year's Gift Exchanges 1559–1603*, Records of Social and Economic History New Series 51 (Oxford: Oxford University Press for The British Academy, 2013), that includes transcriptions of all the extant Elizabethan New Year's Gift Rolls, essential primary sources for this assignment.

4. Lisa M. Klein, "Your Humble Handmaid: Elizabethan Gifts of Needlework," *Renaissance Quarterly* 50, no. 2 (1997): 459–493. My own work includes, Catherine L. Howey, "Dressing A Virgin Queen: Court Women, Dress and Fashioning the Image of England's Queen Elizabeth I," *Early Modern Women: An Interdisciplinary Journal* 4 (2009): 201–208 and "Fashioning Monarchy: Dress, Gender and Power at the Court of Elizabeth I," in *The Rule of Women in Early Modern Europe, 1400–1700*, ed. Anne J. Cruz and Mihoko Suzuki (Champaign, IL: University of Illinois Press, 2009), 142–156 and (under my married name) Catherine Howey Stearn, "Critique or Compliment?: Lady Mary Sidney's 1573 New Year's Gift to Queen Elizabeth I," *The Sidney Journal* 30, no. 2 (2012): 109–127.

5. See bibliography.

6. If your library has access to the catalogue of Early English Books Online (EEBO), students can directly access Geoffrey Whitney's 1586 *A Choice of Emblemes and other devices*. I often go over in class how to use emblem books.

7. See Karen Hearn, ed., *Dynasties: Painting in Tudor and Jacobean England 1530–1630* (London: Tate Gallery, 1995) and Susan Doran, ed., *Elizabeth: The Exhibition at the National Maritime Museum* (London: Chatto & Windus in association with the National Maritime Museum, London, 2003). The bibliography includes both sources.

Bibliography

Auerbach, Erna. "Portraits of Elizabeth I." *The Burlington Magazine* 95, no. 603 (1953): 196–205.

Bellsey, Andrew, and Catherine Bellsey. "Icons of Divinity: Portraits of Elizabeth I." In *Renaissance Bodies: The Human Figure in English Culture c.1540–1660*, edited by Lucy Gent and Nigel Llewellyn, 31–58. London: Reaktion Books, 1995.

Content, Rob. "Fair Is Fowle: Interpreting Anti-Elizabethan Composite Portraiture." In *Dissing Elizabeth: Negative Representations of Gloriana*, edited by Julia M. Walker, 229–251. Durham, NC: Duke University Press, 1998.

Doran, Susan, ed. *Elizabeth: The Exhibition at the National Maritime Museum*. London: Chatto & Windus in association with the National Maritime Museum, London, 2003.

Goldring, Elizabeth. "Portraits of Queen Elizabeth I and the Earl of Leicester for Kenilworth Castle." *The Burlington Magazine* 147, no. 1231 (2005): 654–660.

Haigh, Christopher. *Elizabeth I*. 2nd ed. New York: Longman Press, 1998.

Hearn, Karen, ed. *Dynasties: Painting in Tudor and Jacobean England 1530–1630*. London: Tate Gallery, 1995.

King, John N. "Queen Elizabeth I: Representations of the Virgin Queen." *Renaissance Quarterly* 43, no. 1 (1990): 30–74.

Levin, Carole. *"The Heart and Stomach of a King": Elizabeth I and the Politics of Sex and Power*. Philadelphia, University of Pennsylvania Press, 1994.

McManus, Caroline. "Reading the Margins: Female Courtiers in the Portraits of Elizabeth I." *ELR* 32, no. 2 (2002): 189–213.

Montrose, Louis A. "Idols of the Queen: Policy, Gender and the Picturing of Elizabeth I." *Representations* no. 68 (1999): 108–161.

Nevinson, J.L. "New Year's Gifts to Queen Elizabeth I, 1584." *Costume* 9 (1975): 27–31.

Stump, Donald, and Susan Felch, eds. *Elizabeth I and Her Age*. A Norton Critical Edition. New York: W.W. Norton & Company, 2009.

30
ANALYZING THE SOCIAL FUNCTIONS OF DRESS IN DIFFERENT HISTORICAL ERAS

*Amber M. Chatelain,
Eastern Kentucky University*

Contextualization

Fashion studies is an interdisciplinary field of research with ties to economics, politics, psychology, culture, art, sociology, technology, and more. While clothing is not always necessary for survival, most cultures adorn some semblance of costume. Historically, clothing has been manipulated to denote status; and through silhouette, cut, and drape, clothing serves as a means to decorate the body (Tortora and Marcketti, 2015). Fashion and clothing reflect and communicate a society's cultural beliefs and standards (Eicher and Evenson, 2014), and by studying the origins and evolution of fashion and appearance, we are able to chronicle a changing society (Johnson, Tortore, and Eicher, 2003).

In traditional pedagogies for teaching fashion history, an instructional methodology of lecture-based content has passively transmitted information to students (Cumming, 2004). However, Sara Marcketti's (2011) research on fashion history instruction emphasized active learning strategies, including student-focused and student-led projects, which yield higher levels of student satisfaction in and enthusiasm about fashion history classes.

Cooperative-based and collaborative learning strategies and their effectiveness have been well documented in pedagogical literature (Farr et al., 2005; Gam and Banning, 2011). Students who engage in these kinds of learning activities increase their communication skills and problem-solving abilities (Carpenter and Fairhurst, 2005), and attain a deeper understanding of course materials (Farr et al., 2005). The goal of this assignment is for students to work in a team-based environment for the purpose of conducting investigative research to determine the influencers of fashion changes over time.

Appropriate courses and course levels for the assignment: As this assignment addresses the influences of society, politics, culture, economics, technology, gender, and art on fashion, it is appropriate for a variety of introductory and upper-level courses. Suggested courses would include art history, history, sociology, and women, gender, and sexuality studies. For those utilizing this assignment for upper-division courses, it is suggested the instructor modify the assignment to require a more thoughtful analysis and discussion of each section by adding additional process questions. For example, instructors of an upper-level art history course may expand the *Sources of Evidence for Costume* section of this assignment, requiring students to research specific artists of their chosen period or era, and provide an analysis on how that artist's work tells the story of dress.

Appropriate class size: This assignment could be used in both small or large class sizes, and should be completed in a group setting, ideally with four to five students per group.

Estimated time required: This assignment should take a minimum of two weeks to complete outside of class. It is also recommended that students be allowed the opportunity to work on the assignment in class for duration of at least one hour in one block of time in one class meeting. Allowing students in-class time to work on their group presentation "provides opportunities for greater teacher-to-student mentoring, peer-to-peer collaboration and cross-disciplinary engagement" (Roehl, Reddy, and Shannon, 2013: 44).

Required materials: Students will need access to a computer, the Internet, their campus library, and PowerPoint software.

Learning goals

- Understand the social construction of gender and its influence on clothing design in the United States and Europe.
- Examine the relationship between politics, social issues such as stratification, classism, racism, or gender differences, the economy, culture, and art to costume history.
- Provide a critical analysis of the evolution of men's and women's clothing design through US and European history.
- To work as an individual and as a member of a team toward a shared, common goal and to develop effective communication and leadership skills.

Assessment

The method by which this assignment is evaluated will be dependent upon the particular sections of the assignment the instructor chooses to use. As indicated in the following text, this assignment can be tailored and adjusted depending on the course and materials covered. However, assessment methods should have a similar approach, evaluating on organization of materials, content and analysis, and the oral presentation.

Student materials should be organized, ensuring the presentation is appropriate for its audience, and that information is presented in a logical order. References must be cited and/or clearly documented in the presentation.

The written content should clearly analyze the social functions of dress in different historical eras and thoroughly explain each assigned section in detail. The presentation should contain accurate information and fully address and answer each question assigned.

Students should additionally be assessed on their oral presentation skills. Speakers should maintain good eye contact with their audience and use a clear, audible voice. Excellent language skills and pronunciation should be used. The visual aids (PowerPoint) should be well prepared, informative, effective, and not distracting. Information should be well communicated to the audience.

Guidelines for instructors

This assignment can be tailored and adjusted dependent upon the course and materials covered. For example, if used in a women, gender, and sexuality studies course, an emphasis could be placed on issues of gender differences of dress, or sexuality and costume. If used in a history course, emphasis could be placed on major historical events and their impact on clothing during the specific historical era being considered.

The instructor will decide which time period or era students should focus on for this assignment, ensuring the time period or era coincides with the course materials. For example, the assignment could focus on the 1930s, Ancient Greece and Rome, etc. While a basic understanding of US and European fashion history is helpful for the completion of this assignment, it is not necessary. Through research and exploration of key websites and books (typically available through a university's library), students will easily learn how to draw concepts from history to costume.

The assignment begins with instructor-led discussions about the various course topics that influence costume and design: climate, geography, historical events, politics, art, technology, social conditions, etc. (Tortora and Eubank, 2015). This discussion provides students with a framework of the assignment and encourages them to consider and discuss possible factors that influence dress and clothing choices.

This assignment can be administered and used in several ways. I encourage instructors to adjust the assignment as necessary. This assignment could be a midterm or final course project, completed individually or in a group, or presented weekly to coincide with course lessons. Traditionally, I have had students present weekly to (1) serve as a fun introduction to our course topic for the day they present, (2) break up the monotony of exclusively faculty-led instruction, and (3) ensure that I do not have several course days devoted only to student presentations.

The time period, era, and/or region that students research and present should correlate with the instructor's course instruction and topics. Here is a sample of time periods, eras, and regions I have successfully used in the past:

- Ancient Egypt: 2620–1087 BC
- Crete and Greece: 2900–300 BC
- The Byzantine Period: 330–1453
- The Late Middle Ages: 1300–1500
- The Eighteenth Century: 1700–1800
- The Crinoline Period: 1850–1869
- The Edwardian Period: 1900–1920
- The Twenties: 1920–1930
- The Thirties: 1930–1940
- The Sixties: 1960–1970

Instructors may either assign students to groups and time periods or eras or let students choose their own groups and time periods or eras. I like to let them choose whom they want to work with, and the period or era they find most interesting.

Cautionary advice for instructors

- This assignment requires students to investigate, research, and draw conclusions about one particular assigned time period or era. Therefore, students only have extended in-depth knowledge of one time period, resulting in a potentially unbalanced understanding of fashion history. However, they will ideally learn more about different periods and eras from the class overall and from classmates' presentations.

Copy of the assignment

Analyzing the social functions of dress in different historical eras

Objective: While clothing is not always necessary for survival, most cultures adorn some semblance of costume. Historically, clothing has been manipulated to denote status; and through silhouette, cut, and drape, clothing serves as a means to decorate the body (Tortora and Marcketti, 2015).

Costume can be influenced by a number of variables: economics, politics, psychology, culture, art, sociology, technology, and more. In this assignment, you will be tasked to research and discover more about the influencers of dress over time.

Materials: You will need access to a computer, the Internet, our campus library, and PowerPoint software.

Due date: TBD

ANALYZING THE SOCIAL FUNCTIONS OF DRESS IN DIFFERENT HISTORICAL ERAS

Points Possible: 100

Instructions: In teams of four to five, create a PowerPoint presentation relating to your assigned time period to present to the class. You are encouraged to include visuals, videos, and other enhancements (handouts, in-class activities for your classmates to engage in, etc.) for your presentation. You should be informative about your topic, but also have fun! Be engaging! Really consider the dynamics of your topic and think of how to effectively relate it to your peers.

Your PowerPoint and discussion should take a total of fifteen minutes to complete with five minutes for questions (twenty minutes per group total), so plan your materials and practice your presentation accordingly.

Identify the following in your presentation:

1. **Assigned time period/years**
   a. Example: The 1960s, the Early Middle Ages, and the Victorian Era
2. **Chronology/major historical events**
   a. What were the major historical events that occurred during your time period in your region? Consider economic, political, technological, psychological, or artistic events of the time. Explain in detail.
      i. Example: The November 22, 1963, assassination of President John F. Kennedy Jr. changed the United States politically and culturally, television became the primary news source over newspapers, conspiracy theories were popularized, citizens distrusted the Federal Government, and the United States escalated its involvement in Vietnam (Giokaris, 2013).

3. **Social functions of dress: Gender differences of dress**
   a. What were the primary differences between the dresses of men and women during this time period? Describe the types of behaviors generally considered appropriate and acceptable for men and women based on the societal norms during your time period/era. Were some styles considered traditionally masculine or feminine? If so, which ones? Explain.
      i. Example: In Ancient Rome, only men could be considered citizens of society, and familial life was patriarchal. Women cared for the children and the household. A traditionally masculine costume, only men were allowed to wear the garment known as the *toga*, which women were forbidden to wear (Tortora and Marcketti, 2015).

4. **Social functions of dress: Designation of status**
   a. What role did dress play in designating the class and economic status of the wearer? Consider, for example, how uniforms, religious costume, or clothing differentiated between social classes. Why was this important?
      i. Example: Upper-class ancient Egyptians wore costumes constructed of luxury fabrics with intricately decorated jewelry and belts. This costume

differentiated them from the middle- and lower-class Egyptians, who wore modest jewelry with simplistic loincloths for men and loosely fitted tunics for women (Tortora and Marcketti, 2015).

5. **Social functions of dress: Cross-cultural influences**
    a. What styles of dress from your time period have cross-cultural and global influences? What are they? Where did they originate? If applicable, what was the symbolic meaning of the original style or garment, and how was it reinterpreted for wearers during your time period?
        i. Example: In 1966, the traditional Indian jacket, the Nehru jacket, was a short-lived style for American men. Popularized by fashion designer Pierre Cardin after a trip to India, the jacket featured a standing collar (Tortora and Marcketti, 2015) and intricate designs that influenced the wearing of beaded necklaces by young men in the later 1960s (Lutz, 2015).

6. **Social functions of dress: Sexuality and costume**
    a. How did clothing enhance sexual attractiveness of the wearer, or minimize the idea of sexuality through coverage and/or restriction? (Hint: research costume historian James Laver's theory of shifting erogenous zones.)
        i. Example: In the 1930s, the emphasis of women's evening and day dresses shifted from the legs to the back. For the first time, garments were meant to be seen from the back, featuring bared backs and waists, and emphasized the shape of the buttocks (Laver, 1995).

7. **Popular clothing styles for men and women**
    a. What were some of the primary popular clothing styles for men and women during your time period? What were the popular silhouettes, fabrications, colors, etc.?

8. **Sources of evidence for costume**
    a. How do we know what people wore during your time period? What sorts of artifacts are left behind to tell the story of dress?
        i. Example: Historic artifacts, paintings, illustrations, photographs, magazines, etc.

A few useful resources to consult

Websites

- http://www.fashion-era.com/index.htm
- http://www.costumes.org/
- http://www.costumepage.org/

Books

- DK (2012), *Fashion: The Definitive history of costume and style*, London, England: DK.
- Laver, J. (1995), *Costume & Fashion*, New York, NY: Thames and Hudson Inc.

Typical results and reflections on the assignment

- This assignment has received positive feedback over the years. Students are required to analyze and critically evaluate ideas, concepts, and historical events to draw conclusions and inferences about their impact on costume choice. In doing so, they develop a broader understanding of and appreciation for the elements that shape different societies and human expression.
- While there is the occasional and inevitable student grumble about having to work as a team, students learn cooperation, leadership, and teamwork skills through undertaking this collaborative project.
- Through the examination of historical events and the social functions of dress, students gain an appreciation and understanding how factors such as gender, class, race, sexuality, and socioeconomic status shape and influence our dress. By understanding how costume is influenced historically, it helps students to understand how our dress is shaped by these factors today.

Bibliography

Carpenter, Jason, and Ann Fairhurst. "Delivering Quality and Value in the Classroom: The Use of Problem-based Learning in Retail Merchandising Courses." *Clothing and Textiles Research Journal* 23, no. 4 (2005): 257–265.

Cumming, Valerie. *Understanding Fashion History*. New York, NY: Costume and Fashion Press, 2004.

Eicher, Joanne, and Sandra Evenson. *The Visible Self: Global Perspectives on Dress, Culture, and Society*. 4th edn. New York, NY: Bloomsbury, 2014.

Farr, Cheryl, Shiiretta Ownbey, Donna Brandon, Huantian Cao, and Cathy Starr. "Multimedia and Problem-based Instruction in Textiles Laboratory." *Clothing and Textiles Research Journal* 23, no. 4 (2005): 360–367.

Gam, Hae, and Jennifer Banning. "Addressing Sustainable Apparel Design Challenges with Problem-based Learning." *Clothing and Textiles Research Journal* 29, no. 3 (2011): 202–215.

Giokaris, J. "5 ways JFK's assignation changed America forever," Mic, 22 November 2013. Available online: http://mic.com/articles/74069/5-ways-jfk-s-assassination-changed-america-forever#.WWkmw8qWU.

Johnson, Kim, Susan Tortore, and Joanne Eicher. *Fashion Foundations: Early Writings on Fashion and Dress*. Oxford: Berg, 2003.

Laver, J. *Costume & Fashion*. New York, NY: Thames and Hudson Inc., 1995.
Lutz, H. "Nehru jacket," Love to Know, 2015. Available online: http://fashion-history.lovetoknow.com/clothing-types-styles/nehru-jacket.
Marcketti, Sara. "Effective Learning Strategies in the History of Dress." *The History Teacher* 44, no. 4 (2011): 547–568.
Roehl, Amy, Shweta Reddy, and Gayla Shannon. "The Flipped Classroom: An Opportunity to Engage Millennial Students Through Active Learning Strategies." *Journal of Family and Consumer Sciences* 105, no. 2 (2013): 44–49.
Tortora, Phyliss, and Sara Marcketti. *Survey of Historic Costume*. 6th edn. New York, NY: Bloomsbury, 2015.

31
COSTUME IN HISTORICAL CONTEXT

Catherine Bradley, McGill University

Contextualization

Costumes do not exist in a vacuum; they respond to social and political factors specific to the era in which they were created. They are inextricably linked to the art and architecture of their day as they are to the current political and moral beliefs. A micro miniskirt comments on the sexual mores of the 1960s as succinctly as any treatise on sexual liberation. We, along with *Webster's Dictionary*, use the term "costume" to mean a style of clothing, ornaments, and hair used especially during a certain period, in a certain region, or by a certain class or group.

The structure of this exercise will alternate between one class where the instructor presents costume information and the following class where a designated group of students will respond with an oral presentation to contextualize the styles of the era. The instructor will present the costume history of each specific era through images, example pieces, and embodied learning (which means volunteers get to try on corsets, walk in hoop skirts, and dance the Charleston in a fringed flapper dress with an accompanying feather boa in order to understand how the physicality of costumes effect movement). The instructor's main lecture tool is a PowerPoint presentation with fashion images drawn directly from each period.

In an effort toward inclusion, images in each era reflect not only the stereotypical archetypes, but also reflect diversity in race, gender, sexual orientation, and class. Fashion images tell only part of the story: the full narrative is achieved by inclusion and celebrating difference. This can take the form of acknowledging the contributions of traditionally overlooked minority figures, including images of all strata of society, or charting the path of gender equality and civil rights during the instructor's lectures.

In the next class, students will present their oral projects, which respond to the specific era. Each student in the presentation group will handle one specific topic relating to the era. Topics for presentations include art, music and dance, science and technology, popular culture, and historical context. Additional optional topics include architecture, furniture design, politics, and advertising.

By listening to their fellow students' presentations, the class as a whole will be able to answer questions such as the following: What is the common aesthetic between furniture and clothing design of the Victorian era? How does the music of the 1920s effect dance and, in turn, clothing styles? How do the political and economic realities of the Great Depression impact fabric usage during the 1930s? Historical overview of costumes will be enhanced by an inquisitive look at the link between clothing and the culture that created it. The goal is to see the bigger picture of the interrelated nature of different disciplines, and how each impacts the system as a whole. Although this exercise specifically relates to fashion, it is also a way of seeing and understanding larger cultural, social, historical, and political contexts.

A final note to underpin the exercise comes from a quote by James Laver, in his autobiography: "After studying the What and When, I began to wonder about the How and Why."[1] This exercise provides the wider context in which the students uncover the "How and Why" through their own research, in order to contextualize the instructor's lecture about the "What and When" of changing clothing styles.

Appropriate courses and course levels for the assignment: This assignment is adaptable to all level of survey courses in history of fashion, history of costume, and museum studies. The exercise could also be assigned in a history, sociology, or cultural studies course, and would be useful for studies of particular periods, for instance in a costume design course or in a practical setting such as preparatory costume research for a film or a theater production.

Appropriate class size: This exercise is adaptable for classes of between five and fifty students, with a presentation group of five students per time period. Suitable for weekly presentation groups within a semester-long course or for a single project with one presentation group of five students.

Estimated time required: Two classes, one for the instructor to present and one for the group of five students to present. It is possible to split a three-hour class period between instructor and presentation group, or to cover the material over two class periods of approximately an hour and a half each. Subject material is adaptable; simply divide the amount of time available equally between the number of student presenters, leaving ample time for questions at the end. I make the students themselves responsible for staying within the allotted time, and give up the question period if presentations run long. Within each presentation, the students must play a sampling of influential music of the era, and teach the class a period specific dance, which everyone participates in. One of the highlights in a group presentation on the 1950s occurred when a student played her guitar and had everyone clap in syncopated rhythm while dancing to Elvis Presley's rendition of *Hound Dog*. The group learns valuable skills in timing a presentation with such eclectic, but also highly memorable, offerings.

Required materials

- Data projector and screen.
- Internet connection is useful but not essential.

Learning goals

- Fashion does not exist in a vacuum. Be able to identify the different social, cultural, and political forces that cause it to change.
- Gain awareness of the interrelated nature of different disciplines, and how each impacts the system as a whole.
- Understand the zeitgeist of a particular time period, as well as how the zeitgeist changes over time.
- Understand and be able to anticipate the cyclical nature of fashion.
- Be able to identify and contextualize the changing ideals of beauty and body image. Gain understanding of the constantly shifting nature of the idealized figure type, and translate that into a more accepting notion of body positivity.
- The dance lesson provides a chance to incorporate a physical and auditory reinforcement of the material, and it gives a fun break from listening and note-taking.

Assessment

The students' oral presentations are graded using the following rubric, which is shared with the students in advance. The completed rubric gives the students feedback on their competencies and adds fairness to the grading process by diminishing instructor bias and the appearance of subjectivity. It also supplies a platform for instructors and teaching assistants to give uniform feedback. Most importantly, a well-defined rubric reflects the assignment goals and provides a quick and easy way for the instructor to give feedback that is both objective and specific.

Guidelines for instructors

I typically use this exercise as the framework for a twelve-week class on history of costume, and have time for ten fashion periods. It can work with anything from the ancient civilizations to more contemporary periods. It can also work as a freestanding module with the goal of understanding a particular period. It is useful for instructors to prepare sign-up sheets for each era, including presentation date and topics. (Example is provided in the "Copy of assignment" section.)

Discussion questions

- While researching the presentation topics, which factors are most revealing about the period in question? For instance:

Rubric for oral group presentations: Contextualizing costumes

Criteria	Excellent 5 points	Very Good 4 points	Good 3 points	Fair 2 points	Poor 0 to 1 point
Content	All content highly relevant to the topic. Excellent visual support of subject matter.	Most content was highly relevant to the topic. Images well chosen and supportive of text.	Most content was good. Images well selected, although one or more contained attribution errors.	Some content lacked relevance to the topic, and/or contained inaccuracies.	Content not directly relevant to the topic, and/or contained factual errors.
Quality of research	Used a wide variety of peer-reviewed sources from established researchers.	Used mainly peer-reviewed sources with a few secondary or unreliable Internet sources.	Used a mix of peer-reviewed sources and other secondary or unreliable Internet sources.	Used mainly nonpeer-reviewed sources found through Internet search engines.	Research contained significant attribution errors, and lacked academic rigor.
Clarity	Information conveyed with a high degree of clarity and engagement.	Very good clarity of information.	Most information conveyed with clarity.	Occasional difficulty with clearly conveying information.	The presentation lacked clarity. Audience disengagement evident.
Group score	All assignment criteria met with excellence.	The group functioned well and executed a very good presentation.	Some minor difficulties, but overall good work as a group.	The group missed one or more assignment criteria.	The group missed multiple important assignment criteria.

Overall Score	Excellent 18 or more	Very Good 15 to 17	Good 11 to 14	Fair 7 to 10	Poor 0 to 6

- Which scientific discoveries had the greatest impact on people's lives, hopes, and aspirations?
- What political factors have the most profound influence on the era?
- Which artistic styles are the most innovative in each period? How do these artistic styles manifest themselves in design of architecture, furniture, and other aspects of material culture?
- What type of entertainment is popular, and why? Is it used as an escape from reality, or a celebration of prosperity?
- What are the most popular types of music, and how do they translate into dance styles? What does the dance style say about modesty and changing societal values?

Students should use the above-mentioned questions to direct choices about what to include in their oral presentations, and are encouraged to remember that they are creating a snapshot of a specific time, and to use the elements of their composition wisely.

General questions for students to consider in preparing their own presentations and listening to their classmates' presentations:

- Is there a difference between cultural appropriation and global fashion influences?
- How is fashion used to control conformity?
- How can fashion be used to disrupt power structures?
- When is fashion used as a political statement?
- How can fashion be used to disrupt or challenge stereotypes?

Cautionary advice for instructors

- Decide in advance whether to allow recreations of previous periods rather than primary or secondary source material (i.e., students will often want to use the latest period film or television show as part of their presentations, and instructors will need to decide whether or not this is acceptable). I do not allow this, unless students have asked specific permission to do so in advance, and there is a solid justification for doing so.
  - Decide in advance how strict to be about use of YouTube and other easily accessible Internet sources. I do allow this for primary sources, but always with the disclaimer that the student must check the reliability of the source.
  - I suggest minimizing the pitfalls of group presentations by making each student responsible for their own portion of the presentation (and the greatest proportion of the marks awarded for their individual portion). A nominal amount of marks goes to the group portion, in order to keep the group motivated to hand in a cohesive project as one submission.

- Set a tone of acceptance within the classroom: given the opportunity, students will share personal insights about clothing, body image, peer pressure, discrimination, and gender identification, and will appreciate the notion of safe space.

Copy of the assignment

Oral group presentations: Contextualizing costumes

This is one of the most important assignments of the semester, since the quality of the oral presentations have major impact on the learning experience for the entire class.

The class will divide evenly into five groups of five students each. Each group will select one historical time period from the list.

Presentations:
- Victorian I: 1850–1869
- Victorian II: 1869–1899 (The Bustle)
- Edwardian 1900–1910
- 1911–1919 (The "Teen Years")
- 1920s

Topics: Each student in the presentation group will cover a specific topic or topics. Each student will be graded primarily on his or her own topic(s). Topics that *must* be covered in the presentations are as follows:

- Art: What are the most influential art movements of the era? How do art and clothing of a particular era echo or influence each other?
- Events of major historical impact: What important historical figures or actions influenced the design style of their times?
- Music and dance: How do they relate to clothing and the capacity for movement?
- Advancements in science and technology: How does new technology effect clothing production? What are the most significant scientific discoveries of the era?
- Popular culture: What groups influenced the style of an era, and how? Who/what were the iconic images of the era, and how did they influence fashion?

Optional topics: The topics vary in priority depending on the particular period, and *may* be covered at the discretion of the group:

- Architecture: How does architectural style of an era reflect clothing or vice versa?
- Color palette and fabrics: popular fabric motifs, treatments, and color combinations. Briefly discuss commonly used fabrics of the era.

- Furniture design: How are clothing trends reflected in furniture design? What political influences fostered or hindered clothing? What was their impact?
- Miscellaneous: students may add a topic of particular relevance to the period in question.

Format: There are four components to the project

1. Oral presentation: Fifty to seventy minutes total (it is imperative that each member of the group have the opportunity to complete their presentation within the allotted time)
2. PowerPoint: Video and audio links are to be imbedded, and images credited and handed in to instructor on a memory key at the beginning of their class presentation day.

    Images *must* be produced in the period that they depict. Latter-day recreations (such as a modern film or image depicting the Victorian period) are not permitted without express permission of the instructor.
3. Music/dance: Demonstrate and/or show footage of a dance particular to the period, accompanied by music of the era. Comment on movement as influenced by clothing. Lead the class in the dance.
4. Electronic summary: Sample images and representative text submitted by each team as a *single* document. The electronic summary is to be e-mailed to the instructor on the presentation day.

Mark value: Twenty marks total
Individual portion of the grade: Fifteen marks

Individual students are graded separately on their own portion of the presentation. The grade is based on relevance and cohesion of content, quality of research, images, clarity, and insight.

Each student compiles their own portion of the summary document, and the group submits *one* group report electronically.

Group portion of the grade: Five marks

The group is marked on the quality of the PowerPoint presentation, demonstrations, and cohesion of the overall presentation. Normally, the group mark will be the same for each individual in the group. Both the group and the individual will be penalized if an individual portion is missing from the electronic submission. Include each student's typed notes that accompany their visuals. The document must represent the entire group's work, with individual portions clearly identified.

Sample sign-up sheet

Oral group presentations: Victorian I: 1850–1869

Topics: Each student in the presentation group will cover a specific topic or topics. Each student will be graded primarily on his or her own topic(s).

Topics that *must* be covered are as follows:

Events of major historical impact:
___

Art:
___

Music and dance:
___

Advancements in science and technology:
___

Popular culture:
___

Optional topics: These vary in priority depending on the particular period, and *may* be covered at the discretion of the group:

Architecture:
___

Political influences:
___

Color palette and fabrics:
___

Furniture design:
___

Miscellaneous:
___

Typical results and reflections on the assignment

- Greater understanding of, and respect for, the interconnections between disciplines, for example, breakthroughs in science and technology (such as the 1960s space race) have profound impact on seemingly disconnected spheres like architecture, art, and fashion.

- Deeper understanding of fashion phenomena, as they are rooted in a larger contextual social, political, cultural, and historical picture, rather than individual, seemingly unconnected facts.
- Better retention of information, based on facilitating different learning styles.
  - Visual learners: image-heavy PowerPoint presentations, passing around actual examples of clothing or other period items, images available for study.
  - Auditory learners: oral presentations, period music, class discussion.
  - Experiential learners: volunteers trying on actual costumes and walking around the classroom so that everyone can experience garments like hoop skirts by proxy and by observation.
  - Kinesthetic, embodied learning: getting up and dancing, testing period-specific garments like hobble garters in a timed race (with spotters for safety).
  - Engaging the senses of smell and taste: at times, the presentation groups bring in examples of period-specific foods (such as cucumber sandwiches for the Victorian era).
- Increased ability to accurately identify period clothing, settings, and artistic movements, and to place them within a meaningful cultural context.
- As an instructor, I strive to foster greater acceptance of different body shapes and sizes coupled with the awareness that "ideal body shapes" change over time, and therefore lose their power as absolute standards by which to judge oneself. This learning outcome is primarily derived from the accompanying lecture rather than the student project. It seems to resonate strongly with particular students, as evidenced by student feedback.

Note

1 James Laver, *Museum Piece: Or, The Education of an Iconographer* (Boston: Houghton Mifflin, 1963), 250.

Bibliography

Barnard, Malcolm. *Fashion Theory: An Introduction*. New York: Routledge, 2014.
Barnard, Malcolm, ed. *Fashion Theory: A Reader*. London: Routledge, 2007.
Brown, Susan. *Fashion: The Definitive History of Costume and Style*. New York: DK Publishing, 2012.
Harwood, Buie, Bridget May, and Curt Sherman. *Architecture and Interior Design: An Integrated History to the Present*. Upper Saddle River, NJ: Pearson Prentice Hall, 2012.
Kaiser, Susan B. *Fashion and Cultural Studies*. London: Bloomsbury, 2012.
Steele, Valerie. *Fifty Years of Fashion: New Look to Now*. New Haven: Yale University Press, 2000.
Tortora, Phyllis G., and Sara B. Marcketti. *Survey of Historic Costume*. New York: Fairchild Books, 2015.

32
CULTURE AND CLOTHES IN PREMODERN LITERATURE

*Patricia Lennox, Gallatin School,
New York University*

Contextualization

This exercise comes from a course titled "Fashion's Fictions: the Texts of Clothing." The emphasis in the course is on the varied ways that ancient and early modern texts use clothing, as signifiers of gender, occupation, belief systems, power, sexuality, marketing and consumption, and economic and social status (which are, of course, not always the same thing): in other words, the same issues as those in the current discourse on modern dress. Dress historians usually place the appearance of fashion as a concept in the French court of around 1320, but this course emphasizes cultural constructs of clothing across a broader historical range that includes (but is not limited to) fashion. It starts with a readily available early text: the *Epic of Gilgamesh* (Mesopotamia, *c*. 1500–700 BC). During a fourteen-week semester, students also read Longus's *Daphnis and Chloe* (fourth century), the *Lais of Marie de France* (late twelfth century), *Sir Gawain and the Green Knight* (*c*. 1400), Chaucer's prologue to *Canterbury Tales* (1400), Thomas More's *Utopia* (*c*. 1530), Shakespeare's *As You Like It* (1599), and Emile Zola's *The Ladies' Paradise* (*Au Bonheur des Dames,* 1833).

These texts are chosen as representative of historical periods, but also because each of them can be studied with a focus on specific dress issues: power (*Gilgamesh*), sexuality (*Daphnis and Chloe*), identity (*Lais of Marie de France*), dress as metaphor (*Gawain*), social/economic status (*Canterbury Tales*), politics (*Utopia*), gender (*As You Like It*), and marketing/consumerism (*The Ladies' Paradise*). "Luxury" is a consistent presence in all the texts, as it is in contemporary fashion marketing. None of the premodern readings is specifically about dress or fashion, although these elements are important in the texts as signifiers and the signified. The final reading assignment takes a 300-year leap forward to Zola's novel. This fictionalized (but accurate) account of a Paris department store contains all of the issues discussed throughout the semester and brings us to the beginning of modern marketing, which completes the trajectory we started in ancient Mesopotamia.

In addition to the primary texts, students are assigned theoretical and historical articles and excerpts from books relevant to clothing issues. The general plan of action for the assignments is: match a commentary with the literary text as a way to open class discussion, but also to develop students' awareness of the larger discourse, and to help them develop a critical vocabulary needed to articulate their own ideas. The contents of the course are flexible and can be shaped in numerous ways. I have taught a trimmed-down version of this as the "academic" portion of a "Practicum in the Fashion Business" for all levels and have also adapted the assignments for study-abroad programs. It works equally well with any historical period and with films as well as books. The important thing is capturing, organizing, and analyzing the data in order to see the extent of the presence of clothing.

Appropriate courses and course levels for assignment: The course is intended for upper-division undergraduates. It proves especially useful for second- and third-year students because, in addition to offering a range of premodern literature, the pedagogy includes transferable skills in managing comparative data. The course's method of using charts to record and organize information for analysis is applicable to a wide range of studies beyond histories of fashion and dress and other fashion courses. The technique used to chart the presence of clothing references and categorize their usage is fully applicable to all areas of study and research, including contemporary literature and theater, but also political, sociological, global, economic, religious, gender, consumer, and cultural studies. Because of its wide application, it is also an exciting way—especially for the fashion or dress-focused student—to fulfill assignments in courses on nearly every subject. Many of my students have done this with very good results.

Appropriate class size: Seminar-style classes with groups of twenty-five or under is ideal for this assignment.

Estimated time required: Preparing the chart adds about 20 percent more time to reading the text. With the exception of the final novel, each primary text is approximately 100 pages and the critical readings accompanying it are approximately 30 pages.

Required materials: Copies of the primary texts and two reference books. For some books a specific edition is required.

- *Gilgamesh*, trans. E.K. Sanders Penguin
- *Daphnis and Chloe* by Longus, trans. Ronald McCall, Oxford World's Classics
- *Lais of Marie de France*
- *Sir Gawain and the Green Knight*, trans./editor Simon Armitage, Norton
- *Canterbury Tales* by Geoffrey Chaucer
- *Utopia* by Thomas More
- *As You Like It* by Shakespeare
- *The Ladies' Paradise* (*Au Bonheur des Dames*) by Emile Zola
- *Costume & Fashion: A Concise History* by James Laver et al.
- *Adorned in Dreams* by Elizabeth Wilson
- Other reading is provided through handouts, scans, or online sites.

Learning goals

- Ability to conduct close readings of literature and film with appropriate awareness of strategic use of clothing and accessories in narratives.
- Understanding ways that clothing represents a range of cultural and historical influences.
- Familiarity with theoretical approaches used in a range of academic disciplines for clothing-related discourse.
- Ability to evaluate fashion and clothing culture using interdisciplinary theoretical approaches.
- Fluency in articulating ideas on clothing and fashion representation, past and present.

The goal is twofold: to make these early texts familiar and accessible to the students, also to build, step-by-step, an awareness of the previously unexamined presence of dress in literature. I want the students to understand how clothing is used in ways that coordinate with current critical studies of fashion and dress. The center of the assignments is the students' charts for each of the premodern texts. As they read, the students record on the chart every reference to clothing, textiles, jewels, accessories, or clothing-related trade present in text. The goal of the charts is to approach these texts in the same way an archeologist approaches a dig: recording every shard. The charts, when the "shards" are collected carefully and fully, allow the student to see the thick layering of clothing references in texts.

Assessment

There are two parts to the assessment component for this course. The first is fulfillment of the five learning goals: (1) familiarity with theoretical approaches used in a range of academic disciplines for clothing-related discourse; (2) ability to evaluate fashion and clothing culture using interdisciplinary theoretical approaches; (3) understanding ways that clothing styles represent a range of cultural and historical influences; (4) fluency in articulating clothing and fashion representation, past and present; (5) ability to conduct close readings of literature and film with appropriate awareness of strategic use of clothing and accessories in narratives.

The second part of the assessment component is fulfillment of the following more generic requirements: overall acquisition of knowledge that is deep and comprehensive. Clear, thorough, and fully articulated understanding of material covered in each of the reading and viewing assignments. Thorough and comprehensive knowledge with in-depth articulation of ideas is presented in both written and spoken formats. Charts must show complete documentation of all textual references to clothing, textiles, and accessories. Papers must present appropriate argument and exploration, having a convincing thesis, command of methodology, in-depth development, and sound research skills, as required.

Work must be relevant, accurate, and on topic. The documentation for the student presentation must be professional, full, and with appropriate documentation.

For the final grade, weight given to assignments is as follows: 25 percent for charts; 30 percent for two reader response papers (five to seven pages each); 25 percent for final research paper (twelve to fifteen pages); 15 percent for in-class presentation (ten to fifteen minutes); and 5 percent for discussion topic. There is no final exam.

Guidelines for instructors

My class met once a week for three hours; in addition to discussion of the assigned text, each session included two fifteen-minute student presentations focused on the relation between contemporary dress or fashion issues and that class's assigned readings.

The goals listed earlier are met through constructing a scaffold where each section added reflects the critical issues in the current reading assignment. For example, nudity works in different ways; in *Gilgamesh* it is an issue of identity, while in *Daphnis and Chloe* it has a subtext of sexuality. Or, as another example, there are the political uses made of clothing. In *Gilgamesh*, the king's robes signify one type of power, while the politics of More's *Utopia* demand unified dress for all citizens to remove socioeconomic differences. For the scaffold, new issues or new approaches build upon previous ones, while repeated references to the same issue, such as luxury goods or gender defined through dress, are also tracked. The syllabus is organized to align the premodern texts with issues or themes as follows (some texts are covered in two class meetings, while others in only one):

- A two-part introduction: why we wear clothes and why we have fashion: introduction to the fashion system and its theoretical discourse:
  Reading: Montaigne's essay "Why we wear clothes"

- Foundations of fashion theory:
  Reading: "Fundamental Motives" in *The Psychology of Clothes* by J.C. Flugel and "Fashion"; by Georg Simmel

- Adornment: identity, power, communication, commerce, and branding: reading *Gilgamesh* and "Cloth for the Caravan" in *Women's Work: the First 20,000 Years* by Elizabeth Wayland Barber.

- Sexuality, nudity, and nakedness:
  Reading Longus's *Daphnis and Chloe* and Anne Hollander on "Nudity" and "Nakedness" in *Seeing Through Clothes*.

- Armor: protection, masculine identity, social class, and aesthetics:
  Reading: *Sir Gawain and the Green Knight* and "Gender and Identity" in Elizabeth Wilson's *Adorned in Dreams*.

- Medieval/early modern: markets, class, occupation, identity, and consumption:
  Reading: Prologue to Chaucer's *Canterbury Tales* and selection from "The History of Fashion" in *Adorned in Dreams*.

- Politics, religion, law, and the control of dress:
  Reading: Thomas More's *Utopia*, Part 2, and Elizabethan Sumptuary Laws (handout) and "Fashion, Dress and Social Change" in Joanne Entwistle's *The Fashioned Body*.

- Gender: when a boy actor plays a girl playing a boy—and more ….:
  Reading: William Shakespeare's *As You Like It* and "The Stylish Shepherd" by Russell Jackson in *Shakespeare and Costume*.

- Constructing modern consumerism:
  Reading *The Ladies' Paradise*

Between 30 and 50 percent of the pages of our premodern texts contain clothing-related references. When analyzing the results of their charts, students find patterns in the issues as well as the actual number of references. It becomes clear that although historical period and place affect different uses of clothing, those uses always have a current-day equivalent. Writers in the ancient world, the medieval and Renaissance Europe, for example, used items of clothing, textiles, and accessories to identify power, wealth, economic, or social status, political or religious affiliation, gender, individuality, conformity, and rebellion. Students learn how important clothing has always been to individual and cultural identity, and learn to watch for this in their studies in other fields.

Cautionary advice for instructors

- Since the length of most of the readings is approximately 100 pages long, preparing the chart can be painstaking work, but is nonetheless a practical and doable pedagogical component.

- There may be initial resistance to making the charts, but once students see the patterns of references to clothing the charts reveal, it does work. My students were used to being required to write a reading response for most assignments in most classes, so this assignment fit a familiar expectation. The only difference was that it required a very careful close reading.

Copy of the assignment

Charts for *summary reading reports*: you are asked to hand in a chart that provides a detailed reading summary report for each of the primary texts, except for *The Ladies' Paradise*. The goal is to record every reference related to clothing, accessories, textiles, and clothing trade or business. This "archaeological" chart works to establish the significant presence of clothing in the text and its relation to current critical discussions in dress theory. Have this chart with you for reference during the class discussion and hand in, or e-mail, your chart at the end of class. A sample chart is provided in the following text. This is the format to follow for all of the early texts. The column "Purpose" could be the way this reference functions in the plot and/or why the author seems to include the information. "Your Analysis" column can be an overall summary and does not have to be for every page and/or reference. It may also be written as a separate document.

Page #	Your Name	Book / Author	Your Analysis
	Quote—if long use key phrase............	Purpose of clothing	

Typical results and reflections on the assignment

- Each of the premodern texts opens new areas of reflection for the students about the always/already presence of clothing. The basic critical issues given earlier function as a scaffold that can be added to, both going forward and in retrospect as new ideas enter the discussion and build upon previous ones. Most of the material is new to the students but, if they have read the text before, this offers a fresh perspective. For example, many of the students know the story of *Gilgamesh*, but have never considered how often the storyteller refers to clothing and gems. We discuss these and the story's other markers of civilization, including the commercial importance of the flourishing trade of weaving in Ancient Mesopotamia, clothes as symbols of power, but also as signs of personal identity even in the ancient world. For example, when the grief-stricken king in *Gilgamesh* goes on a quest, naked except for a lion's skin, having thrown off the robes and gems that are the markers of his rank, no one recognizes him. Identity and dress become a recurring theme, but one that is repeated in different times and places with variation. Dress and identity played a different role in *Daphnis and Chloe*, where the reader is constantly reminded that the eponymous characters though lovingly raised as peasants were born to a higher class and are dressed beneath their rank. In *As You Like It*, both Celia and Rosalind hide their identity: one loses status by dressing as a countrywoman, and the other gains liberation by dressing as a young man.

- Students see that trade and marketable goods are a common theme. The luxurious textiles and gems, seen briefly in *Gilgamesh*, play increasingly significant roles in both *Daphnis and Chloe* and *Lais of Marie de France*, where beautifully woven pieces of cloth from Constantinople, wrapped around abandoned babies, later serve to prove parentage. This cloth is rare in the late twelfth century, but texts from the end of the fourteenth century make it clear that a steady and prosperous trade has developed with the Near East—*Gawain's* Green Knight sleeps in a bed swathed in imported silk.

- Clothing—and the removal of clothing—with resulting frissons of sexuality occur in *Daphnis and Chloe*, as well as the three attempted seductions in *Sir Gawain*.

- Socioeconomic issues in an early modern sense become clear with Chaucer where several of his pilgrims have connection with trade. While *Gawain* is a fairy tale set in the court of King Arthur, the nearly contemporary *Canterbury Tales* paints an accurate picture of the social and gender hierarchy within an emerging middle class, *c.* 1400. Describing his group of pilgrims, Chaucer plays close attention to establishing them through their appearance—hair, complexion, and body type—but especially their clothes that reflect their occupation and social status. For students, this begins discussions about today's concepts of "dress for success."

- Students find the sixteenth-century texts even more approachable in terms of equivalent modern issues. More's imagined Utopia, where any form of conspicuous consumption is forbidden in order to achieve universal harmony, is partially achieved through same clothing for everyone and making jewels babies' playthings.

- *As You Like It* deals with the cultural construction of gender and plays with the exhilarating sense of freedom felt by a young woman pretending to be male. Throughout students are encouraged to make connections with contemporary fashion and its context and conventions, so this play works particularly well in terms of the body, clothing, and social expectations.

- The final novel in some ways disrupts the flow of historical momentum, but it serves as a capstone for the trajectory of marketing that is visible in all of the texts, beginning in ancient Uruk, followed slowly, but steadily, by an ever-increasing flow of global trade, culminating in the creation of the department store in 1860s Paris—and for us now even expanding on the Internet.

- Throughout all the reading, the relation of clothing to wealth, power, dress, sexuality, socioeconomic, and gendered roles is always a present theme. One other, unexpected, element was the connection between clothing and love—a mother, being separated from her baby, wraps it in rare Constantinople cloth; another places a necklace on a child; rings are exchanged in love and in friendship; a lover ties a knot in his shirt that only his true love can untie; Gilgamesh covers the face of his beloved dead friend with a bridal veil. *The Ladies' Paradise* has a love story at its center that includes a shared understanding of stunning retail display and modern marketing techniques. It is a reminder that among the many issues that an interdisciplinary study of clothing invites us to consider there is also the human element.

Bibliography

Anon. *Gilgamesh*. Trans. N.K. Sandars. London: London: Penguin, 1973.
Anon. *Sir Gawain and the Green Knight*. Trans. Simon Armitage. London: Faber & Faber, 2007.
Chaucer, Geoffrey. *Canterbury Tales*. Ed. Jill Mann. London and New York: Penguin, 2005.
Entwistle, Joanne. *The Fashioned Body*. Cambridge: Polity Press, 2000, 2nd edn. 2015.
Flugel, J.C. *The Psychology of Clothes*. London: Hogarth Press, 1930. Reprint New York: AMS Press, 1976.

Hollander, Anne. *Seeing Through Clothes*. Berkley: University of California Press, 1978.
Laver, James et al. *Costume and Fashion: A Concise History*. London: Thames and Hudson, 1995, rev. edn. 2014.
Longus. *Daphnis and Chloe*. Trans. Ronald McCall. Oxford: Oxford World's Classics, 2009.
Marie de France. *Lais of Marie de France*. Trans. Keith Busby. London: Penguin, 1999.
Montaigne, Michel de. *Essays*. Ed. John Cohen. London: Penguin, 1993.
More, Thomas. *Utopia*. Ed. Ronald Herder. New York: Dover, 1997.
Shakespeare, William. *As You Like It*. Ed. Alan Brisenden. Oxford: Oxford, 1998.
Simmel, Georg. "Fashion." *American Journal of Sociology* 62 (May 1957): 541–558.
Wilson, Elizabeth. *Adorned in Dreams*. London: Virago Press, 1985, rev. edn. 2013, I.B. Tauris.
Zola, Emile. *The Ladies' Paradise* (*Au Bonheur des Dames*). Trans. Brian Nelson, Oxford: Oxford World Classics, 1998.

DISCIPLINE GUIDE

This discipline guide is designed to help instructors seeking assignments especially relevant to them, providing insight into which chapters focus on exercises in the following disciplines:

Art History: Chapters 2, 11, 12, 28, 29, 31
Business and Economics: Chapters 5, 6, 7, 8, 9, 10, 22, 24
Consumer Studies: Chapters 1, 4, 7, 9, 10, 24
Cultural Studies: Chapters 3, 4, 15, 18, 19, 20, 25, 26, 28, 29, 31, 32
Design: Chapters 1, 3, 4, 7, 11, 16, 17, 30, 31
Environmental Studies: Chapters 15, 22, 24
Ethics: Chapters 22 and 24
Ethnic Studies: Chapters 20, 23, 30
Global Studies: Chapters 1, 5, 24, 27, 32
History: Chapters 1, 2, 3, 15, 17, 27, 28, 29, 30, 32
Labor Studies: Chapter 27
Literature: Chapters 15 and 32
Marketing, Merchandising, and Management: Chapters 5, 6, 7, 8, 9, 10, 17, 22
Material Culture: Chapters 2, 11, 12, 13, 15, 18, 21, 25, 29
Media Studies: Chapters 4, 19, 23
Museum Studies: Chapters 8, 11, 12, 14
Sociology/Anthropology: Chapters 1, 4, 13, 23, 26, 27, 30
Theater: Chapter 31
Visual Arts: Chapters 5, 11, 16, 31
Women's, Gender, and Sexuality Studies: Chapters 1, 2, 13, 18, 19, 20, 21, 25, 26, 27, 29, 32

AUTHOR BIOGRAPHIES

Holly M. Kent is Associate Professor of History at the University of Illinois-Springfield, where she teaches classes in US women's history, fashion history, and the history of slavery and abolition. She is the author of *Her Voice Will Be on the Side of Right: Gender and Power in Women's Antebellum Antislavery Fiction*.

Alyssa Dana Adomaitis is Assistant Professor and Director of The Business of Fashion and Technology program at the New York City College of Technology, CUNY. She holds a PhD from the University of Minnesota. Her research interests include beauty prejudice, perceptions of dress, impression management, and advertising's impact on consumers' behavior.

Jody Aultman holds a PhD in the Apparel, Merchandizing, and Design Program from Iowa State University. Her work has included surface design, digital textile printing, and apparel design. Her research areas of interest include surface design, quilting and how quilting relates to STEM, and apparel design.

Eileen Boris is the Hull Professor of Feminist Studies and Professor of History, Black Studies, and Global Studies at the University of California, Santa Barbara. She is the author of *Home to Work: Motherhood and the Politics of Industrial Homework in the United States*. Her latest books are *Caring for America: Home Health Workers in the Shadow of the Welfare State* (with J. Klein) and *Women's ILO: Transnational Networks, Global Labour Standards, and Gender Equity*, coedited with D. Hoehtker and S. Zimmermann.

Jay McCauley Bowstead lectures in Cultural and Historical Studies at London College of Fashion and writes on fashion, gender, and visual culture. His recent publications include the monograph *Menswear Revolution* for Bloomsbury Academic, an educational book for A&C Black and an article on Hedi Slimane for *Critical Studies in Men's Fashion*.

Catherine Bradley is Resident Costume Designer and Head of Wardrobe at McGill University, where she teaches Costuming. She is founder of the *Textile Resource Center*, an open access initiative housing a Textile Dictionary and Weave Guide. Her costume practice has taken her from Canada's Maritimes to the Rocky Mountains.

Kiara Bulley is Lecturer at Queensland University of Technology, teaching in both fashion practice and theory units. She is also codirector of The Stitchery Collective, a not-for-profit fashion collective which explores ideas of engagement, experience, and community in fashion. Bulley has worked extensively in both fashion and costume production and design.

Charity Calvin Armstead is a doctoral student in Apparel, Merchandizing, and Design at Iowa State University. She has a master's degree in Textiles, Merchandizing, and Interiors from the University of Georgia. She teaches dress history at Lipscomb University and manages Lipscomb's fashion archive.

Amber M. Chatelain is Assistant Professor of Apparel Design and Merchandizing and Child and Family Studies at Eastern Kentucky University. Her teaching interests include dress and culture, visual merchandising, retail management, and gender issues. Her research has focused on Generation Y shopping behavior and on student perceptions of faculty dress and gender.

Alexandra van den Berg Christensen taught early modern European fashion history through the Experimental College at Tufts University, and has worked with costume collections at the American Textile History Museum and the Slater Memorial Museum. She currently lives in China, where her interests are expanding to include global fashion.

Patricia Dillon, AAA, is an instructor at New York University where she teaches *Historical Costume and Textiles.* She is a certified appraiser in American Decorative Arts and president of Putnam Art Advisors and Consultants, Inc., where she works with museums, historic sites, corporations, and private collectors in collection management.

Lili Golmohammadi lectures at Goldsmiths, University of London, and London College of Fashion. She is a designer, researcher, and design educator. Her interdisciplinary practice encompasses performance, print, garment design, websites, jewelry, podcasting, photography, and installation. She has worked for design and trend forecasting companies including Zara, Pull & Bear, and WGSN.

Jennifer Farley Gordon is an independent researcher, writer, and curator. She earned a PhD in Apparel, Merchandizing, and Design at Iowa State University. She formerly worked as an assistant curator at The Museum at FIT in New York and is coauthor of *Sustainable Fashion: Past, Present, and Future* (Bloomsbury, 2015).

Michele Granger recently retired as a full professor in Fashion and Entrepreneurship at Missouri State University. She has authored several textbooks, including *The Fashion Intern, Case Studies in Merchandising Apparel and Soft Goods*, and *Fashion: The Industry and its Careers*, and coauthored *Fashion Entrepreneurship: Retail Business Planning*.

June-Ann Greeley is Associate Professor in the Department of Theology and Religious Studies at Sacred Heart University. Her areas of scholarship and publications include women's spirituality in Christianity and Islam, eco-feminism in feminist theology, environmental justice studies, liberation theology and human rights, and religion and ethical inquiry in popular culture.

AUTHOR BIOGRAPHIES

Anna Green is a doctoral candidate in the English Department at Michigan State University. Her dissertation "The Aesthetics of Urban Precarity" explores the dialogic relationship between the precarious subject positions of woman artists and their engagements with collage and collage adjacent methodologies. She has a chapter forthcoming in *Wharton and Hemingway, Architects of American Modernism.*

Shipra Gupta is Assistant Professor of Marketing at the University of Illinois-Springfield. She holds a PhD in Marketing from University of Nebraska-Lincoln. Her research interests include consumer behavior, gender issues, retail management, and sustainability. Her teaching interests include retail management, marketing management, research methods of marketing, and international marketing.

Anya Kurennaya serves as part-time faculty at Parsons School of Design, The New School. She teaches Parsons' introductory fashion studies survey course, and has taught courses on fashion and celebrity culture, fashion and language, hip-hop culture and style, and zine culture.

Patricia Lennox has taught fashion-related courses at New York University's Gallatin School and NYU Global sites in London and Florence. Recent publications: coeditor *Shakespeare and Costume*, exhibition reviews *Studies in Costume and Performance*, articles on Shakespeare performance and films. Before academia she was personal assistant to Diana Vreeland at the Metropolitan Museum's Costume Institute.

Mel Michelle Lewis is Associate Professor and Program Director of Ethnic Studies at Saint Mary's College of California. Her research explores intersections of race, gender, and sexuality, addressing black queer feminist thought, femme studies, and performance as critical pedagogical praxis.

Diane Maglio is Master Faculty at Berkeley College, Larry L. Luing School of Business, Fashion Department. She specializes in menswear and has published in academic journals of the Costume Society of America and the Textile Society of America. She received a grant from the Fashion Institute of Technology to continue her study of resort wear in France.

Sara Marcketti is professor in the Apparel Program and Associate Director of the Center for Excellence in Learning and Teaching at Iowa State University. Her coauthored books include *Survey of Historic Costume, Textiles* and *Knock It Off: A History of Design Piracy in the U.S. Women's Ready to Wear Apparel Industry.*

Ingrid Mida is a curator, dress historian, and lecturer at Ryerson University at Toronto. She is the lead author of *The Dress Detective: A Practical Guide to Object-Based Research in Fashion* (Bloomsbury Academic 2015).

Alice Payne is Senior Lecturer in Fashion at Queensland University of Technology. Her research interests include the fashion design process, the Australian mass-market fashion industry, and the problem of design for sustainability within the fashion context. Payne is an award-winning designer and has exhibited her work in Australia and overseas.

Diana Saiki is Associate Professor at Ball State University. She teaches history of costume and the fashion industry. She also works with the university's apparel and textile collection, the Beeman Historic Costume Collection.

Katherine Schaefer is Assistant Professor in Fashion Studies at Columbia College Chicago. She received her MBA from DePaul University and BA from Indiana University. Schaefer primarily teaches Fashion Business courses. She oversees the visual merchandising curriculum and spearheaded the Fashion Studies department's online course offerings.

Amanda Sikarskie is Lecturer in Art History at the University of Michigan-Dearborn. She is a historian of fashion and textiles, and her first monograph, *Textile Collections: Preservation, Access, Curation and Interpretation in a Digital Age* (Rowman & Littlefield), came out in 2016.

Laura Snelgrove holds an MA in Fashion Studies from Parsons The New School for Design, where she has taught courses in Art and Design History and Theory. She has published on topics including wedding dresses, sunglasses, and how conflicting models of time are manifested in the pages of fashion magazines.

Catherine Howey Stearn is Associate Professor of History at Eastern Kentucky University. She teaches classes on World Civilization, Early Modern Europe, Tudor England, and Early Modern Women. She incorporates dress history into her scholarship on the women who served at the court of Elizabeth I, Queen of England, 1558–1603.

Elizabeth J. Stigler is a doctoral candidate in Women, Gender, and Sexuality Studies at the University of Kansas, where she also teaches courses on the Politics of Physical Appearance. Her dissertation explores the role of food as it relates to memory, labor, and cultural knowledge within Chicago's Czech American community.

Sarah Wiggins is Professor of History at Bridgewater State University. Her area of expertise is gender in modern Britain and her research and teaching interests include women in politics and higher education, the history of sexuality, and the history of fashion and material culture.

INDEX

Abnett, Kate 62
accessories 53–7, 285
Adobe Illustrator 142, 145
Adobe Photoshop 142
Adomaitis, Alyssa Dana 43–50
Adorned in Dreams (Wilson) 229–30
aesthetic economy, the 34, 35
Aesthetic Economy of Fashion, The (Entwistle) 33
African American culture 34
Africana studies 176
agency 159, 163, 179
Anatomy of Fashion, The (McDowell) 150
Ancient Greek costume. *See* classical era
Appadurai, Arjun 131–2
apparel 53–4
apparel design, historical influences 25–6
Appleford, Katherine 138
appraisal 70
Apsaalooke Nights 201
Arnold, Janet 257
artifacts 96, 97
Ashelford, Jane 257
ateliers 237–8
Atlantic, The 202
auction 70
Aultman, Jody 141–6

Baker, Josephine 175, 180
Banning, Jennifer 26
Barthes, Roland 168
Baudelaire, Charles 229
Bean, John C. 18
Belafonte, Harry 175
Benjamin, Walter 229, 230
Beyoncé 45, 175, 180
Beyond Design: The Synergy of Apparel Development 150
black fashion 175–80, 237
Blanc, Odile 10
blogging 183–9, 213, 214, 237, 238

Blumer, Hebert 11
body image 18, 115
body shape 61
body shaping 114–15, 116, 117, 119
body type 62
Book of the Practice of Tailoring, Measuring and Marking Out 142
Boris, Eileen 237–44
Bourdieu, Pierre 33, 34, 221, 223–4
Bowstead, Jay McCauley 33–41
Bradley, Catherine 273–81
branding 193, 194, 195–7
Brannon, Evelyn L. 43–4
bubble up 33, 34
Buckley, Cheryl 221
business overview 87
business plan 83
Butler, Judith 168

Changing Clothes in China (Finnane) 10
Chatelain, Amber M. 265–71
Chaucer, Geoffrey 283, 284
Christensen, Alexandra van den Berg 9–15, 113–21
Clark, Hazel 221
classical era 25–6, 249–55
classic forms/styles 149–54
Cline, Elizabeth 62
clothing design 266, 267
clothing styles 154
Clough, G. Wayne 123
code 167
collection 62
collective selection 33
communication 168, 170, 172, 176
community 127
complex reasoning 43
computer-aided design 142
consumer behavior 77, 78, 80, 210, 213, 237–44
Consumer Culture (Lury) 33

contemporary fashion, historic fashion as inspiration 25–6, 188
contradiction 168
Corbin Limited 110
corporate accountability 210
corporate social responsibility (CSR) 194, 195
corset/corsetry 113–21
Corset: A Cultural History, The (Steele) 114
Corsets and Crinolines (Waugh) 115
Cox, Laverne 175
creative assignments 257
Crenshaw, Kimberlé 159
critical thinking 43–5, 50
Crusades, the 10
cultural appropriation 201–7
cultural capital 33, 34, 35
cultural factors 65
cultural intermediaries 34
culture, influence of 265–6, 283–9
customer target 62

Dandridge, Dorothy 175
databases 25–8
Davis, Fred 168
de Certeau, Michel 229
De La Haye, Amy 131
demographic trends 35
description 95, 96, 97, 99, 104
design, elements and principles 143, 144–5
design experimentation 151
Dewey, John 43
digital presentation 123
Dillon, Patricia 69–75, 123–9
distance learning 123–9
DIY practices 138
Douglass, Frederick 176
drawing 95, 96–7, 99, 100
dress 221
Dress Detective: A Practical Guide to Object-based Research in Fashion, The (Mida and Kim) 95
dress practice 159, 163, 189, 221–7

economics, influence of 265–6
Elements of Teaching Writing, The (Gottschalk and Hjortshoj) 18
Elizabeth I 257–62
embodied learning 273, 281
embodiment 159, 160, 189, 221–7, 230–1
emotional intelligence 103–11
Engaging Ideas (Bean) 18
Entwistle, Joanne 33, 34, 229

environment 193, 195, 197, 199
environmental ethics 209–15
everyday life 221–7, 229–35
experiential learning 114–15, 281
exploitation 209, 210, 242, 243
extant garments 25

fashion
  analysis of 131
  definition of 10, 45
  evolution of 265, 266
  mechanics of 10–11
  in premodern literature 283–9
  and STEM skills 141–6
  symbolic meaning 149, 150, 151, 153
  and urban space 229–35
Fashion: A Philosophy (Svendsen) 168
fashion capitals 238
fashion consumption 113–14, 138
fashion cultures 149, 150, 151
fashion cycle 11, 15, 47
fashion design, classic forms/styles 149–54
Fashioned Body, The (Entwistle) 229, 230–1
fashion forecasting 43–50
  databases 45
  object analysis and emotional responses 103–4
  steps in 43–5
fashion history
  classical era 25–6
  historical influences in contemporary fashion 25–6
  theoretical context 9–10
fashion media 167–73, 183–9
fashion product 86
Fashionsnoops 45
fashion studies
  key approaches 3–5
  material culturist approach 131, 221–2
  traditional educational models 3
  and WGSS courses 167–8
fashion system, definition of 10
fashion theory
  historical perspective 9–10
  scholarship 9–15
fashion transmission 33
fast fashion 62, 209–15
feasibility decision 87
feasibility study 83, 87
feminism 167–73
financial assessment 87
Finnane, Antonia 10

INDEX

"first-world" privilege 210, 211
flâneur 229, 230, 231, 232, 233
Fleming, E. McClung 104
forecasting. *See* fashion forecasting
Foucault, Michel 168, 170
French Revolution 10, 250, 254

Gam, Hae Jin 26
garment, as gift 257–8, 260, 262
garment patterns 115–17, 118, 120
garment styles (fashion styles) 151
gaze, the 170
gender 4, 8, 11, 18, 41, 94, 104, 108, 110, 114, 115, 129, 157, 158, 159, 160, 163, 164, 167–73, 180, 184, 185, 187, 202, 214, 231, 234, 237, 238, 239, 240, 240, 247, 254, 265–6, 267, 269, 273, 278, 283, 284, 286, 287, 289
gift-giving 257–8, 260, 262
globalization 210, 230
global warming 209
Golmohammadi, Lili 33–41
Gordon, Jennifer Farley 25–8, 138
Gottschalk, Katherine 18
Granger, Michele 61–8, 83–92
Great Depression 274
Greeley, June-Ann 209–15
Green, Anna 131–8
group presentation 273–81
group project 266, 268
grunge 34
Gupta, Shipra 77–81

habitus 34, 221, 224
handling costumes 126
hands-on strategy 249–55
Harvey, Karen 18
hegemony 159, 163
Herpen, Iris Van 142
Hill, Colleen 138
hippies 34
historic costume 123–9, 249–55, 265–70, 273–81
historiography 9
Hjortshoj, Keith 18
Hollander, Anne 116–17, 149
home products 53–4, 103

iconography 257–62
image 61, 62, 103
Indian Country Media 201
indigenous fashion 201–7

Industrial Revolution 10
injustice 209, 210, 211
inspiration 25
interdisciplinary 274, 275, 280
international students 124
Internet 21, 43, 64, 65, 71, 72, 113, 124, 178, 185, 188, 258, 277, 289
intersectionality 159–65, 176

jewelry 56, 260, 262
Jolles, Marjorie 167–9

Kaiser, Susan 159, 164, 165
Kauffman Foundation 83
Kearny Museum 104
Kent, Holly M. 3–5, 183–9
Kim, Alexandra 104
kinesthetic learning 3, 115
King, Jr., Martin Luther 176
Kokon to Zai (KTZ) 201
Kopytoff, Ivan 104
Koskela, Hille 229
Kurennaya, Anya 159–65, 221–7

labor 199, 210, 237–8
Laver, James 270, 274
Lawson, Jane A. 257–8
Lee, Joohyeon 104
Lemire, Beverly 10
Lennox, Patricia 283–9
Lewis, Mel Michelle 175–80
Life Cycle Assessment (LCA) 193
local collections 126–7
Lurie, Alison 168
Lury, Celia 33

Maglio, Diane 103–10
Marcketti, Sara 25–8, 141–6
market 70
market assessment 87
marketplace 72
Marzec, Evangeline 83
material culture 18, 277
Material Sustainability Index 193
McDowell, Colin 150
mentoring 17, 18, 19, 20, 21, 22, 266
merchandise management 77
Merleau-Ponty, Maurice 230
"Metropolis and Mental Life, The" (Simmel) 230
Mida, Ingrid 95–101, 104
Minaj, Nicki 180
model making 249–55

monetary worth 69–70
Montgomery, Charles F. 104
More, Thomas 283, 284, 286, 287, 289
multiculturalism 124, 125
Murphy, Deirdre 25
music 45, 50, 164, 177, 178, 179, 180, 273, 274, 277, 278, 279, 280, 281

Nevinson, J.L. 260
New Year's gift list 260
Nyong'o, Lupita 175

object analysis (object-based research)
    emotional engagement with 103–10
    of personal closet 186–7
    role of 95
    slow approach to 95–101
observation 95, 96, 97, 99
Okuma, Jamie 201–2
Okuma, Sandra 202
online fashion culture 189
online learning 127, 129, 249
online shopping 142
operations and management assessment 87
oral history 186
oral presentation 17, 18, 19, 20, 21, 22, 87, 242, 259, 267, 275, 278–9, 281
Overdressed: The Shockingly High Cost of Cheap Fashion (Cline) 62

Painter of Modern Life, The (Baudelaire) 229
Parisian couture 201
patternmaking 142
Paul, Richard 43
Payne, Alice 149–54, 193–200
Pearce, Susan 95
peer review 17–18, 19, 20, 21, 22
Pham, Minh Ha T. 202
photography 95, 105, 109, 160, 227, 244
plagiarism 205
political events, and fashion 45
political power 257
politics, influence of 18, 213, 248, 257, 258, 265–6, 267, 273, 283, 286, 287
popular culture 34, 175–6, 273, 277, 278
portraiture 257–8
Practical Guide to Sustainable Fashion, A (Gwilt) 194
premodern literature, fashion in 283–9
primary sources 17, 18, 19–20, 21, 22, 43, 103, 107, 257, 261, 277

product development 61–8
production 237–44
Project Runway (TV show) 132
Prown, Jules 103
public image 257–62
punk 34
purchasing decisions 62

Qing Dynasty 45
queer culture 34, 183, 220, 235, 237, 239, 241, 243

race/racism 4, 84, 157, 158, 159, 167, 168, 169, 171, 172, 175, 184, 185, 189, 202, 238, 248, 259, 266, 271, 273
recycling 138, 193–4, 197–8, 199
Reflection as a Meaning Process (Dewey) 43
Reillo, Giorgio 10
Renaissance 10
repurposing clothing 138
research project 17–22
retail anthropology 77–81
retail management 77, 81
Roche, Daniel 131
Rogers, Carol 43–4
Ross, Diana 175
rote memorization 43

Said, Edward 168
Saiki, Diana 249–55
scaffolding 18, 19–20, 31, 45, 286
Schaefer, Katherine 53–7
science, technology, engineering, and mathematics (STEM) 141–6
scientific discoveries, and fashion 45
Scriven, Michael 43
seasonal trend predictions 53–4
secondary sources 17, 18, 19–20, 21, 22, 37, 106, 257, 261, 277
secondhand clothing 131–9, 237
seeing. See slow approach to seeing
Seeing Through Clothes (Hollander) 116–17
self-reflexivity 138
sexuality 4, 11, 18, 110, 113, 115, 132, 152, 157, 160, 164, 167, 169, 175, 176, 178, 179, 184, 222, 231, 248, 266, 267, 270, 271, 273, 283, 286, 288, 289
Shakespeare, William 283, 284, 287
shopping habits 77, 81
Sikarskie, Amanda 201–7
silhouette 62

INDEX

Simmel, Georg 11, 230
slow fashion 214, 215
slow approach to seeing 95–101
Snelgrove, Laura 229–35
social media 183, 185
spatial visualization 116, 118
sports, and fashion 45
square breathing 108
'squaw' fashion 202
start-up business 83–4
Stearn, Catherine Howey 257–63
Steele, Valerie 114
Stigler, Elizabeth 167–73
strategy, retail 77, 81
Strauss, Valerie 104
street fashions 45
student work 36, 84, 260
student writing 17, 19, 20, 21, 22
subcultural capital 33–4
subcultures 41, 131, 238
subjectivity 160, 163
subject position 157, 159–65, 168–9, 222, 225
subversion 150, 168, 175
sustainability 33, 34, 94, 132–3, 138, 193–200, 209–15
Svendsen, Lars 168
symbolism/symbols 149, 150, 151, 153, 257–63, 270

tacit aesthetic knowledge 34, 35
target market 61
taste, notions of 33, 34, 36, 37, 108, 126, 239
Technical Sourcebook for Designers 150
technology, influence of 38, 94, 106, 110, 123, 124, 125, 126, 141–6, 251, 252, 254, 265–6, 267, 268, 273, 278, 280
Tham, Mathilda 33, 34
thick description 93, 96, 99
Thom Browne 110
Thornton, Sarah 33
3D printing 142

timeline 44–5, 113–14, 115, 117
trend(s)
    and product development 62
    seasonal 53–4
trend forecasting
    accessories 53–7
    taste and trends 33–41
trend research 44–5, 53–4
trickle down 33
Tubman, Harriet 176

undergraduate research 17–22
upcycling 138, 195
urban space 229–35

Valdez, Louis 138
valuation 69–70
value 69–70
Veblen, Thorsten 7, 11, 15, 33
Victorian era 113–14
vintage black glamor 175–80
visual merchandising 77, 78
vlogs (video-blogs) 133–4

Washington Post, The 104
waste 138, 193, 195, 198
Waugh, Norah 115
web-based learning. *See* distance learning
WGSN/Stylesight 45
Whitehead, Shannon 62
Wiley, Kehinde 175
Wilson, Elizabeth 229–30, 284
women, gender, and sexuality studies (WGSS) 167–8, 176
worth 69
written communication skills 43, 60

Yellowtail, Bethany 201
Young, Agnes 11

zeitgeist 103, 275
Zola, Emile 283, 284
Zoot Suit (Valdez) 138

www.ingramcontent.com/pod-product-compliance
Lightning Source LLC
Chambersburg PA
CBHW081800300426
44116CB00014B/2189